The Anatomy of Racial Attitudes

The Anatomy of Racial Attitudes

Richard A. Apostle
Charles Y. Glock
Thomas Piazza
Marijean Suelzle

University of California Press

Berkeley
Los Angeles
London

128031

University of California Press
Berkeley and Los Angeles, California

University of California Press, Ltd.
London, England

© 1983 by
The Regents of the University of California

Printed in the United States of America

1 2 3 4 5 6 7 8 9

Library of Congress Cataloging in Publication Data
Main entry under title:

The Anatomy of racial attitudes.

Includes bibliographical references and index.
1. United States—Race relations—Public opinion.
2. Racism—United States—Public opinion.   3. Social
surveys—United States.   4. Public opinion—United
States.   I. Apostle, Richard A.
E185.615.A678   305.8′00973   82–4867
ISBN 0-520-04719-2   AACR2

Contents

Acknowledgments

Much social science research these days is made possible because large numbers of people are willing to contribute their time and energy, usually without recompense, answering questions about themselves. This contribution is rarely acknowledged, yet it is crucial to the social scientific enterprise.

In this respect, the authors of this volume owe a debt to more than two thousand people—the respondents to the several research instruments employed in the pursuit of our inquiries. To accommodate us, these people agreed to participate in a long, open-ended interview or a lengthy structured interview. Alternatively, they filled out a questionnaire, which, as can be inferred from Appendix D, where the questionnaire is reproduced, was no easy task. We promised these respondents anonymity, so we cannot thank them by name. To one and all, however, we express our deep appreciation.

We are also grateful to those who assisted us in data collection—the advanced undergraduate students at the University of California who conducted the in-depth interviews and the interviewing staff members of the University's Survey Research Center who took responsibility for administering the structured interviews. Among the latter, Charlotte Coleman, who supervised the interviewing, was especially helpful. Acknowledgment is also due to the Center's computing staff, especially then Chief Programmer Harvey Weinstein, and to Heidi Nebel, for generating the data files on which the analysis was based.

William L. Nicholls II, then Executive Officer of the Survey Research Center and now with the Bureau of the Census, was responsible for the design and construction of the sample of the Bay Area Survey. We are also grateful to him for technical assistance afforded during analysis.

As this book will report in more detail, our research on racial attitudes was part of a larger project being conducted by the Survey Research Center to develop model social indicators. This project was funded by the National Science Foundation under grant No. Soc 72-05214. J. Merrill Shanks, then Director of the Center, was Principal Investigator of the larger project. Other participants included Jack Citrin, Gertrude Jaeger, Herbert McCloskey, Karen Paige, Paul Sniderman, and Arthur Stinchcombe. These colleagues helped us in their responses to our plans and progress reports in a project seminar.

Our original plans for our studies of racial attitudes included a laboratory component, which was to be directed by Richard Ofshe. He and a research assistant, Richard Conley, participated actively in early phases of our project and made contributions both to its formulation and to the construction of research instruments. When it became clear that the funding necessary to support the experimental phase of the project would not be forthcoming, Ofshe and Conley withdrew. We benefited considerably from their interaction with us, however, and we are pleased at this opportunity to acknowledge their help and express our gratitude for it. Clifford McGlotten was also a research assistant on the project in its early phases. He was of particular assistance to us in formulating the versions of the research instruments that were administered to black respondents. To our regret, McGlotten for personal reasons was unable to continue as a member of our project group.

As to our own contributions to the project, we consider them roughly equal, as signaled by the alphabetical listing of our names as authors. However, though we participated equally we played different roles, and it is appropriate here to distinguish among them.

Glock originated the idea for the project and wrote the prospectus that yielded the funding. He recruited the staff and functioned as overall project director.

All four authors, as well as those individuals mentioned above, contributed to the formulation of the research instruments. Suelzle, however, took specific responsibility for the racial attitudes component of the interview schedule used in the Bay Area Survey, which served as a part of the larger Survey Research Center program on social indicators. She also oversaw the data collection of the Bay Area Survey insofar as it bore on racial attitudes. She supervised the coding of the racial attitude questions and the construction of the computer tape on which the results were recorded. Suelzle was also responsible for an extended initial analysis of the Bay Area Survey data, a write-up of which subsequently became her Ph.D. dissertation.

Apostle assumed a similar role with respect to the study undertaken to follow up on the results of the Bay Area Survey. He assumed responsibility for putting together the questionnaire, oversaw the data collection and coding operations, and supervised the construction of the computer tape on which the data were recorded. Apostle did an extended initial analysis of the follow-up study data, which subsequently became his Ph.D. dissertation.

The present manuscript draws heavily on the initial analyses conducted by Apostle and Suelzle. It also reports on the results of extensive additional analysis, especially of the follow-up data, undertaken by Glock and Piazza. Piazza reanalyzed all the sets of items in the follow-up study and created most of the summary measures used in the present analysis. He and Glock jointly developed the ex-

planatory-mode typology described in the text. Glock produced the first draft of the present manuscript, except for
Appendices A and B, which were initially drafted by Piazza. Apostle, Piazza, and Suelzle reviewed the initial manuscript draft, in some instances making extensive suggestions for revision. Glock then incorporated their
suggestions into subsequent drafts of the manuscript.

We also benefited from critical comments provided by
Raymond Currie and Robert Wuthnow. Karen Garrett,
Jeanette Roger, and Ann Stannard served consecutively as
secretary to the project over its course. We are grateful to
Carole Lowinger for her fine contribution to the editing of
the manuscript and to Bonnie Milligan for yeoman help in
getting the manuscript typed and to the printer.

June 1981   R. A. A.
                                                                  C. Y. G.
                                                                  T. P.
                                                                  M. S.

Chapter 1 *The Components of Racial Prejudice*

Chances are good that if white Americans were questioned, a majority of them would speculate that less racial prejudice exists in America today than in the past. The response of black Americans to the same question is harder to predict. Given that they are still discriminated against and that their social status relative to whites has not improved substantially over the last decades, black Americans might express some skepticism in response to the assertion that racial prejudice has declined.

In fact, it is not known for sure whether the extent of racial prejudice is greater or smaller now than in the past. This topic has not been regularly monitored by the nation's data collection machinery in a systematic way.

If such monitoring were to be undertaken, how might it be done? It appears that the means are already at hand. Investigators could survey periodically equivalent samples of the white population to collect information on which to judge the prevalence of racial prejudice. What is not so self-evident, on reflection, is just how racial prejudice should be defined for such an enterprise. What questions should researchers ask and how should they put answers together to produce a valid measure that would reliably and accurately indicate how much racial prejudice exists in America, both at any one point in time and over time? This book reports on a research project designed to try to resolve such issues and, in the process, to gain a better understanding of the anatomy of white racial attitudes in America today.

The idea of monitoring change in racial prejudice has its origins in a more general concern among social scientists and policy makers to extend the nation's data collection machinery in order to produce information on a wider range of social topics. Social scientists want a more extensive body of social data so as to enrich opportunities for advancing knowledge and understanding of social change. The relative absence of longitudinal data on many topics has been the major obstacle to testing the rather substantial body of theory about change. Governmental policy makers, including some Congressmen, have become interested in expanding the scope of social indicators to enable the more effective monitoring of the nation's physical, economic, and social health. There is a growing sensitivity to the inadequacy of current measures to assess the quality of American life in other than narrowly economic terms.

Interest in social indicators is not new in America. Indeed, as shown by the Constitutional provisions for the conducting of a decennial census and for a presidential report to Congress from time to time containing "information on the State of the Union," the topic was of concern to the founding fathers. Since then other periods have been characterized by increased interest in assessing the state of the society. Most notable in this regard was President Hoover's commissioning of a Research Committee on Social Trends, which resulted in the 1933 publication of the highly regarded *Recent Social Trends*.[1]

Current interest in social indicators was stimulated significantly by the book of that title edited by Raymond Bauer and published in 1966.[2] Challenging what it termed

1. President's Research Committee on Social Trends, *Recent Social Trends in the United States* (New York: McGraw-Hill, 1933).
2. Raymond A. Bauer, ed., *Social Indicators* (Cambridge, Mass.: M.I.T. Press, 1966).

the "economic philistinianism of the U.S. Government's present statistical establishment," *Social Indicators* set forth a blueprint for a comprehensive assessment of where Americans have been, where they are, and where they are going. Its publication struck a highly responsive chord in both academic and government circles. Almost immediately, social indicators became a major topic at meetings of professional societies. At least three professional journals devoted special issues to the topic. Then President Johnson commissioned the Department of Health, Education and Welfare to develop a blueprint setting forth what the government might do to develop indicators of societal change beyond the economic ones. This effort produced the publication, in 1969, *Towards a Social Report.*[3] At about the same time, Congress was passing The Full Opportunity and Social Accounting Act of 1967 and the Social Accounting Act of 1969, which provided for the President to prepare an annual social report.[4]

More recent developments have included the establishment in 1972 of a Center for Research on Social Indicators under the auspices of the Social Science Research Council. In 1974 an international journal, *Social Indicators Research*, was launched. And in 1977 a separate research division on social indicators was established within the National Science Foundation.[5]

All this activity has stimulated the growth of a sizable theoretical and methodological literature on social indicators.[6] It has not resulted, however, in the kind of major

3. U.S. Department of Health, Education and Welfare, *Towards a Social Report* (Washington, D.C.: U.S. Government Printing Office, 1969).
4. See Ralph M. Brooks, "Social Planning and Societal Monitoring," in Leslie D. Wilcox, Ralph M. Brooks, George M. Beal, and Gerald E. Klonglan, *Social Indicators and Societal Monitoring: An Annotated Bibliography* (San Francisco: Jossey-Bass, 1972), for a report on social indicator developments through 1970, pp. 1–30.
5. See Kevin J. Gilmartin, Robert J. Rossi, Leonard S. Lutomski, and Donald F. B. Reed, *Social Indicators: An Annotated Bibliography of Current Literature* (New York: Garland, 1979), for a report on social indicator developments since 1970.
6. Wilcox et al., and Gilmartin et al.

overhaul of governmental data collection envisioned by
Bauer and his associates. Some progress has been made in
organizing existing data to increase their usefulness for
social indicator purposes. Witness, for example, the reports
entitled *Social Indicators 1973: Selected Statistics on Social
Conditions and Trends in the United States* and its sequel,
Social Indicators 1976.[7] Using existing data, these docu-
ments report on trends in health, public safety, education,
employment, income, housing, leisure, and population
growth with the sequel adding chapters on the family and
social mobility and participation. Since 1975, the National
Center for Education Statistics has been publishing an annual compendium of statistical data on education covering
such topics as number of students and educators, school-
ing outcomes, and school finance.[8] Also included are comparisons between education in the United States and other
countries. Once again, these reports simply put existing
data in new form.

So far the innovations in new data collection that the
social indicator movement has stimulated have been primarily experimental rather than permanent. A National
Crime Survey conducted by the Bureau of the Census for
the U.S. Department of Justice has sought, through month-
ly surveys of the nation's population and of the nation's
business firms, to assess the incidence of crime through
self-reports of victims.[9] A periodic national survey of the

7. Executive Office of the President, Office of Management and Budget,
*Social Indicators 1973: Selected Statistics on Social Conditions and Trends in the
United States* (Washington, D.C.: U.S. Government Printing Office, 1973);
Executive Office of the President, U.S. Department of Commerce, Office of
Federal Statistical Policy and Standards, Bureau of the Census, *Social Indica-
tors 1976: Selected Statistics on Social Conditions and Trends in the United States*
(Washington, D.C.: U.S. Government Printing Office, 1977).

8. National Center for Education Statistics, *The Condition of Education*
(Washington, D.C.: U.S. Government Printing Office, published annually
since 1975).

9. U.S. National Criminal Justice Information and Statistics Service, *Criminal Victimization in the United States: A National Crime Panel Survey Report*
(issued irregularly).

knowledge, skills, understanding, and attitudes of young Americans in ten different subject areas has also been launched recently by the U.S. Office of Education under the title *National Assessment of Educational Progress.*[10] Neither of these projects, however, is to be continued indefinitely. In addition to such federal efforts, state governments have done some experimentation with social indicators. By and large, however, the social indicator movement has not yet succeeded in its broader ambition to effect, through Congress, a wide-ranging revision and extension of national data collection that would enable a truly comprehensive assessment, over time, of national well-being.

There are political reasons why these ambitions have not been realized. There is in government disagreement as to how social measurement may best be improved as well as concern that any increase in data collection, aside from being costly, would place the individual's right to privacy in jeopardy. More fundamentally, perhaps, no one has presented a plan for expanding the range of social indicators either comprehensively or in a step-by-step fashion that has gained wide support. This is not because of a lack of trying—many people have been devoting a lot of energy to social indicator development—but because the conceptual and operational problems have proven difficult to solve.

The project to develop social indicators of racial prejudice is part of a larger program of social indicator development being pursued at the University of California, Berkeley.[11] Under grants from the National Science Foundation, the University's Survey Research Center is seeking to develop model social indicators in three subject-matter ar-

10. *The National Assessment of Educational Progress* (Washington, D.C.: U.S. Government Printing Office, 1975).
11. J. Merrill Shanks is Principal Investigator of the larger social indicators project.

eas—racial prejudice, political alienation, and the status of women—and is also working to advance the general methodology of social indicators measurement. The larger Center program was launched in the belief that one way to move the social indicator movement forward is through projects that demonstrate the feasibility and utility of social indicators for studying the quality of life in the society.

Racial prejudice was chosen as a topic for such an attempted demonstration because it continues to be among the nation's virulent social diseases. Moreover, more so than in many other subject matter areas, the quest to understand the nature and etiology of racial prejudice has been hampered by the absence of time-series data. There has been no way to assess the direction and extent of change in racial prejudice, nor to test theory about the sources of change. Thus there is the promise that the development of social indicators of racial prejudice will serve both public policy and academic goals.

What follows is a report on our endeavors to develop social indicators of racial prejudice or, as the task was later redefined, to comprehend the anatomy of white racial attitudes.[12] We chose a chronological form for several reasons. First, the ideas that originally informed our project were modified as the project proceeded. Documenting the modifications as they evolved was deemed an important demonstration of the interplay in research between ideas and data. Second, the chronological form recommended itself for instructional reasons. We are under no illusions that we made all the right decisions as we proceeded. Still, other students of race relations, especially young research workers, may find it useful to see how the research project unfolded step by step. Third, we wanted to demonstrate

12. The following dissertations are also products of the Social Indicators of Racial Prejudice project: Richard Alexander Apostle, "White Racial Perspectives in the United States," Ph.D. dissertation, Department of Sociology, University of California, Berkeley, 1975; and Hilda Marijean Ferguson Suelzle, "Social Indicators of White Racial Attitudes," Ph.D. dissertation, Department of Sociology, University of California, Berkeley, 1977.

the difficulties that can arise in developing social indicators. There are lessons to be learned from our experience, we thought, for social indicator development generally.

Our first efforts were given to concept specification; that is, at the outset, we tried to identify exactly what racial prejudice means.

Concept Specification

On what grounds is it justifiable to conclude that a person is racially prejudiced? Posing the question this way assumes that there are some people who are prejudiced and some who are free of prejudice. An alternative approach might be to assume that people vary as to the degree of their prejudice. With this assumption, the question becomes how to determine the degree of a person's prejudice. A third possibility is that distinctions in kind need to be made rather than, or in addition to, distinctions in degree. This approach would apply if, irrespective of whether some individuals are found to be free of prejudice, those who exhibit it do so in distinctly different ways. A fourth possibility is that prejudice is not a defensible social science concept and that another construct must be substituted for it to describe how racial groups relate to one another in America.

If we look to the literature, it is almost immediately evident that the use of the term *prejudice* is controversial.[13] It is uniformly acknowledged that the term is pejorative. For some, this connotation rules out the term for social scientific use. Most often, among those who hold this

13. Especially important to codifying the work done on prejudice have been B. M. Kramer, "Dimension of Prejudice," *Journal of Psychology* 27 (1949):348–451; J. Harding, B. Kutner, H. Prochansky, and I. Chein, "Prejudice and Ethnic Relations," in G. Lindzey, ed., *Handbook of Social Psychology*, vol. 2 (Cambridge, Mass.: Addison-Wesley, 1954), pp. 1021–1061; J. Harding, H. Prochansky, B. Kutner, and I. Chein, "Prejudice and Ethnic Relations," in Lindzey, ed., *Handbook of Social Psychology*, 2nd ed., vol. 5 (Reading, Mass.: Addison-Wesley, 1969), pp. 1–76; and Howard J. Ehrlich, *The Social Psychology of Prejudice* (New York: John Wiley, 1973).

view, *racial attitudes* is substituted for *racial prejudice*. For other researchers, social science cannot be value free; therefore, for them it is not an obstacle that *prejudice* connotes something undesirable so long as it is investigated with unbiased methods.

While disagreeing about the use of the term *prejudice*, proponents of the two approaches address problems of conception and measurement in similar ways. This similarity is explained by the fact that those who study racial attitudes distinguish between positive and negative attitudes, which is not very different from distinguishing between prejudiced attitudes and unprejudiced ones. In the following discussion, we use the term *prejudice* in reviewing past work on conceptualization and measurement.[14]

Investigators of prejudice overwhelmingly reject a specification that simply classifies persons as prejudiced or unprejudiced. It is uniformly acknowledged that people may be more or less prejudiced, with the question left open, or subjected to empirical resolution, of whether there is anyone who is not prejudiced at all. At the same time, it is recognized that prejudice may be expressed in more than one way. The identified modes of expression have been labeled the cognitive, affective, and conative.[15] All the

14. It will be noted that the rather voluminous literature on racism is not cited in this discussion. Virtually none of this literature is germane because it is concerned with racism at the societal or institutional rather than the individual level. No attempt is made to classify individuals according to the extent or character of their racism. Included among well-known works on racism that do not address the task of concept specification at the individual level, if they address it at all, are Jacques Barzun, *Race, A Study in Superstition* (New York: Harcourt, Brace, 1937); Pierre L. van den Berghe, *Race and Ethnicity, Essays in Comparative Sociology* (New York: Basic Books, 1970); Robert Blauner, *Racial Oppression in America* (New York: Harper and Row, 1972); Michael Banton and Jonathan Harwood, *The Race Concept* (New York: Praeger, 1975); and Oliver C. Cox, *Race Relations, Elements and Social Dynamics* (Detroit: Wayne State University Press, 1976). Perhaps the major exception to this general tendency is David T. Wellman's *Portraits of White Racism* (Cambridge: Cambridge University Press, 1977), which does examine the racist attitudes of individuals and which we shall have occasion to cite as the discussion proceeds.

15. Harding et al.

ways prejudice may be expressed have been judged classifiable into one of these three types.

At the cognitive level, prejudice has been judged to be indicated principally by the harboring of negative beliefs (stereotypes) about an out-group. Negative feelings about out-group members are held to constitute prejudice at the affective level. Conatively expressed prejudice has been identified where there is a willingness to engage in discriminatory behavior towards members of an out-group. Although not the equivalent of discriminatory behavior itself, this latter form of prejudice is the set of ideas and attitudes that countenance discrimination.

Our initial concern was to assess the suitability of this specification of prejudice for our research aims. To begin with, the omission of discriminatory behavior suited us. While we wanted our measure of prejudice to be a good predictor of discrimination, we saw prejudice as attitudinal and discrimination as behavioral and felt the distinction was worth retaining. Moreover, we saw no way to measure discriminatory behavior through a research instrument administered by an interviewer or through a self-administered questionnaire.

Of the three dimensions of prejudice identified in past research, we chose to include the cognitive and the conative but to omit the affective. We acknowledge that whites can be distinguished from one another with respect to their emotional responses to blacks. Moreover, it is possible that people may feel prejudiced toward blacks while rejecting prejudice intellectually. However, feelings are difficult to measure even in a laboratory situation. There are presently no means for doing so accurately in an interview or questionnaire, and we did not feel ourselves equipped to develop such a measure.

With respect to our decision to retain the cognitive component in our own efforts to measure prejudice, we elected, because we believe it makes for greater clarity of expression, to employ the term *perceptions* rather than *cognition* to describe what is to be measured. By perceptions, we include individuals' ideas about similarities and dissimilarities between blacks and whites in American society. Thus, the term is used not in a literal psychological sense, but rather to refer to what people *believe, think,* and *conceive* racial differences to be.

Among investigators whose work has focused on measuring the cognitive element in prejudice, an underlying assumption is that racial prejudice is the harboring of negative and presumably false perceptions of blacks. Many measures of prejudice are grounded in this and the additional assumption that the degree of prejudice is a function of the number of racial stereotypes and, sometimes, the intensity with which these opinions are held.

Among well-known measures of prejudice based on the relative tendency of subjects to engage in negative racial stereotyping are Katz and Braly's Measure of Racial Stereotyping, Schuman and Harding's Scale of Prejudice and Rationality, and Matthews and Prothro's Racial Stereotype Index.[16] Sometimes, as for example in the Matthews and Prothro index, the degree of prejudice is determined by simply adding up the number of negative stereotypes attributed to blacks. In other instances, as with the Schuman and Harding scale, the mode of scale construction takes into account the possible accuracy of the stereotypes. This adjustment is made by distinguishing between the accept-

16. Daniel Katz and Kenneth Braly, "Racial Stereotypes of One Hundred College Students," *Journal of Abnormal and Social Psychology,* no. 28 (October–December, 1933):280–290; Daniel Katz and Kenneth Braly, "Racial Prejudice and Racial Stereotypes," *Journal of Abnormal and Social Psychology* 30 (July–September 1935): 175–193; Howard Schuman and John Harding, "Prejudice and the Norm of Rationality," *Sociometry* 27 (September 1964):353–371; D. R. Matthews and J. W. Prothro, *Negroes and the New Southern Politics* (New York: Harcourt, Brace and World, 1966). See also Angus Campbell, *White Attitudes toward Black People* (Ann Arbor: Institute for Social Research, University of Michigan, 1971).

ance of "rational" positive or negative ascriptions of blacks and "irrational" ascriptions. Still, however sophisticated the measure, the common assumption is to associate negative ascription with prejudice.

Stereotyping has also been the grounds for judging prejudice in studies using less refined measures. For example, national polling data have been used to demonstrate a reduction of prejudice in the United States based on the evidence that the proportion of whites who accept the stereotype that blacks are inferior to whites has declined.[17]

For our purposes, it seemed self-evident that how racial differences are perceived must be taken into account in any measure of prejudice we developed. Clearly, what whites think about blacks is partly made up of how, if at all, they perceive blacks to be different from whites. For theoretical as well as practical reasons, however, we were extremely wary of relying exclusively on a perception-based measure.

First of all, unlike many past investigators, we saw no reason to ignore the possible truth of negative ascriptions.[18] Doing so could create the anomaly of an accurate perception of group differences being labeled prejudiced and an inaccurate one, unprejudiced. For example, is the perception that in America blacks on the average are more

17. Paul B. Sheatsley, "White Attitudes toward the Negro," *Daedalus* 95 (Winter 1966):217–238.

18. Early investigators of stereotypes, while recognizing that they are not necessarily false in particular instances, took the position that they are false as generalizations. For example, in an article, "An Experimental Study of Some Problems Relating to Stereotypes," *Archives of Psychology*, 270 (June 1942), Nathan Schoenfeld concluded that the demonstration of personal name stereotypes—Cuthbert is a "sissy," Agatha is middle-aged, Richard is good-looking—proved that not every stereotype necessarily depends on a kernel of truth. Otto Klineberg in a monograph, *Tensions Affecting International Understanding*, Social Science Research Council Bulletin no. 62 (New York, 1950), cites studies that revealed the development of stereotypes independently of any factual basis. The conclusion was drawn that rather than examine stereotypes for their truth content, investigators should treat the stereotype itself as a real psychological phenomenon.

likely than whites to get into trouble with the police prejudice or an accurate perception of a fact of contemporary
life?

But once this matter of a perception's truth or falsity is
raised, new problems arise. Often the evidence necessary
for judging objectively how much truth there is to a perception does not exist. Just what constitutes "objective"
evidence is also ambiguous. Perceptions may be true in
some settings and not in others. Unless the setting is taken
into account—and often this is not possible—it is difficult
to judge whether the harboring of a negative perception
constitutes prejudice, accurate perception, both, or neither.[19]

Presuming such problems were resolvable, the additional weakness of relying exclusively on a perception-based
measure, at least to develop social indicators, is that stereotypes are subject to change without underlying attitudes
necessarily being affected. A decline in the acceptance of
one stereotype may merely be the result of another one
coming into vogue; for example, the decline in the incidence of the stereotype that blacks are inferior to whites
was accompanied by an increase in the stereotype that
blacks are militant. Under such circumstances it is difficult
to decide—on the basis of changes in the acceptance of
negative perceptions alone—whether prejudice has increased, decreased, or remained the same.[20]

19. Stereotypes, it is to be recognized, are sometimes expressed in relative and sometimes in absolute terms. The possibility that a "kernel of truth"
exists in a stereotype would appear to be greater where the stereotype is
stated in relative rather than absolute terms. However, from a measurement
point of view, to rely on a research instrument built exclusively to determine
the extent to which absolutely stated stereotypes are accepted would produce more problems than it would solve. Respondents who acknowledged
relative differences but denied that they were absolute would score as unprejudiced no matter how negative their relative perceptions may be.

20. A further problem with relying on perception-based measures of
prejudice is that the meaning of a stereotype may change over time. For
example, to perceive blacks as aggressive may not have the same meaning
during a period of racial calm as during a period of racial strife. In their

The weaknesses of perception-based measures of prejudice cannot be entirely compensated for by attending to the conative, or what we shall hereafter call the prescriptive, component. In a number of well-known scales or indices, prejudice is judged according to the extent to which subjects are willing to countenance discriminatory behavior toward blacks and/or to reject actions whose effect would be to help reduce discrimination. Perhaps the best known of such scales is the Ethnocentrism Scale developed by Adorno et al. in connection with their study of the authoritarian personality and the Bogardus Social Distance Scale.[21]

The Ethnocentrism Scale is intended as a general measure of prejudice, although a subset of its items is directed to tapping racial prejudice. As can be seen from the selection of racial items from this scale reproduced below, subjects are asked essentially to choose between tolerating or disapproving of discrimination.

> Negroes have their rights, but it is best to keep them in their own districts and to prevent too much contact with whites.

> It would be a mistake ever to have Negroes for foremen and leaders over whites.

---

analysis of the Detroit area data from 1956 to 1971, Duncan, Schuman, and Duncan observe that variation in answers to the same question may be due to changes in underlying attitudes, to changes in the meaning of the question over time, or to both. See Otis Dudley Duncan, Howard Schuman, and Beverly Duncan, *Social Change in a Metropolitan Community* (New York: Russell Sage Foundation, 1973).

21. T. W. Adorno, Else Frenkel-Brunswik, Daniel J. Levinson, and R. Nevitt Sanford, *The Authoritarian Personality*, pts. 1 and 2 (New York: John Wiley, 1950); Emory S. Bogardus, "Measuring Social Distances," *Journal of Applied Sociology* (March–April 1925):299–308. It is also to be noted that among more recent efforts to assess racial prejudice, there is a tendency to rely on questions that are prescription- rather than perception-based. See especially the questions on prejudice asked in National Opinion Research Center, University of Chicago, *General Social Surveys, 1972–78, Cumulative Codebook*, distributed by Roper Public Opinion Research Center. See also Campbell.

Manual labor and unskilled jobs seem to fit the Negro mentality and ability better than more skilled and responsible work.

The Social Distance Scale also represents an attempt to get at the prescriptive or conative component of prejudice. Unlike the Ethnocentrism Scale, which deals primarily with social policy questions, the Social Distance Scale taps prejudice in terms of what individuals are willing or unwilling to do by way of personal interaction with members of an out-group. Sometimes implicitly and sometimes explicitly, measures combine indications of both negative perceptions and negative prescriptions. Note, for example, the last item from the Ethnocentrism Scale quoted above. Its acceptance would imply both the negative perception—blacks are mentally deficient and have less ability than whites—and the negative prescription—blacks should be kept in low-status occupations.

Prescription-based measures of prejudice ordinarily have greater face validity than perception-based measures; that is, what constitutes a prejudiced response and an unprejudiced one is less ambiguous in prescription-based than perception-based measures. This is because items in prescription-based measures are invariably matters of opinion. In perception-based measures, as we have already indicated, it is often unclear whether the items are opinions or facts.

With both perception-based and prescription-based measures, it is virtually impossible to invent items that are not time-bound. The items cited above from the Ethnocentrism Scale, for example, are very old-fashioned. That items get dated are signs, of course, that changes are taking place. But does the impression that the Ethnocentrism items are out of date mean that there has been a decline in tolerance of discrimination since the late 1940s when the items were formulated, or is the explanation simply that modes of discrimination have changed?

To be used as a social indicator, any measure of prejudice should include means to assess how whites perceive
blacks as well as how whites respond to discrimination
against blacks. But is this information enough to enable
one to infer a person's degree of racial prejudice? We
thought not. Our reservations stemmed, in part, from the
just mentioned difficulty that perceptions and prescriptions may change without signifying a change in basic
racial attitudes. We were concerned also about how to construct a perception-based measure that would overcome
the truth-content problem, and we were disturbed that
prescription-based measures appeared to tap the consequences of prejudice more than the phenomenon itself.

The Explanatory Component

At this point in our deliberations, we were guided by
some insights gained from an earlier study of prejudice
among adolescents on which one of us had been engaged.[22]
The result of that study, addressed to adolescent anti-Semitism as well as racial prejudice, suggested that the ways
people respond to an out-group are less dependent on
perceived differences than on how the perceived differences are explained.[23] Thus, for example, if blacks are per-

22. Charles Y. Glock, Robert Wuthnow, Jane Allyn Piliavin, and Metta
Spencer, *Adolescent Prejudice* (New York: Harper and Row, 1975). The present
inquiry was also informed by earlier work of the second author on the role
ideas about the way reality is structured have played in maintaining social
stability and in fostering social change. See Charles Y. Glock, "Images of
Man and Public Opinion," *Public Opinion Quarterly* (Winter 1964); Afterword
in Earl R. Babbie, *Science and Morality in Medicine* (Berkeley and Los Angeles:
University of California Press, 1970); "Images of 'God,' Images of Man, and
the Organization of Social Life," *Journal for the Scientific Study of Religion* no.
11, 1 (Spring 1972); and "Consciousness among Contemporary Youth: An
Interpretation," in Charles Y. Glock and Robert N. Bellah, eds., *The New
Religious Consciousness* (Berkeley and Los Angeles: University of California
Press, 1976).
23. The explanatory component of prejudice, we learned later, has also
been identified by Donald T. Campbell, "Stereotypes and the Perception of

ceived as lazy, the attitude indicated by the perception is quite different if the laziness is accounted for as an innate black character trait than if it is understood to be the result of blacks having been denied for many generations access to opportunities to achieve.

It is probably true, as the earlier study suggests, that outright negative perceptions that have no genuine empirical support—that blacks are lazy, for example, or that they are sloppy or untrustworthy compared with whites— are likely to be explained in racist terms. But the correspondence between such perceptions and the way they are explained is not perfect. Sometimes negative perceptions are not accompanied by racist explanations. By examining

---

Group Differences," *American Psychologist* 22 (October 1967):817–829; and by Henry Tafjel, "Cognitive Aspects of Prejudice," *Journal of Social Issues* 25 (Autumn 1969):79–87. In neither article is there an attempt to specify types of explanations. The explanatory component is also implicit in William Ryan's *Blaming the Victim* (New York: Random House, 1971). The burden of Ryan's book is that the privileged in society are able to live comfortably with poverty and discrimination because they consider these phenomena to be caused by their victims. In effect, "the poor are poor because they choose to be poor," and "blacks could be as successful as whites if only they would try." Ryan does not consider possible other explanations that individuals may hold to account for poverty and discrimination, a task which is central to our own work. Also of relevance is the already mentioned book by David Wellman, *Portraits of White Racism.* Wellman's principal theme is that, as he puts it, "how people explain [racial inequality] is at the heart of racial thinking" (p. 37). This theme is pursued principally through the medium of indepth interviews with whites about their responses to racial inequality. Like Ryan, Wellman does not specify the range of explanations that Americans invoke to account for racial inequality. The explanatory theme has also been pursued in studies of poverty but again without a systematic effort to order the range of alternative ways in which poverty is explained. (See Joan Huber and William Form, *Income and Ideology: An Analysis of the American Political Formula*, [New York: The Free Press, 1973] and Joe R. Feagin, Charles Tilly, and Constance W. Williams, *Subsidizing the Poor: A Boston Housing Experiment*, [Lexington, Ma.: D.C. Heath, 1972].) Attribution theory in cognitive psychology has also given attention to how particular forms of behavior are accounted for. However, the phenomena which subjects have been asked to explain has been primarily the behavior of individuals (for example, why a child acts aggressively towards another child), rather than social differences. To our knowledge, no effort has been made in attribution research to identify the causal agents which are operative in the explanation of racial differences.

explanations as well as perceptions, investigators can determine the amount of correspondence.

A more important advantage of including the explanatory component, the earlier study suggests, is that knowing how a perception is accounted for makes it less crucial
to establish the accuracy of the perception. Even a clearly
false negative perception is subject to an explanation that
may indicate a positive rather than a negative attitude. The
person in the example just cited who attributes a perception of black laziness to white oppression is not expressing
a hostile racial attitude. Moreover, knowing how racial
differences are explained is also helpful in interpreting
attitudes in cases where perceptions can be shown to be
true—for example, that black teenagers do less well in
school on the average than white teenagers.

In the earlier study the discovery of the importance of
what we shall call *explanatory modes* was serendipitous; it
grew out of research findings rather than being built into
the study design. Moreover, the discovery was made too
late in the research process to enable the researchers to
explore, and hence to specify, the full range of explanatory
modes that accompany the perception of group differences. It was clear that one mode of accounting for racial
differences is a genetic one—"Racial differences are a result of the genetic superiority of whites over blacks." It
was also evident that for the teenagers studied the principal counterpart of the genetic mode was one in which
racial differences were conceived of as deriving from some
combination of cultural, historical, and social factors. The
earlier study did not make clear if there were other modes
of explaining racial differences.

Summing Up

By this point in our evolving project we had specified
that racial prejudice—or more accurately stated, perhaps,

racial attitudes—is composed of three elements—perceptions, explanations, and prescriptions. In effect, white racial attitudes are made up of how black-white differences are perceived (perceptions) and accounted for (explanations) and how the deprived status of blacks in the society is responded to (prescriptions).

This distinction among perceptions, explanations, and prescriptions has not informed previous research on prejudice. Consequently, no studies have sought simultaneous measurement of the three components and no evidence exists about the interconnections among the three. At the stage of research we are now describing, our opinion was that in the socialization process racial differences are probably perceived before there is any attempt to explain them. In turn, prescriptions probably follow after individuals decide upon explanations. During their lives, we presumed, individuals will have formulated for themselves, however tentatively, crudely, and unconsciously, answers to the questions that are raised by the existence of racial differences: What are they, how did they come about, and what, if anything, is to be done about them? We suspected that answers would be found to vary widely and to be expressed more articulately by some than by others. We also assumed that in all settings in which racial differences are salient—which in the United States would be virtually everywhere—all three components of the set would be present. A possible exception, of course, would be people who honestly perceive no differences between the races. For them, obviously, there would be no occasion to address the second and third questions. If they existed in the United States, such persons would be extremely rare, we suspected, and would be found principally among persons living in isolation from the larger society, and among very young children.

At this early stage, we judged explanations to be the most fundamental and central element of the attitude set for social indicator purposes. We arrived at this conclusion because (1) we felt that knowing how racial differences are understood is necessary in order to interpret the meaning of particular perceptions; (2) we believed that prescriptions follow from explanations rather than the other way around; and (3) we conceived that a change in explanation, unlike a change in perception or prescription, would unambiguously indicate a fundamental change in racial attitude.

The specification of racial attitudes as comprising perceptions, explanations, and prescriptions left unanswered the question of what constitutes prejudice. We rejected the conventional wisdom that prejudice consists of the harboring of negative perceptions or beliefs about an out-group. We also denied that it can be judged, for social indicator purposes, on the basis of a person's tolerance of existing discriminatory practice (prescriptions). We suggested that in order to comprehend a person's racial attitudes it is necessary to take his or her explanation of racial differences into account. As yet, however, we had not addressed the question of whether some explanations can be judged unambiguously to constitute prejudice and others to indicate its absence.

Chapter 2 *Modes of Explaining Racial Differences*

Do people try to account for the racial differences they perceive? If so, what modes of explanation do they come up with? Are the explanations idiosyncratic to each person or do they encompass only a limited range of alternatives? To answer these questions, we conducted exploratory in-depth interviews with more than 200 persons from various walks of life residing in the East Bay of the San Francisco metropolitan area. No strict sampling scheme was followed in selecting respondents. Rather, those conducting the interviews were instructed to choose their respondents so as to ensure some distribution by age, sex, and educational status.[1] At this early point in the research process, the aim was to establish the existence and to determine the range of explanatory modes rather than to estimate their frequency in any population. That latter task would follow, should the exploratory interviews demonstrate the validity of the explanatory-mode concept.

The interview guide called for the interviewers to pursue three themes in sequence: (1) respondents' *perceptions* of racial differences, (2) their *explanations* of how these differences came about, and (3) their *prescriptions* for what,

1. Interviewers were instructed that half their interviews were to be with women, half with men; half with persons 40 years of age and older, half with younger persons; and half with persons with more than a high school education, half with less educated persons.

if anything, should be done to bring about greater racial equality. Interviewers were instructed to introduce each of these themes by asking a very general question. For example, to introduce the first theme (perception of differences), a suggested question was "How, if at all, do you think black people living in the United States are different from the white population?" To initiate discussion of the second theme (explanations), it was suggested to interviewers that they say, "You've mentioned a number of different ways in which blacks and whites differ from each other. How do you account for these differences? What brought them about?" Finally, on the third theme (prescriptions), the following question was recommended as a way to get started: "What, if anything, do you think ought to be done to bring about greater equality between the races?"

At the outset, the interviewer explored each theme with respondents in as nondirective a manner as possible. Responses to the first question, for example, were followed by such nondirective probes as "Anything else?" or "Do you have anything more to add?" Or the interviewer might remain silent for a moment to give the respondent time to think of additional things to say. Once questioning along such lines was no longer productive, interviewers were instructed to engage in more directed probing in relation to the three themes.

When respondents no longer had anything spontaneous to say about their *perceptions* of racial differences, they were asked about possible differences in areas they had not mentioned. Thus, for example, if respondents had not mentioned differences in income, housing, or intelligence in the nondirected part of the interview, they were asked whether or not they believed the two races to be different in such respects and, if so, how.[2]

2. One of the readers of the manuscript for the University of California Press raised the possible objection that the directed questioning about per-

Probing about *explanations* was directed at learning what respondents believed to be the original source of racial differences. Interviewers were cautioned not to be satisfied with responses such as "The reason black youngsters do not do as well in school as white youngsters is that black families are less encouraging of their children's education than white parents are," or "The reason blacks are more likely to engage in crime than whites is because they are discriminated against in getting jobs." Responses of this kind were to be followed up by such questions as "Well, how does it happen that black families are less supportive of their children's education than white families?" or "Why is it that blacks are discriminated against in the job market?" Probing along such lines was to be repeated until respondents offered an explanation of the origin of racial differences or until, in the interviewer's judgment, they had really expressed all they had to say on the subject.

Questioning about *prescriptions* also called for the interviewer to ask how respondents felt about relevant matters that they had not mentioned spontaneously in response to nondirective questions. Thus, for example, if respondents had not brought up school integration as a means to help bring about greater racial equality, they were asked whether they favored or opposed school integration.

Interviews lasted from twenty minutes to more than an hour. They were spotty in quality since the student interviewers varied both in experience and conscientiousness. All in all, however, as the following report on the results

---

ceptions may have influenced the respondents' later formulations of "explanations." This was not a matter that we considered in formulating the interview guide; nor did we engage in any pre-test to try to find out what the effects, if any, might be. Comparing the results obtained from persons who were subjected to varied amounts of directed questioning about perceptions, we were unable to discern any differences in explanations attributable to the amount of directed questioning. This comparison does not resolve the matter entirely, of course, and if further inquiries are conducted along these lines, more systematic effort to assess the effects of directed questioning would be called for.

attests, the interviews served the purposes for which they were undertaken.

Identifying Explanatory Modes

The exploratory interviews make evident that people do hold certain explanations—however crude and unsophisticated—for the racial differences they perceive. Several respondents denied vehemently that the races were in any way different, thus making it impossible to question them about the sources of racial differences. With these few exceptions, however, all respondents both perceived differences and were able to offer some accounting of how these differences came about. The same perceived differences were often explained in quite different ways. Even perceptions that on the surface cast blacks in a negative light were explained in different ways.

The mode of explanation, it was discovered, is dependent on the forces conceived of as controlling agents. On the basis of the interviews, six controlling processes or, as we have come to call them, explanatory modes, were identified. Two of these modes attribute black-white differences to the operation of forces beyond human control. The first of these we termed the *supernatural mode*. God is believed to be the creator of racial differences. The following quotations taken from the interviews illustrate the ways in which a supernatural explanation is expressed.

> Negroes are just different. I don't know why but I suppose it is something God saw fit to do. God believes in differences.

* * *

Interviewer: Do you think black people are just as well off as white people?

Respondent: No.

I: What do you think keeps them from being as well off?

R: They don't want to work for anything. Oh we got some good working colored guys at the plant but most of them are lazy niggers.

I: Why do you think they are this way?

R: They just are. It's the way they were put together.

I: How were they put together like this?

R: That's just how the race is. That's how God made them.   *   *   *
Well, it goes back to the Bible, where the good angels were colored white, whereas the devil is black. Black was related to evil. So you see, it goes back a long way in history.

*   *   *

R: God made the races different.

I: Why?

R: For his own reasons which he hasn't revealed to us.

A second force beyond human control that some respondents consider to be responsible for racial differences is the laws of nature. Although respondents did not use this terminology, we infer that that is what is meant when someone asserts that "blacks are by nature different than whites," or conveys the idea that the differences are genetic in more pejorative terms. The *genetic mode*, as we shall call it, is illustrated by the following exchanges between interviewers and respondents.

I: What do you feel are the essential differences between the races?

R: Whites are obviously of the higher intellectual quality. This is proved by the fact that mostly whites have high governmental positions. Blacks tend to be lazy and live on welfare. They seem to have little intellectual capacity except in athletics. Orientals are quiet and work hard. There are definite physical differences.

I: Are you saying that whites are generally superior to minority groups?

R: Oh, certainly. All the great thinkers have been white. Leaders too.

*   *   *

I: Why aren't they [blacks] ambitious?

R: It's in their genes—their makeup. Blacks have no in-
born achievement. They are not energetic, not self-starters.

*   *   *

I: Generally, do you think colored people are poorer
than white people?

R: Yes, they are.

I: Why do you think this is so?

R: They haven't had the advantages that other people
have had. Color is more obvious than being Jewish. Now
they are getting better off, though. Now they are seen on
TV, the radio, all over.

I: So, it's because they haven't had the same advantages
that blacks are different from you or me?

R: Well, they say it's only skin color, but in the hospitals
they can tell a difference in the blood.

I: Then you think there is something different in their
blood?

R: Well, as a race, they are inferior.

Whereas both the supernatural and genetic modes conceive of racial differences as innate, a third mode, which
we called the *individualistic mode,* conceives of differences
as being under the individual's control. The key assumption underlying this perspective is that everyone possesses
extensive free will and has the capacity, consequently, to
control his or her own destiny. Black-white differences are
judged to be the result of blacks failing relative to whites to
use their free will to better themselves. Common to the
observations of those who use this individualistic mode of
explanation are such statements as the following: "If I can
make it so can they"; "Blacks would be as well off as
whites if only they would try harder"; and "Some blacks
make it; they all could if they wanted to." Here are two
examples of the individualistic mode, expressed in more
detail.

I [after respondent has observed that whites generally fare better in American society than blacks]: I wonder if you could tell me why it is like that.

R: Well, that's because most of them are so lazy. It's their own fault that they don't have so much. Their blood is just as red as ours; the only difference is that they have darker skins.

I: Are they lazy because they are colored or does it have anything to do with their race?

R: No, there are some white folks that are just as lazy. It depends on the individual. Those colored folks down by the river don't have to be there. They can help themselves if they want. It is just that they are too lazy to do it.

*   *   *

I: So you think that the best qualified person should get the job. Why would you say blacks are less qualified to take these jobs than whites?

R: Well, if I answered that, I probably would be accused of being discriminating but, by God, it goes back to the old saying that most . . . Well, the new ones coming up today aren't trying to work and don't want to work on something that takes manual labor. But, as to why they aren't qualified . . . well, they should be. Let me reverse it—why shouldn't they be as well qualified? They have the equal opportunity for education as anybody else. Now if they fail you would say the same thing for a white boy. If a white boy fails it is because he lacks ambition and he's lazy. . . . But if a black boy or man fails you can't say those things because you'd be discriminating. But it is the same blessed thing—he just doesn't want to do it. He has got the same opportunity as everybody else. . . . There should be no reason why he can't. My only explanation is to forget the race on that issue. It's the same reason for both races—they're not trying hard enough.

It might seem that someone who perceives blacks as not trying as hard as whites and explains this condition as something blacks decide on for themselves would adopt another mode of explanation when asked *why* he or she thinks blacks as a group try less hard than whites as a group. Some respondents, under such probing, do acknowledge that the differences are due to innate racial differences, but others do not, insisting to the end that it is for the individual to decide and that race makes no difference.

In effect, respondents who are this strongly committed to an individualistic perspective refuse to acknowledge the possibility that other factors limit the individual's free choice. This tenacity is illustrated by the respondent just cited, who, when questioned further by the interviewer, continued to assert that not trying harder is a matter of individual blacks failing to make the "right" choices.

I: You think, then, that if they really wanted to, blacks could attain better jobs and living conditions?

R: Yes, I would say that probably before my time that there was discrimination . . . I don't really know; I wasn't there. That is why to accuse me of discrimination when I don't know what it is, is wrong to me. But during my lifetime I think the Negro, if he wanted to, could have progressed a lot more rapidly if he had the ambition to do so.

I: Then, it is not genetic, it is rather . . .

R: How you apply yourself. You don't acquire intelligence by going out and yelling about it. You have to put a little effort into it. If you are too lazy to go to school you won't get educated, and that goes for everybody.

I: You have stressed the blacks not applying themselves and not making use of their faculties. Why don't they apply themselves more?

R: Why did some of the Southern whites do the same thing? Maybe it was just hereditary. Maybe it was just laziness on their part. I don't know. To call it hereditary for a Southern white is all right but to call it hereditary for a black, then I'm prejudiced. I would say that in the past I don't think they had the ambition.

I: How much of the difference is hereditary?

R: Thirty or forty years ago I don't know. But I think now they are pretty equal now. I think it's just that blacks don't try hard enough.

Two additional explanatory modes identified from the exploratory interviews, the *radical* and the *environmental*, cite social forces as the source of racial differences. Both modes recognize the relatively deprived condition of blacks in American society and regard that deprivation as originating in slavery. They differ, however, in their interpretation of how the deprivation has been sustained over the intervening period.

From what we called the *radical* perspective, whites, especially whites in power, were the conscious perpetrators of slavery and of the oppression of blacks in America ever since. In effect, in this view, the social and economic structure has been, and continues to be, manipulated by powerful whites to keep blacks down. Implicit, if not always explicit, in this accounting of racial differences is the belief that whites conspire to ensure that social arrangements keep "blacks in their place." Those who adopt a radical explanation of racial differences are disposed to use terms such as *oppression, racism,* and *suppression* to convey their understanding of racial inequality, as is seen in the following quotations from some of the interviews.[3]

Yes, all failings in the black community are directly attributable to white oppression.

People in power are the white racists. It's these people in power that are making decisions that are f_____ minorities.

The whites have exploited blacks since the beginning of slavery.

The power structure, of course, being white, helps perpetuate all these myths because it becomes very convenient for them to do so, both economically and socially. So the economic exploitation follows directly from the structure of the American capitalistic system.

3. We experienced difficulty in finding an appropriate label for this mode. We considered calling it the *conspiratorial mode* but finally rejected that label because it might have suggested that those adopting this mode uniformly conceived whites to be consciously conspiring to keep blacks down. The term *radical* was finally settled upon as a compromise.

In contrast to these are respondents who, while they see social forces at the root of racial differences, do not interpret those forces as being manipulated consciously by whites to maintain their relatively privileged positions in society. Rather, blacks and whites are both seen as being subject to these social currents. Poor whites and poor blacks both have to struggle to get ahead, and social conditions make it difficult for them to do so. That whites are generally better off than blacks is traced to slavery, and those in this mode condemn slavery. They are not disposed, however, to blame succeeding generations of whites, especially this one, for black difficulties. On the other hand, those holding this view do not accept the status quo as inevitable. Rather, they believe that greater racial equality can be achieved as we come to understand better the social bases of inequality. The following excerpts from some of the interviews exemplify how this explanatory mode, hereafter called the *environmental mode*, is expressed.

> The living conditions of blacks are well below standard, with most living in rat-infested one-room tenements. Blacks are only able to get the most menial jobs and consequently can find no way out of the ghetto. . . .
>
> * * *
>
> *I:* How do you think these differences you've mentioned come about?
>
> *R:* I think it is a social thing. Society has brought it about.
>
> *I:* What do you mean?
>
> *R:* Naturally a lower-class person doesn't have money for medical things or a clean house and they're going to live in filth. . . . I would say it goes back to blacks being lower class. * * *
>
> *I:* Why do you think that blacks on the average are poorer than whites?
>
> *R:* Formal education has failed to achieve its goals for both blacks and whites. . . . But I feel that it has failed more for blacks. Part of this is also informal education which

educates the preschool child and, naturally, the more educated the parents, the more varied the environment the child will get.   *   *   *

I: You've said that blacks have less education, less income, worse jobs, and can't get as good homes as white people can. Why do you think that blacks are less well off in these ways?

R: Well, I think it's one of those things that just sort of happened. Back in the days when the black man was a slave, people believed he was inferior. Things like that are just slow to change.   *   *   *

I: What are the reasons for differences in the education of blacks as compared to whites?

R: I think in the past it has been a result of segregated schools. The black kids were going to poorly funded, ill-equipped schools which provided them with a poor education. Integration of the schools has helped, but there are still some predominantly black schools in the bigger cities that face the same problems. Part of the problem is due to the training that the children get from their parents. I don't think black parents are as likely to stress the importance of a good education as white parents are.

                              *   *   *

I: If blacks do not have equal opportunity, why do you think that is?

R: This is a very complex question. They don't have equal opportunity because of their origin in the United States. The blacks were brought here as a slave population and, unlike every other group that came to America who came here to better themselves, the blacks were imported to this country for the purpose of working as legal chattels on the plantations and in other menial jobs for white masters who owned them. So there developed in the U.S. a feeling of contempt for the black population as being people who belonged to a lesser breed outside the law. Now the blacks themselves, because of their slavery in part, developed as most people who are the subjects of discrimination do (over a period), a kind of slavish mentality and they began to acquire some of the very defects for which they were blamed by their white owners. Apart from that, in slave days the blacks were very often not permitted to marry simply because if a black couple married and had children it became much more difficult to separate them. For instance, to sell the husband into slavery to one owner and the wife to another and the children to a third meant much more friction than if they were not married and there were no family feelings. So the black family unit became very weak and when the family unit is weak the children grow up without the sense of security and affection that they need. And the result is that you have a black population which becomes rather shiftless and has no ambition. This puts the black at a disadvantage with the white in competition for jobs and then because he has no job he has to continue living under ghetto conditions. So it's a kind of vicious circle.

A sixth explanatory mode conceives of black-white differences as stemming primarily from cultural dissimilarities. Sometimes, this mode, which we call the *cultural mode*, is given expression through reference to the African roots of black culture, as compared with the European background of white culture. At other times, as in the following interview excerpt, the focus is on the difference between contemporary white and black culture.

R: . . . there are many middle-class Negroes who apparently share the same values and life styles that comprise the American middle-class myths, but undoubtedly there exists a black subculture in America, which in very many respects is in conflict with the American middle-class myth.

I: In what way is the black subculture in conflict with the American middle-class myth?

R: The black subculture isn't obsessed with the Protestant ethic. On the other hand, material possessions are very highly regarded. This in part explains the high incidence of crime and its relative respectability in the black subculture. Secondly, the black subculture emphasizes aggressiveness and physical prowess. Obviously they don't place the same values on the middle-class family structure. There seems to be no stigma attached to illegitimacy.

I: Do you think that blacks are responsible for this subculture or that this subculture would create similar conditions for other ethnic groups?

R: I don't think you can apportion blame. Usually a culture is not something consciously created nor something
created in a short period of time, and it's something that is
inherited. It's not all a result, I believe, of the white society. In fact, isn't it the case that they value black culture,
that black is beautiful? That is, they value black culture.
And I believe that many of them recognize that integration in a true sense, that is cultural integration by definition, spells doom for the black subculture.

Not all respondents fit distinctly into one explanatory
mode. Explanations sometimes included several modes,
and the most sophisticated respondents often seemed to
prefer a multi-causal explanation. When asked to choose
from among alternative explanations, however, most individuals were able to select one dominant explanatory
mode.

In sum, the in-depth interviews support the assumption
that people try to explain the racial differences they perceive. Consequently, any effort to comprehend what was
defined earlier as the cognitive component of prejudice
must take such explanations into account.

Perceptions and Explanations

In addition to allowing us to explore the ways in which
racial differences are accounted for, the in-depth interviews also permitted us to examine how explanations and
perceptions go together and how the two, individually
and in combination, affect responses to the problem of
discrimination. To begin with, we were able to confirm
our expectation that there is not a perfect correspondence
between how racial differences are perceived and how
they are accounted for. The same perceived difference is
frequently accounted for in different ways, especially

when the social situation of blacks is perceived to be different from that of whites. Observations of the following kind are subject, by different people of course, to the whole range of explanatory modes just cited: that blacks are less well off financially than whites, that they live in poorer housing, that they more often get into trouble with the police, and that they do less well in school. When blacks are alleged to be intrinsically different from whites, the correspondence between perception and explanation appears to be somewhat greater than when the differences perceived are not intrinsic. For example, perceptions that blacks are lazier or less intelligent or less trustworthy than whites were usually, although not always, accounted for in the genetic mode.

Earlier it was speculated purely on logical grounds that in the socialization process people *observe* racial differences before attempting to explain them. Explanation, it would seem, cannot occur if there is nothing to explain. Because they were conducted at one point in time and on an adult population, the exploratory interviews afford no firm test of this speculation. However, the interviews do suggest that, once formulated, the explanatory modes within which people operate influence any further perception of racial differences. In effect, observations of differences may initially precede explanation, but once an explanation has been formulated, the process becomes interactive.

Explanations and Prescriptions

More adequate data than those yielded by these preliminary in-depth interviews were required to learn more precisely what the explanatory modes implied regarding people's responses to the problem of discrimination and the actions they would support to eliminate it. These data did afford, however, some initial insights into the policy significance of the modes. These insights are reported here in a tentative way, with the understanding that they will be checked against more adequate data as we proceed.

The interviewers were instructed to ask respondents about the kinds of governmental action they would be willing to support and what they would be willing to do on a personal basis to reduce discrimination and to help bring about greater equality between the races. Interviewers pursued the governmental theme by asking what the government might do to help reduce discrimination in employment, in education, and in housing; they approached the personal aspect by asking about support for black political candidates, intermarriage between the races, living next to a black family, and the like.

The greatest resistance to doing anything to bring about racial equality is expressed by the geneticists—those who conceive of white-black differences as genetically produced. For people in this mode the races are unequal because blacks are naturally inferior, and it is not conceivable to them that anything can or should be done to bring about greater racial equality. The geneticists are the most hostile in their response to blacks and the least likely to be sympathetic to black causes.

The supernaturalists—those who see God as the original source of racial differences—also exhibit resistance to governmental or personal efforts to bring about racial equality, but their resistance is weaker than that of the geneticists. While members of both explanatory modes consider racial differences to be innate and therefore presumably immutable, the image of God as the agent apparently encourages a more sympathetic response than when the differences are judged to be caused by the impersonal laws of nature.

The individualists—those who see individuals as having control over their own destinies—are strongly resistant to governmental efforts to improve the condition of blacks. Their view is that "blacks should pull themselves up by

their own bootstraps." More so than the geneticists, however, individualists are receptive to helping black people
who try hard and to removing laws that create artificial
barriers preventing blacks from getting ahead. Individualists express hostility to blacks whom they perceive as not
trying hard enough to improve their condition.

Those in the environmental mode—persons offering an
essentially sociological explanation of racial differences—
could be called reformist in their ideas about what might
be done to bring about racial equality. They approve of
greater governmental efforts to break down barriers and
are personally open to help bring about change. They do
not tend, however, to support compensatory programs. In
part, they may withhold such support because they don't
see themselves as responsible for the discrimination that
blacks in America have experienced historically.

Persons whose explanation of racial differences is classified as the radical mode tend to hold an almost conspiratorial theory of racial inequality. Accordingly, they tend to
adopt a more radical stance about what needs to be done.
Among all modes, the radicals are the strongest advocates
of reformulating government policy to bring about racial
equality.

The culturalists—people who believe racial differences
to be culturally based—appear to disagree among themselves more than adherents to the other modes concerning
what ought to be done about discrimination and racial
inequality. Their responses to the prescriptive questions
are divided between support for social reforms and opposition to them. The opposition comes from culturalists
who express a distinct preference for white over black
culture; the support comes either from culturalists who are
neutral in this respect or from those few whites who express a preference for black culture. For some people, a
cultural explanation for racial differences may be a means
of disguising or suppressing a more fundamental belief

that the differences are basically genetic. This ambiguity makes it difficult to establish the validity of the cultural explanation as a distinct type of explanatory mode. Whether this type should be refined or abandoned was a matter for attention as we proceeded.

Implications for Social Indicator Development

These results cast into question the desirability of retaining the term *prejudice* to designate what we hoped to measure. It was not self-evident which explanatory modes warranted the designation *prejudiced* and which *unprejudiced*. Designation could be made arbitrarily, but it was unlikely that those persons called *prejudiced* would willingly accept that designation. Moreover, given the pejorative nature of the term *prejudice*, more general objections might be raised as to its acceptability as an objective scientific concept. It seemed wise at this juncture to abandon the term *prejudice* in favor of *racial attitudes*.[4]

The exploratory interviews advanced our task of measurement by tentatively identifying what appeared to be the major modes of accounting for racial differences. They also provided some initial justification for conceiving of white racial attitudes as including elements of perception, explanation, and prescription. Still on the agenda, however, was finding reliable and valid ways of asking about the three elements, especially explanatory modes, in a structured research instrument. We also had to establish, in a more rigorous fashion than the exploratory interviews allowed, that the explanatory element is as central to the

4. We also considered the possibility of adopting the term *racism* to designate what we were seeking to measure. We decided against this term, in part because of its pejorative nature. More importantly, as was reported in a footnote to Chapter 1, investigators who have utilized the term *racism* have either not sought to specify it in a way to make it operationalizable or have adopted a specification that fails to recognize the variety of ways in which whites may respond to blacks.

measurement of white racial attitudes as we claimed. Also, we needed to give attention to determining whether modes of explaining racial differences are issue-specific or, rather, constitute ways of accounting for a wider range of phenomena. Finally, we had to establish the stability of the modes.

These tasks could have been accomplished in a variety of ways. At that point in our work, however, we had the opportunity to participate in a cross-sectional survey of the adult population of the San Francisco Bay Area. Our research group was invited to be a party to this survey and was given control over developing questions for a fifteen-minute segment of the interview schedule.

Fifteen minutes was hardly sufficient for collecting enough data for working out all our measurement problems. However, participation in the survey afforded us an efficient means of finding out whether the conceptual ideas that had emerged from the exploratory interviews could be measured in the context of a fixed-question survey. Moreover, before committing ourselves more fully to the position that explanatory modes lie at the root of what is ordinarily meant by *prejudice*, it seemed wise to gather some quantitative evidence to support or refute that position. The next chapter reports on the results of our participation in this Bay Area Survey.

Chapter 3 *Preliminary Attempts to Measure Racial Attitudes*

Interviewing people in depth to identify their modes of explaining racial differences is a feasible procedure, as demonstrated by the results reported in Chapter 2. Is it possible to fulfill the same purpose through a limited set of questions asked uniformly of respondents in a structured survey? If so, are the modes that people adopt to explain racial differences related, in the directions suggested by the in-depth interviews, to how they respond to the social deprivations that blacks experience in American society? These were the principal questions addressed through our group's participation in the Bay Area Survey (hereafter BAS), conducted by the University of California's Survey Research Center on behalf of the larger Social Indicators project.

The BAS involved approximately 1,000 structured interviews lasting from an hour to an hour and a quarter in length with a probability sample of the adult population of the San Francisco Bay Area.[1] The three parts of the project—political alienation, status of women, and racial prejudice—were each apportioned fifteen minutes of the interview. An additional quarter hour was shared by the three subprojects to ask commonly desired background ques-

1. A fuller description of the design of the Bay Area Survey is provided in Appendix A. See also William L. Nicholls, *Bay Area Survey 2—Social Indicators Project Study Codebook* (Berkeley, Calif.: University of California Survey Research Center, 1975).

tions, mostly demographic in nature. Of the 1,000 respondents, 698 were white. Except where otherwise indicated, the analysis reported upon in this chapter is based on these white respondents.[2]

Given the time constraint, we were able to ask only a limited number of questions. Therefore, it was not expected that the BAS would solve all our measurement problems. Essentially, we hoped for some further evidence by which to judge (1) whether focusing on the *explanations* that persons give for their attitudes is a fruitful approach for understanding these attitudes, and (2) whether it is feasible to measure explanations in a structured instrument.

Asking about Explanatory Modes

In framing questions for the BAS we followed two different approaches. The first approach called for the interviewer to make the following prefatory remarks:

> We have asked questions like this of quite a few people by now, both blacks and whites, and they have given very different ideas about why on the average white people get more of the good things of life in America than black people.
>
> I will read you some of the reasons people have given, including some things that other people don't agree with at all. For each I'd like you to tell me whether you agree strongly, agree somewhat, disagree somewhat, or disagree strongly. Here are the answers on this card. [Respondent is handed cards on which the answer categories agree strongly, agree somewhat, disagree somewhat, disagree strongly are listed.]

The statements read to respondents represented an attempt to make operational the six explanatory modes identified from the in-depth interviews. After the six state-

2. Where the N for tables in this chapter is smaller than 698, it is due to missing data.

ments had been read and the respondents' answers recorded, the interviewer then went on to ask, "Which do you think is the most important reason why whites are better off than blacks?"

The first statement read to the respondent was intended to represent the radical mode of explaining racial differences. It read, "Powerful and wealthy white people purposely act to keep black people down." The second statement, "God made the races different as part of his divine plan," was designed to give those in the supernatural mode an opportunity to express themselves. The succeeding statements are recorded below together with the explanatory mode each represents in parentheses.

> It's really a matter of blacks not trying as hard as whites. If blacks tried harder they'd be just as well off.   (*Individualistic*)

> Generations of slavery and discrimination have created conditions that made it difficult for black people to work their way out of the lower class.   (*Environmental*)

> Blacks come from a less able race and this explains why blacks are not as well off as whites.   (*Genetic*)

> Black Americans teach their children values which are different from those which are required to be successful in America.   (*Cultural*)

The purpose of first asking people to express their degree of agreement with each of the six statements was to ascertain the extent to which respondents would accept more than one way of accounting for racial differences. One function of the follow-up question was to learn how many respondents would resist having to choose only one of the six explanations as paramount.

The second approach we used to ask about respondents' explanatory modes called for the interviewer to hand the respondent a card on which were set forth six different reasons why blacks do not seem to do as well on intelligence tests as whites. After respondents read the statements, they were asked, "Which statement comes closest to expressing your view of why whites tend to do better on intelligence tests than blacks?" The six statements appeared on the card in the order shown below; in the following list the explanatory mode depicted by each statement has been added in parentheses.

White people purposely design intelligence tests to favor themselves. (*Radical*)

God gave different gifts to different races for reasons we cannot understand. (*Supernatural*)

Black people score less well than white people because they do not try hard enough. (*Individualistic*)

The tests are made for middle-class white people and the tests turn out to be unfair to black people. (*Environmental*)

By nature black people are less intelligent on the average than white people. (*Genetic*)

In general black people don't put much value on doing well on intelligence tests. They're more interested in other things. (*Cultural*)

In formulating the question in this fashion, we wanted to discover, among other things, how much resistance might be generated when respondents were obliged to choose from a number of different explanations without being given the initial opportunity, as in the previously described approach, to express their relative agreement or disagreement with each individual statement.

We did not anticipate that these questions would satisfy the ultimate goal of providing a valid basis for classifying respondents by their explanatory mode. This would require experimenting with a larger number of questions in a more varied format, a task that the BAS, with its time limitation, was not suited to accomplish. We expected, however, that responses to the two questions would reveal whether a general population sample would experience discomfort or confusion in answering questions of this kind and, if it did, how much. The answers would also allow the consistency of responses and the adequacy of the question wording to be checked. In addition, answers would provide a measure of the distribution of the different explanatory modes in a meaningful population sample, which was not accomplished by the in-depth interviews.

Table 1 reports the distribution of answers by white respondents in the sample population to the question eliciting their relative agreement or disagreement with each of six statements purporting to explain why whites are better off than blacks in America.

Looking initially at the first column of Table 1, which reports the percentage expressing strong agreement with each mode statement, we see that the environmental explanation gains the greatest support (42 percent) and the genetic explanation the least (6 percent). A substantial minority strongly agree with the supernatural (21 percent) and individualistic (19 percent) explanations; the radical (11 percent) and the cultural (7 percent) explanations obtain considerably less support. Adding up the percentages in the first column produces a total of 106 percent. Making the assumption that every respondent gave at least one "strongly agree" response, this figure would suggest that only 6 percent of the respondents strongly agreed with more than one of the six explanations. Considerably greater openness to multi-causal explanation is indicated, however, upon examination of the third column of the table, which reports a subtotal of those agreeing strongly *or* moderately with each statement. The total for this column is 259 percent, signifying that, on the average, respondents expressed some agreement with close to three of the six statements.

Table 1 **Relative Agreement with Six Statements Purporting to Explain Why "White People Get More of the Good Things in Life in America than Black People"**

EXPLANATION	LEVEL OF AGREEMENT						
	Agree Strongly	Agree Somewhat	(Subtotal: Agree)	Disagree Somewhat	Disagree Strongly	Can't Say; No Answer	Total
Individualist	19%	24	(43)	26	28	3	100
Genetic	6%	17	(23)	18	55	4	100
Supernatural	21%	14	(35)	10	49	6	100
Environmental	42%	34	(76)	11	10	3	100
Radical	11%	32	(43)	29	24	4	100
Cultural	7%	32	(39)	26	14	21	100

N = 698

Some insight into the pattern of multi-causality is provided by examining in Table 2 the correlations between the degree of acceptance accorded each of the explanatory modes.

Table 2 **Correlations among Modes of Explaining Racial Differences in Socio-Economic Status**

EXPLANATIONS	EXPLANATIONS				
	Individualist	*Genetic*	*Supernatural*	*Environmental*	*Radical*
Genetic	.40				
Supernatural	.33	.31			
Environmental	−.44	−.18	−.26		
Radical	−.23	−.04	−.06	.30	
Cultural	.18	.19	.02	−.01	−.05

Correlations are Pearson's r.

Accepting an environmental explanation of racial differences is positively associated with agreeing to a radical explanation, although the correlation is only moderate in strength. Support for these two modes, however, is negatively associated with support for the remaining causal agents. The supernatural, individualistic, genetic, and cultural modes all correlate positively with each other. In each instance, the correlations are, at best, of only moderate strength; nevertheless, they indicate that some people explain racial differences in a multi-causal way.

Despite the apparent openness of some respondents to multi-causal explanation, only 3 percent of respondents balked when asked to choose the most important reason why whites are better off than blacks in America. The question asking why blacks do not seem to perform as well as whites on IQ tests was also answered without protest by more than 97 percent of respondents.

Even when formulating the two questions, we did not expect responses to them to be entirely consistent. For one thing, some discordance would occur because of the usual experience in surveys that some respondents do not pay careful attention to the interviewer's instructions or mis-understand them. For another, it seemed unlikely that in this first attempt we would succeed in portraying the ex-planatory modes in precisely equivalent ways in the two questions—a necessary condition, obviously, to allow com-plete concordance in response. Moreover, given the evi-dent disposition to multi-causal explanation on the part of some respondents, it is possible that they would choose a different mode in the two questions because they were obliged by the question form to give uni-causal responses.

Still, while we did not anticipate perfect concordance, we did expect that consistency among responses to the two questions would be considerably greater than that attribut-able to chance. Clearly, a total lack of consistency in mode responses would raise serious questions about the viability of the concept.

Table 3 affords a means to judge the degree of consisten-cy in responses. The total column reports the distribution of responses to the question asking respondents to cite the most important reason for socio-economic differences be-tween blacks and whites. The total row does the same for responses to the question on IQ. In the body of the table is reported the joint distribution of responses to the two questions. Thus, for example, 5.3 percent of all white re-spondents gave an individualistic response to both the SES question and the one on IQ. Concordant responses, located on the diagonal of the table, have been circled.

Fifty percent use the same mode in their responses to the two questions; this figure is obtained by adding up the percentages in the circled, diagonal cells. It is very unlikely that this much concordance could have occurred by chance. Still, these figures do indicate that a substantial number of people believe that socio-economic differences between blacks and whites stem from a source other than differences in IQ-test performance.

We reported these results to interviewers, asking them

Table 3   *Correspondence between Explanation of Racial Differences in Socio-Economic Status (SES) and Explanation of Racial Differences in Performance on IQ Tests*

EXPLANATION OF SES DIFFERENCES	EXPLANATIONS OF RACIAL DIFFERENCES ON IQ TESTS						
	Individualist	Genetic	Supernatural	Environmental	Radical	Cultural	Total
Individualist	5.3%	3.2	2.1	3.0	.6	5.0	19.2
Genetic	.6	1.3	.3	.7	.0	.4	3.3
Supernatural	1.9	1.1	4.0	2.0	.2	2.1	11.3
Environmental	2.7	1.9	2.9	37.2	1.2	5.3	51.2
Radical	.6	.0	.1	5.1	.8	1.3	7.9
Cultural	.8	.9	.4	3.0	.0	1.6	6.7
Total	11.9	8.4	9.8	51.0	2.8	15.7	99.6%

N = 624
χ^2 = 249.2 df = 25 p < .001

to speculate about the reasons for inconsistent responses. We also examined whether types of discrepant answers formed patterns that might derive from some respondents conceiving of racial differences as multiply caused. Finally, we examined for clues the association between responses to the IQ question and responses to subparts of the SES question.

This activity did not fully clarify the sources of discrepancy in the responses. Nevertheless, it demonstrated that we had not achieved equivalence in representing the explanatory modes in the two questions. On this score, interviewers were especially critical of the wording used to depict the radical mode. It was considerably easier, they claimed, for respondents to conceive of "powerful and wealthy white people purposely act[ing] to keep black people down" in answer to the SES question than to imagine that the scientists who compose IQ tests were purposely biasing them to favor whites. The interviewers' intuition is supported by the evidence—7.9 percent supported the radical explanation in response to the SES question as compared with 2.8 percent in answer to the IQ question. Interviewers also felt that the wording of the cultural response in the IQ question was less harsh than its wording in the SES question, making the latter therefore more attractive to respondents. This observation is also consistent with the evidence—6.7 percent gave the cultural response to the SES question as compared with 15.7 percent to the IQ question.

It also seems likely, based on the in-depth interview results and on a comparison of Table 2 with Table 3, that contributing to the discrepancies in responses to the two questions was, as we suspected, the disposition of some respondents to explain racial differences in multi- rather than uni-causal terms. There is a clear tendency for those who accept an individualist explanation of racial differences to select also a genetic and/or supernatural explanation, and vice versa. A similar overlapping tendency exists between the radical and environmental social modes.

This tendency is reflected in Table 3, which reveals that those who answer the first question in an individualistic, genetic, or supernatural way are strongly inclined to do the same in answer to the second question. Judged in this way, the consistency in responses to the questions is 66 percent, and the response consistency is even higher—82 percent—for those who give an environmental or radical response to the first question. No similar pattern is revealed for the cultural mode; those who respond in this mode in answer to the first question are about as disposed in the second question to choose an environmental or radical response as they are to choose a genetic, supernatural, or individualistic one. This result conforms with our suspicion, expressed earlier, that the cultural does not constitute a distinct mode. It appears that some persons who say that racial differences are culturally produced have in mind the superiority of white culture; they hold, but hide, a genetic explanation of racial differences. Others who adopt a cultural explanation, however, use it as a substitute for an environmental explanation.

There was no way, using the BAS data, for us to correct for wording problems, to deal with multi-causality, or to resolve the ambiguities apparently inherent in the cultural mode. These matters had to be set aside for investigation in the next phase of our endeavors. There were other purposes to be served by the BAS data, however, and to these we now turn.

The Generality of the Modes

As reported earlier, we first speculated that modes of explaining racial differences may carry over to other phenomena during the analysis of the exploratory interviews. There was no way to use the interviews to test the idea, however, since this issue had not been anticipated during the designing of the interview guide. For several reasons it was decided that the idea deserved exploration in the BAS phase of our inquiries. Demonstrating that explanatory modes apply to a class of phenomena of which racial differences are only a part would have implications for social science research on these other phenomena. For the study of racial attitudes, such a demonstration would help answer the possible criticism that our conceptual model was tautological. On the other hand, should we find that modes of explaining racial differences do not apply to other phenomena, this conclusion too would shed light on white racial attitudes.

We formulated two structured questions to explore the generality of the modes. One question asked respondents how they accounted for the fact that some people live longer than others. The second asked them to explain poverty in the world. Our choice of subjects for these questions was based on the hypothesis that people's explanations of racial differences might be more closely related to accounting for some kinds of phenomena than others. If so, it was assumed that the correspondence between people's explanations of racial differences and those of poverty would be greater than that between explanations of racial differences and those of life-span differences. Poverty and racial differences bear more distinctly on social inequality than does variation in length of life.

In the length-of-life question, respondents were asked to choose from six possible explanations, listed on a card, of why some people live to a ripe old age while others die in the prime of life. We worded these explanations to capture the same range of control agents that was introduced in the questions about race, except that we found no simple way to make the cultural mode operational and therefore omitted it.

"It's in the hands of God" was intended to tap the supernatural mode; "It's mostly because some people are in a position to buy medical services and others can't," the environmental mode; "It's mostly a matter of the survival of the fittest," the genetic mode; "It mostly depends on how people take care of themselves," the individualistic mode; and "It's mostly because the medical profession has prevented the government from making medical care equally available to all people," the radical mode.[3] Respondents were also offered the additional option, not included in the race questions, of replying that the length of a person's life is simply a function of good or bad luck.

The question on why poverty exists, like that on why socio-economic differences exist between the races, offered respondents first an opportunity to express their relative agreement or disagreement with each of six explanations and then to choose the most important reason from among them. The following phrases were used to portray six different explanations of poverty; the explanatory mode each statement represents follows in parentheses.

> The poor are poor because the wealthy and powerful keep them poor.   (*Radical*)
>
> There are poor people because God made it so.   (*Supernatural*)

3. One of our readers objected that "it is a matter of survival of the fittest" does not necessarily connote a genetic explanation. A subject giving this response may simply mean that some individuals have longer lives than others because they "happen to be fit" or because their particular characteristics are at the moment highly valued. The procedure we used in operationalizing the different modes for this and other questions was to arrive at a formulation about which all members of the project staff agreed. The formulations were then subjected to pre-test by the Survey Research Center's field services staff. The formulations retained were those that withstood the tests of validity incorporated in the pre-tests. It is clear, in retrospect, that not all our formulations were understood uniformly, and in the way we intended them to be understood, by all respondents. For this reason, we do not rely on the more intensive analysis of the explanatory-mode concept, as reported in Chapters 3 through 10, on responses to answers to individual questions, but rather on an elaborately constructed typology of explanatory modes using items judged to be the most valid of those included in our inquiries. See Appendix B for technical details.

Poor people simply don't want to work hard.   (*Individualistic*)

Being poor is the result of having been born without the talents to get ahead.   (*Genetic*)

The poor are poor because the American way of life doesn't give all people an equal chance.   (*Environmental*)

Poor people are used to being poor because they grew up with it and it is a way of life for them.   (*Cultural*)

Table 4 shows the correspondence between the most important reason respondents cited for whites being better off than blacks and their responses to the length-of-life question. As in Table 3, the column and row totals show the distribution of responses to the two questions independently. The figures in the body of the table show the frequency with which different combinations of responses occurred. Responses to the two questions that were consistent are circled.

If we compare the total column with the total row of Table 4, it is immediately evident that the distribution of responses to the length-of-life question differs considerably from the distribution for the race question. The individualistic and supernatural responses together account for 68 percent of the choices on the length-of-life question as compared with only 31 percent on the race question. The environmental mode gains more than 50 percent of the responses on the race question but only 11 percent support on the question about length of life.

Even if we omit the nonoverlapping categories—luck on the length-of-life question and culture on the race question—only 23 percent of the responses to the two questions are consistent. This correspondence is still considerably greater than that attributable to chance, suggesting that there is some similarity in the way people think about the two phenomena. However, even if we take into account possible inadequacies in question wording, a sub-

Table 4 *Correspondence between Explanation of Racial Differences in SES and Explanation of Why Length of Life Varies among People*

EXPLANATION OF LENGTH-OF-LIFE DIFFERENCES	EXPLANATION OF RACIAL DIFFERENCES IN SES						
	Individualist	Genetic	Supernatural	Environmental	Radical	Cultural	Total
Individualist	7.0%	1.6	2.4	21.5	4.7	2.9	40.1
Genetic	1.2	.5	.6	6.0	.3	.8	9.5
Supernatural	8.8	.5	6.6	10.5	.6	1.3	28.3
Environmental	1.2	.2	.8	6.4	1.3	1.2	11.1
Radical	.5	.0	.0	3.6	1.0	.1	5.3
Luck	.9	.2	.7	3.7	.2	.2	5.7
Total	19.6	2.9	11.2	51.7	8.2	6.5	100.0%

N = 657
χ^2 = 103.9 df = 25 p < .001

stantial majority of people see different agents in control of one situation as compared with the other.

Table 5 shows, in its total column and row, the distribution of responses to the poverty and racial-inequality questions independently. In the body of the table, the distribution of alternative joint responses to the two questions is reported.

Thirty-three percent of the responses are wholly consistent. While this degree of correspondence is greater than it was for the length-of-life and racial-inequality questions, it is considerably smaller than the 51 percent correspondence between the two race questions.

What happens if we substitute responses to the question on racial differences in IQ performance for the responses to the SES question as our means for classifying people according to their explanatory mode? The proportion of responses to the IQ question that are consistent with responses to the length-of-life question was 24 percent; the cultural and luck responses were again omitted. The corresponding figure for the IQ and poverty question was 45 percent. Thus, it turns out that on both sets of comparisons there is greater consistency between how people explain racial inequalities and how they account for poverty than between their explanations of racial inequalities and length-of-life differences. In none of the comparisons, however, is the consistency as large as for the responses to the two race questions.

These results about the generality of the modes are not conclusive. The consistency scores are neither large enough to justify a claim of generality nor small enough to justify a conclusion that no relation exists between explanations of different phenomena. Given these results, we decided to explore more fully the question of the modes' generality in the project's next phase.

Table 5 *Correspondence between Explanation of Racial Differences in SES and Explanation of Poverty*

EXPLANATION OF POVERTY	EXPLANATION OF RACIAL DIFFERENCES IN SES						
	Individualist	Genetic	Supernatural	Environmental	Radical	Cultural	Total
Individualist	5.5%	.4	1.1	3.3	.8	1.1	12.2
Genetic	2.3	.8	1.4	5.2	.6	.7	10.9
Supernatural	1.5	.0	2.3	.3	.0	.3	4.4
Environmental	1.3	.8	2.3	17.4	2.0	.7	24.4
Radical	2.6	.2	1.2	9.8	3.9	.4	18.2
Cultural	5.8	.9	2.3	16.9	1.4	2.6	29.9
Total	19.0	3.1	10.6	53.0	8.6	5.7	100.0%

N = 608
x^2 = 166.0 df = 25 p < .001

The Implications of Explanations for Prescriptions

The BAS was also designed to enable a provisional test of the hypotheses derived from the in-depth interviews concerning relationships between explanatory modes and prescriptions. The earlier results, you will recall, suggested that different modes imply quite different prescriptions about what ought to be done about racial inequality in America.

For the provisional test, the BAS questionnaire included a number of questions designed to find out what, if anything, respondents are willing to do to bring about greater racial equality. The time constraints allowed only a limited number of prescriptive questions. In constructing them, we sought to deal with how white respondents felt about more government action to bring about greater social and racial equality. We also sought to assess what respondents would be willing to do and to subscribe to personally to bring an end to racial inequality. The questions and responses are reported in Table 6.

Judging from the distribution of responses to these questions, the white population of the San Francisco Bay Area is in considerable disagreement about what to do about racial inequality. There is substantial support for retaining the status quo, some support for turning back the clock on the progress that has been made, some disposition for reform, and a modicum of support for radical solutions.

Questions of this kind, as suggested earlier, represent efforts to measure the consequences of what is meant ordinarily by *prejudice* rather than the phenomenon itself. It is to be expected, consequently, that if explanatory modes are at the root of what is commonly called prejudice, then they should be strongly related to answers to these questions about consequences. In effect, to make the case for the explanatory-mode concept, it is necessary, although not sufficient, to demonstrate a relationship between how people explain racial differences and what they are willing to do to bring about racial equality.

Table 6   **Wording and Distribution of Responses to Questions about What Ought to Be Done about Racial Inequalities**

Which of the statements on this card [respondent is handed card] comes closest to your overall feelings about how much the Federal and State Governments should be doing to help black people in the United States?

Nothing more, government has done too much already.	5%
Nothing more, what government is doing now is enough.	16
No new laws are necessary, but the present laws against discrimination should be more strictly enforced.	38
New and tougher laws against racial discrimination should be passed and strictly enforced.	18
I think the Federal and State Governments in America are racist and it is unrealistic to expect them to help black people.	6
The government shouldn't be doing anything at all; it should be left up to individuals.	12
Other	2
Don't know and no answer	3
	100

Which of the statements on this card [respondent is handed card] comes closest to your personal feelings about marriage between blacks and whites?

Blacks and whites should marry their own kind.	24%
It's not a good idea for blacks and whites to marry because their children will suffer.	30
People should marry anyone they choose regardless of race.	45
Don't know and no answer	1
	100

Here are some actions—suggested by others—that people could take to help with the racial problems facing our country. Not everyone agrees, of course, that each is really needed. Please tell me for each whether it is something you personally would be willing to do if you had the chance.

Table 6 **(continued)**

| | WILLING TO DO | | | |
	Yes	No	Can't Say	Total
Have a child of yours bused to an integrated school	33%	63	4	100%
Sign a petition urging passage of strong laws to prevent discrimination in housing	69%	27	4	100%
Pay higher taxes to provide job training, better housing, and better schools for black citizens	43%	53	4	100%
Spend more of your free time working in a campaign to get more people to register and vote	46%	51	3	100%
Vote for a qualified black candidate for a local school board	90%	7	3	100%

Suppose you had a child who wanted to marry a black person who had a good education and a good job. How would you feel about this—would you approve, disapprove but keep silent, object, or not care either way?

Approve	25%
Disapprove but keep silent	19
Object	43
Not care either way	8
No answer and don't know	4
Other	1
	100

N = 698 for all sets

With the BAS data, the test had to be provisional, since we had neither a highly refined measure of explanatory modes nor a means to deal with multi-causal explanations. Nevertheless, if results of a crude test supported the proposition that modes are associated with prescriptions, these findings would afford a basis for engaging in further refinement in conceptualization and measurement.

Table 7 presents a special computation designed to show the extent to which respondents in each of the mode types are attracted to or repelled by alternative proposals about

Table 7 **Preferred Government Policy to Reduce Racial Inequality by Mode of Explaining Racial Differences in Socio-Economic Status (in over-under statistic)[a]**

WHAT GOVERNMENT SHOULD DO	EXPLANATION OF RACIAL DIFFERENCES						Total %
	Individualist	Genetic	Supernatural	Environmental	Radical	Cultural	
Leave to individuals	.88[a]	.81	.09	−.43	.48	−.43	12.7
Nothing more; too much already	1.25	2.67	.65	−.63	−1.00	.12	15.1
Doing enough now	.22	1.27	.56	−.36	−.56	1.32	17.2
Enforce laws more stringently	−.21	−.62	−.11	.22	−.25	−.28	40.6
Pass new laws	−.52	−.80	−.31	.26	.47	−.23	18.6
Government is racist	−.52	−1.00	−.69	.19	1.76	−.41	5.8

N = 652
χ^2 = 135.7 df = 25 p < .001
[a](Cell percent − total percent)/total percent

what the government might do to help black people. Assignment into a mode type is based on responses to the question asking for the most important reason that blacks in America are socially and economically deprived relative to whites.

To understand the nature of the "over-under statistic" created to present the results in Table 7, notice that in the first row of the table the proportion of the total sample who believe that the problem of reducing racial inequality should be left to individuals is 12.7 percent. Note also the over-under statistic of .88 for those whose explanatory mode is individualistic. The .88 means that those in the individualistic mode are 88 percent more likely than the average respondent to believe that the problem of racial inequality should be left for individuals to solve. (The corresponding cell percentage of 23.9 is 88 percent higher than 12.7 percent.)[4]

Such a positive over-under score means that a particular response category has been "over-selected" by an explanatory-mode type as compared with the sample as a whole. A negative statistic means that the response category has been "under-selected" by the explanatory-mode type compared with the sample as a whole; the number −.43 in the first row of Table 7 for those in the environmental mode, for example, means that these respondents were 43 percent less likely than the average respondent in the sample to say that the problem of racial inequality should be left up to individuals to resolve. The higher or lower the over-under statistic, the greater the degree of over- or under-selection.

4. It will be observed that the "over-under statistic" suggests that differences are larger than do percentage differences. The former is judged superior to the latter, for present purposes, because it allows comparisons across the rows as well as down the columns of bivariate tables. Percentaged tables would simply not allow such comparisons readily. We have included the percentage distributions for the total sample in all tables so that the reader can judge what is signified by over-under scores of different magnitudes.

The figures in Table 7 can be read either horizontally or vertically. Read horizontally, they report the relative attractiveness of a particular form of government action for each mode type. Thus, for example, looking across the last row of the table shows that the idea that the government is racist gains its greatest support from those in the radical mode, is slightly over-subscribed to by those in the environmental mode, but is under-selected by those in all other modes.

Read vertically, Table 7 compares the attractiveness of proposed alternative government policies within each mode type. Thus, for example, the first column shows that, relative to the total sample, individualists are especially attracted to two kinds of policies—that the government leaves it up to individuals to deal with problems of racial inequality and that the government does nothing new, having done too much already. Compared with those in other modes, individualists are slightly more attracted to the government doing nothing and slightly repelled by the idea of new and tougher laws against discrimination. These respondents find least attractive the proposals that new and tougher laws against racial discrimination be passed and strictly enforced and the assertion that the government is racist.

The table generally confirms the expectations set forth in the previous chapter regarding how the different modes would be found to respond to the problem of racial discrimination. It was expected that because individualists interpret racial differences to be a matter of individual choice, they would favor policies that they think encourage individual initiative. As Table 7 reveals, the individualists, more than any other mode, are attracted to the policy of the government leaving it up to individuals to deal with the problem of discrimination. They also over-select the response that the government has done too much already. The geneticists were also expected to favor a policy of inaction, since they believe that racial differences are immutable and, therefore, that nothing can be done to change them. The geneticists consistently over-select those policies calling for no further government action to reduce discrimination.

The supernaturalists, while sharing with the geneticists the view that racial differences are innate, were expected to respond less harshly than the geneticists because of their commitment to a supernatural being. This expectation is also confirmed in Table 7. The supernaturalists are both less attracted than the geneticists to the government doing nothing and less repelled by the government doing something. On balance, however, the supernaturalists lean to the government doing nothing.

The data confirm our anticipation that those in the environmental mode would favor reformist policies for dealing with racial discrimination. "New and tougher laws against racial discrimination should be passed" and "present laws should be more strictly enforced" are the response categories that respondents in the environmental mode over-select the most. These respondents also tend to over-select the response that the government is racist. The most disposed, by far, to this latter view, however, are those in the radical mode. They are almost three times as likely than the average respondent to say that the government is racist. Surprisingly, however, respondents in the radical mode also show a disposition to over-select the policy that individuals should be left alone to solve the problem of racial discrimination. We suspect that this finding is more a reflection of their antipathy toward government, however, than a sign of resistance to action taken against discrimination.

We have several times expressed our suspicion that the cultural explanation may not form a distinct mode. Some confirmation of this suspicion is afforded by Table 7. Rather than selecting policies that would recognize equality of the two cultures, the culturalists most often chose the policy to retain the status quo.

The trends expressed in the results reported in Table 7 are repeated almost exactly when respondents are assigned explanatory-mode types based on their responses to the IQ rather than the SES question. The results are also about the same when other prescriptive questions are substituted for the question on governmental action.

Perceptions and Explanations

These results demonstrated that the same perception of racial differences can have very different consequences for black-white relations, depending on how that perception is explained. It is to be recognized, however, that in framing both the SES and the IQ questions we imposed a perception on respondents. They were told, in effect, that whites in America are better off than blacks and that whites do better than blacks on IQ tests. None of the respondents disagreed. Still, it cannot be assumed that all perceptions of racial differences are shared. It is eminently clear from other studies that in many instances people do not perceive the same racial differences.

Some effort was made in the BAS to explore the relation between perceptions and explanations of racial differences. At the time, we had not formulated any theory to guide our inquiries on this subject. Nevertheless, we included a few questions on perceptions so we could examine the relationships between responses to perception questions and responses to the questions used to classify respondents into explanatory modes.

In retrospect, our formulation of the questions on perception was less than inspired. We failed to ask a single question designed to assess the degree of acceptance of outright negative stereotypes, for example. In the absence of theory, the questions had no clear underlying rationale.

They were formulated by different members of the project team in a relatively ad hoc fashion and adopted because, at the time, they intuitively seemed to tap perceptions well. We report briefly on these efforts for the record and for the illumination they cast on some matters at issue.

In all, five simple questions were asked about respondents' perceptions of racial differences. The questions and the distributions of responses they evoked among white respondents are reported in Table 8.

Table 8 **Wording and Distribution of Responses to Perception Questions**

Interviewer: I'd like to read you some statements about black people and white people in America. Please tell me for each whether you think the statement is true or false. If you don't know, just say so.

	TRUE	FALSE	DON'T KNOW	TOTAL
The average black child does as well in school in America today as the average white child.	22%	61	17	100%
Black families are more loving and warm toward their children than white families.	11%	63	26	100%
A black person is more likely to get in trouble with the police during his lifetime than a white person.	73%	19	8	100%
Black women usually have a harder time in life than white women.	69%	16	15	100%
The average working black man now earns more than the average working white woman.	32%	28	40	100%

N = 698

It is of incidental interest that on two of the three questions for which there is factual evidence to support or deny the stereotype contained in the question, the majority of respondents give a correct response. Sixty-one percent correctly deny that the average black child does as well in school as the average white child, and 73 percent correctly affirm that "a black person is more likely to get in trouble with the police during his lifetime than a white person." At the time the survey was undertaken, the average earnings of black men exceeded the average earnings of working white women. This fact, however, does not appear to be widely known; note the 40 percent who respond "don't know" and the additional 28 percent who respond "false." We know of no evidence to support or deny the perception that "black families are more loving and warm toward their children than white families." A majority of respondents, however, choose to deny that this statement is true rather than to respond "don't know." Very few, however, aver that it is true. There is also no firm evidence that "black women usually have a harder time in life than white women," although this seems a reasonable inference from the relative economic deprivation of blacks as compared with whites. In any case, a majority of 69 percent make the inference and respond that the statement is true.

It appears from these results that people do attend to the accuracy of stereotypes. This being the case, it is hard to interpret the meaning of the acceptance of a negative but true stereotype. It seems hardly warranted, as in some past research, to assume all negative stereotyping to be prejudice, irrespective of truth content.

As noted above, however, none of these questions gets at outright negative stereotypes that are patently false. Consequently, they do not allow for assessing the relative disposition of the explanatory-mode types to make negative ascriptions of blacks. In some past work, to say that blacks are more likely to get into trouble with the police or that black children do less well in school than white children has been taken as a sign of prejudice. However, given that a factual basis exists for these beliefs, they can hardly be used to assess the relative disposition of the different explanatory-mode types to negative stereotyping.

Indeed, as can be seen in the upper half of Table 9, the proportion of respondents who believe that blacks are more likely to get into trouble with the police varies very little by mode. Those in the supernatural mode are the least likely to accept this assertion, but less than 10 percentage points separate the proportion of believers in the other modes. There are somewhat greater differences by mode in the proportion who consider it false that the average black child does as well in school as the average white child; see the lower half of Table 9. However, a substantial portion of each mode type makes such a denial. Surprisingly, perhaps, the individualists and the supernaturalists, who earlier had been found especially resistant to efforts to reduce discrimination, are here shown to be the most likely of the mode types to affirm that black children do as well in school as white children.

The main contribution of these results was to confirm that the same beliefs about racial differences can be held by people who vary considerably in their understanding of how these differences come about. We still knew very little about the fundamental relationships between perceptions and explanations. In the next phase of our research, we formulated a firmer theoretical foundation for investigating these interconnections and for then going on to explore the interplay among perceptions, explanations, and prescriptions.

Summing Up

The results of the BAS by and large support the idea that explanatory modes are an important element in how whites respond to blacks and to race relations in general.[5]

---

5. For a fuller analysis of the BAS data, see Suelzle, "Social Indicators of White Racial Attitudes."

Table 9 **Responses to Two Questions about Black-White Differences by Explanatory Mode**[a]

			MODE OF EXPLAINING RACIAL DIFFERENCES				
QUESTION	Individualist %	Genetic %	Supernatural %	Environmental %	Radical %	Cultural %	Total %
Blacks more likely to get in trouble with police							
True	76	71	55	79	72	71	75
False	17	24	38	15	21	24	19
Don't know	7	5	7	6	7	5	6
	100	100	100	100	100	100	100
Black child does as well in school							
True	38	10	38	16	25	7	22
False	49	76	32	70	64	79	62
Don't know	13	14	30	14	11	14	16
	100	100	100	100	100	100	100

N = 672
[a] Mode assignment made according to responses to SES question.

The results also make clear, however, that to make the explanatory-mode concept operational it is necessary to distinguish between persons whose explanatory framework is multi-causal and those for whom it is uni-causal. The need to improve the wording of questions used for classifying people into modes is also made evident by the BAS analysis.

The results are ambiguous concerning whether modes of explaining racial differences are issue-specific or are employed by people to explain other phenomena as well. There is some overlap; some people explain different phenomena from the same perspective. Other people, however, interpret different kinds of events in quite different ways. How general the modes may be cannot be finally resolved, the results suggest, until the problem of multi-causality is resolved.

The BAS data analysis casts further doubt on the utility of using the word *prejudice* to designate the phenomenon we are trying to measure or as a more general term to distinguish negative from positive racial attitudes. Indeed, understanding of racial attitudes has probably been set back by the use of the term. While it is unlikely that anything can be done to discourage public custom in this regard, it seems wise to abandon the term *prejudice* for scientific usage.

The BAS affords no sound basis for testing the surmise that once a mode of explanation has been internalized it becomes an influence on new perceptions of racial differences. This issue probably cannot be absolutely resolved with cross-sectional data; in any case, our efforts to this end in the BAS were unproductive. Our failure to measure perceptions adequately also prevented us from exploring the joint impact of perceptions and explanations on prescriptions.

Taken in sum, the BAS experience was more helpful in clarifying our task than in moving it forward. At the BAS's conclusion, there were more major tasks of measurement still ahead than behind us. Nevertheless, the BAS was encouraging in the support it afforded the concept of explanatory modes.

Our next step was to engage in a new, additional data collection operation designed to tackle the outstanding problems. The design of that effort plus a report on how the new data were used to deal with multi-causal explanations is reported in Chapter 4. Chapter 5, using the new data, considers the relationship between explanations, multi- and uni-causal, and prescriptions. Chapter 6 examines, more successfully than this chapter, the interconnections between perceptions and explanations. In Chapter 7, the joint association of perceptions and explanations with prescriptions is taken up. Chapter 8 examines patterns of recruitment to the different modes. Chapter 9 considers the possibility that the relation between modes and prescriptions is spurious. In Chapter 10, the question of the modes' generality is taken up anew, the stability of the modes is assessed, and the suitability of the explanatory-mode concept to an understanding of black racial attitudes is explored. A concluding chapter, Chapter 11, considers the implications of what has been learned for social indicator development, for understanding racial attitudes, and for general attitude research.

Chapter 4 *The Building of an Explanatory-Mode Typology*

The agenda for further work generated by the results of the Bay Area Survey (BAS) was a formidable one. It called for

- refining the concept of explanatory modes to take account of multi-causal explanations;

- making operational the three components of our conceptual modes—perceptions, explanations, and prescriptions—in a more effective way than was possible in the BAS;

- testing, with the new operationalization, the analytic model that had been developed out of the in-depth interviews;

- seeking to account for the sources of different explanatory modes, trying to determine the generality of the modes, and setting forth, finally, the implications of all this for social indicator development.

Besides performing these tasks, which have their origin in the results of the BAS, we also had to investigate the stability of the modes. Specifically, how likely was it that people who were classified as explaining racial differences in a particular way at one time would be similarly classified if measurement were made at another time? Moreover, some exploration of the explanatory-mode concept as it operated in minority communities was called for. It was especially appropriate to inquire how blacks account for the racial differences they perceive.

69

Given these goals, how were they to be accomplished? Were resources unlimited, a series of studies would be ideal, each building on the other to produce ever finer measures of the concepts. Were such efforts to succeed, we might then examine the feasibility of utilizing these measures in repeated national studies of white racial attitudes.

Such an ambitious program was far beyond our means. Indeed, we could not even undertake another BAS devoted entirely to our purposes, at least not one utilizing the services of personal interviewers. However, available resources did permit us to conduct another survey of a sample of the Bay Area using mailback questionnaires instead of personal interviews. We held no illusions that such a survey would allow us to answer all outstanding questions, but because it would afford us complete control of the questionnaire's contents, a survey of this type offered a way to examine outstanding issues in considerably more breadth and depth than had been possible in the BAS.

The study was based on a sample of the adult population of the San Francisco Bay Area roughly equivalent to the sample used in the BAS.[1] Of 993 designated respondents, we received 646 usable questionnaires, a return rate of 65 percent, only slightly smaller than that achieved for the BAS. Of these returned questionnaires, 504 were from white respondents. Except where otherwise noted, the data base for the succeeding analysis is constituted by these white respondents.[2]

The questionnaire for the follow-up study was formulated to meet the goals set forth in the agenda above. Questions concerned respondents' perceptions of racial differ-

1. A fuller description of the design of the follow-up study is provided in Appendix A. See also Apostle, "White Racial Perspectives in the United States."

2. Where tables are based on an N smaller than 504, the discrepancy is a result of missing cases. The discrepancy tends to be larger where tables are based on summary measures whose construction required that respondents answer sufficient items to enable them to be scored.

ences, explanations of these differences, and prescriptions, if any, for reducing racial inequality. In addition to the usual background items, questions were designed to assess the generality of the modes and the extent of respondents' interracial contacts and of their sensitivity to the problem of prejudice. The questionnaire is reproduced as Appendix D.

Framing Explanatory-Mode Questions

We relied on four questions in the new survey to assess the explanatory modes used by respondents to account for perceived racial differences. We repeated, with some modification, the SES question and, with no modifications, the IQ question asked in the BAS. We asked two additional questions to provide a larger body of data on which to build a summary measure of explanatory modes and to assess the character and frequency of multi-causal explanations of racial differences.

The so-called SES question, it will be recalled, invited respondents to assess six reasons presented to them for why "white people get more of the good things in life in America than black people." Respondents were first asked to rank their relative agreement or disagreement with each of the stated reasons and then asked to choose the reason they thought most important.[3] Table 10 compares the distributions of responses to the two parts of the SES question as answered in the BAS and the follow-up samples.

The last two columns of Table 10 show the responses of the BAS and follow-up samples to the question eliciting what respondents considered the most important reason for whites being better off than blacks. The distributions are remarkably similar.

3. We modified the so-called SES version for the follow-up study in order to adapt the BAS version to a questionnaire format and to improve the clarity of the question. The BAS version of the question is quoted on pp. 39–40 of Chapter 3. For the follow-up version, see question 32 in the questionnaire included as Appendix D.

Table 10 Distribution of Responses of the BAS and Follow-Up Samples (FUS) to the Question on the Sources of Racial Differences in Socio-Economic Status

EXPLANATORY MODE	EXTENT OF AGREEMENT						MOST IMPORTANT REASON	
	Agree Strongly	Agree Somewhat	Disagree Somewhat	Disagree Strongly	Can't Say; No Answer	Total	BAS	FUS
Individualist								
BAS	19%	24	26	28	3	100%	18.8%	
Follow-Up	14%	33	24	23	6	100%		20.4%
Genetic								
BAS	6%	17	18	55	4	100%	3.1	
Follow-Up	4%	16	18	55	7	100%		2.9
Supernatural								
BAS	21%	14	10	49	6	100%	10.5	
Follow-Up	10%	16	9	46	19	100%		8.6
Environmental								
BAS	42%	34	11	10	3	100%	50.1	
Follow-Up	43%	35	9	9	4	100%		46.0
Radical								
BAS	11%	32	29	24	4	100%	7.8	
Follow-Up	14%	29	23	25	9	100%		7.6
Cultural								
BAS	7%	32	26	14	21	100%	6.1	
Follow-Up	8%	32	26	22	12	100%		7.9
Other							3.6	6.6
Total							100.0%	100.0%

BAS N = 698
Follow-up N = 504

In the body of the table, which presents the degree to which the two samples accept each explanatory mode, we note that the distributions are again highly similar. Most differences are attributable to the fact that the mailback questionnaire produced a larger "can't say" response than the personal interview. (Mailback questionnaire respondents were given the option of answering "can't say" whereas such a response was not specifically provided to respondents in the BAS personal interviews.) This tendency is especially marked for the supernatural mode, where almost three times as many questionnaire respondents answered "can't say" than respondents to the personal interview. This difference notwithstanding, the table shows more similarities than dissimilarities in results from the two surveys.

Unlike the SES question, the IQ question only asked respondents to choose from among six explanations the one they considered the most important reason why blacks perform less well than whites on intelligence tests. The wording of the IQ question was the same in the two surveys and, as can be seen in Table 11, the results are close

Table 11 **Distribution of Responses of the BAS and Follow-Up Samples to the Question on the Sources of Racial Differences in Performance on IQ Tests**

EXPLANATORY MODE	BAS	FOLLOW-UP
Individualist	11%	14%
Genetic	8	10
Supernatural	9	7
Environmental	46	47
Radical	3	1
Cultural	15	15
Other or no answer	8	6
Total	100%	100%
N	(698)	(504)

to being equivalent also; each mode gets substantially the same support in both surveys. These results afford some assurance that the modes are stable. However, we shall later report further on stability using panel data.

The two additional questions asked in the follow-up study to assess explanatory modes differed in format and content from each other and from the SES and IQ questions. What we shall refer to as the John Smith question asked respondents to account for the experiences of a black man who achieves a reasonable degree of success in his career. In framing this question, we sought to represent in the answer categories all six explanatory modes identified from the in-depth interviews. We also added two explanations for Smith's success to give respondents an opportunity to choose a mode of explanation not included in our conceptual scheme. One of these reasons was "Nowadays most firms want to have a few blacks around. John is probably one of these token blacks." This explanation suggested that despite Smith's success, the social system was essentially discriminatory. The other depicted Smith as an "Uncle Tom": John was probably willing to "knuckle under to do whatever his white employers told him." In effect, these additions were intended as a test of the adequacy of our specification of the modes.

The wording and responses to the John Smith question are presented in Table 12; the first four columns show the proportion of respondents who accepted or rejected each reason as a probable explanation of Smith's success and the proportion who did not answer. The last column shows the distribution of responses when the sample was asked to choose the most important reason for Smith's success.

The results reveal, first of all, a strong tendency for respondents to acknowledge more than one reason for Smith's success. On the average, respondents checked four reasons out of the eight offered to them. Four of the explanations—the radical, the environmental, the cultural, and the individualist—were checked by a majority of respondents. The format of the question undoubtedly contributed to the considerably greater disposition toward multi-causal explanation to this question than to the SES and IQ questions.

At the same time, once respondents were asked to choose the one reason they considered most important for Smith's success, very few—7.0 percent—found it impossible to do so. The individualist explanation gains the most support (32 percent), followed by the environmental (24 percent) and the radical (15 percent). Supernatural and genetic explanations are infrequently chosen (4.5 and 1.7 percent, respectively) as are the two explanations added as a test of the overall conceptual scheme. While the virtual absence of support for the added explanations does not guarantee the inclusiveness of our specification of explanatory modes, it lends support to this conclusion.

The second new explanatory-mode question approached the topic in a wholly different way from the other questions. Implicit in each of the modes, we reasoned, is an assumption about who or what is to "blame" for inequality between the races. The individualists see the fault as located in the black community. Those in the radical mode conceive it to be in the white community. The supernaturalists, geneticists, and culturalists locate the source outside the two communities, as do those in the environmental mode, although it is conceivable that some in this latter mode would place the blame on whites.

Building on this reasoning, we developed a multi-part question asking respondents to rank the roles different control agents play in causing racial differences. Thus, one part of the question asked, "Thinking still of the fact that the average black person is less well off than the average white person, how much do you think this is the fault of white people living today?" In response, 10 percent replied that it is mostly the fault of white people, 73 percent

Table 12 *Wording and Distribution of Responses to the John Smith Question*

John Smith is a 32-year-old black man. He and his family live in a fine house in the suburbs. He has an important job as a manager in an industrial firm and earns an income of $20,000 a year.

There's a lot of talk at the plant where Smith works about how a black man like Smith could have become so successful. Here are some of the reasons offered.

(Instruction to respondent: Please read each reason and place an "X" in column I if you think it might be a reason for Smith's success. If you feel it probably isn't a reason for Smith's success, place a check in column II.)

	I PROBABLY A REASON	II PROBABLY NOT A REASON	NO ANSWER	TOTAL	MOST IMPORTANT REASON
Nowadays most firms want to have a few blacks around. John is probably one of these token blacks. (*Token*)	25%	65	10	100%	1.8%
The reason John Smith prospers is probably because he respects God and lives the kind of life God rewards. (*Supernatural*)	26%	63	11	100%	4.5
John was talented and intelligent enough to get by the whites who were trying to keep him down. If he had been white with his abilities, he would probably have a better job and be earning even more. (*Radical*)	51%	39	10	100%	14.5
Black people as a group are somewhat down on the intelligence scale, but there are a few capable individuals like John Smith. (*Genetic*)	29%	59	12	100%	1.7
There is a lot less discrimination in America than there used to be and it is not at all surprising to find more and more successful black people. (*Environmental*)	80%	12	8	100%	23.7

Table 12 *(continued)*

A large part of it may be due to the fact that John Smith's family and friends were different from most black people in that they encouraged him to develop his talents. (*Cultural*)	60%	30	10	100%	13.5
John Smith became so successful because despite what some people say, anybody who has ambition and works hard in America can make it. (*Individualistic*)	71%	22	7	100%	31.8
John was probably willing to "knuckle under" and do whatever his white employers told him. (*Uncle Tom*)	24%	64	12	100%	1.5
Other/No Answer					7.0
Total					100.0%
N					504

The labels in parentheses were not in the original questionnaire.

said it is partly white people's fault, and 17 percent said it is not at all the fault of white people.

Another part of the question asked, "How much do you think it is the fault of black people that they don't do as well as whites?" To this question, 14 percent replied that it is mostly black people's fault, 74 percent said it is partly their fault, and 12 percent said it is not their fault at all.

Two other parts of the question sought to determine more explicitly how much respondents were disposed to conceive of racial differences either as divinely wrought or as deriving from genetic causes. In response to the question "How do you feel about the idea that, for reasons which we cannot know, God made the races different?" 16 percent replied that they were convinced this was true, 16 percent said they leaned toward believing that this was true, 25 percent expressed doubt but would leave the possibility open, and 42 percent responded that they did not believe this. The question "How about the genetic argument that the forces of nature have created the differences between races that we find today" produced the following responses: 9 percent reported that they were convinced this was true, 32 percent leaned in that direction, 31 percent were doubtful but left the possibility open, and 29 percent were disbelievers.

Building an Explanatory-Mode Typology

Armed with these responses to the follow-up survey questions, we set out to determine their suitability for classifying respondents according to their mode of explaining racial differences. Our aim was to develop a valid and reliable measure that would distinguish those who operate from a multi-causal perspective from those who account for racial differences in a uni-causal way. A further requirement, of course, was that the measure clearly identify both multi-causal and uni-causal modes.

To these ends, we carried out a considerable amount of

detailed analysis of the data, a technical description of which is contained in Appendix B. The first step was to subject the responses to the mode questions to a series of factor and cluster analyses to assess the extent to which they produce factors in accord with those we had arrived at conceptually. The results of this work support the conceptualization, except in their strong suggestion that the cultural mode does not form a distinct type and might wisely be abandoned.

The supernatural items form an independent dimension, as do the items tapping the genetic mode. Each appears to constitute a distinct explanatory style. The clustering of the items designed to distinguish the individualistic, radical, and environmental modes was not so simple, however. We finally concluded that the three sets of items generate two distinct response patterns or dimensions.

One pattern relates to how society is understood to function. At one extreme are those who seem to conceive of social relationships in strictly individualistic terms. They do not recognize the existence of social forces. To them the way society is organized is a result of individual behavior. At the other extreme are those we classify as operating from an environmental mode of explanation. They interpret racial differences in socio-economic status and IQ test scores as the result of ingrained institutional racism that persists even without any deliberate discriminatory intent on the part of whites living today. Unlike the individualists, they are sensitive to the potential in social forces to shape the organization of social life, including the relatively deprived status of blacks in American society. Empirically this first pattern is manifested at the one extreme by acceptance of the individualistic items and the rejection of the environmental ones. At the other extreme, it is characterized by just the opposite—the rejection of the individualistic items and the acceptance of the environmental ones.

The second pattern involves, once again, some of the

individualistic items, this time in their relation to the radical items. The interpretative scheme underlying this pattern is focused less on how racial inequality has come about and more on who is to blame for its existence. At the individualistic end of this continuum are found those who say that if blacks are less well off, it is their own fault because they don't work hard enough. At the other extreme are those who say that black inequality is the fault of whites who even today are keeping blacks from attaining equality. In comparison with the first pattern, this one appears less cognitive and more affective in content.

The relation between these two patterns or dimensions might be conceptualized by the shape of the letter V. At the base of the V, the individualist ends of the two dimensions converge; those who conceive of racial differences in strictly individualistic terms also tend to be the ones who say that the situation of blacks is their own fault. As one moves away from a strictly individualistic interpretation of the social disparities between blacks and whites, however, there are two distinct avenues available. One possibility is to assert that whites, and not blacks, are really to blame. This assertion does not necessarily imply a more sophisticated understanding of society, but it could be expected to lead to support for helping blacks. The other alternative to individualism is a broadening of the notion of how society operates to include an awareness of social constraints on individual behavior. Although this approach is more sophisticated intellectually, it can also be a way for whites to avoid assuming any personal responsibility for the condition of blacks, since the emphasis is placed on impersonal social forces rather than the deliberate discriminatory actions of whites. These two alternatives to individualism are empirically distinguishable in the data. They are not mutually exclusive, however. Some respondents endorse both.

The cultural items, as already noted, were not found to

constitute a distinct explanatory style. Those agreeing with one cultural explanation did not tend to agree with the other cultural explanations to any great degree. Their responses to other explanation items proved to be more indicative of their operating explanatory mode. We do not mean that cultural explanations were uncommon—we have already seen that they were not—but rather that they did not have a consistent meaning. A cultural response was sometimes a substitute for an environmental answer, with culture being seen as equivalent to a social force. At other times, apparently, a cultural response was a means of expressing the opinion that black culture, and blacks in general, are inferior to whites. Given this ambiguity, it seemed best to set the cultural items aside and to assign respondents to a mode according to responses to other items.

After identifying the four dimensions just described—supernatural, genetic, individualist-radical, and individualist-environmental—we built separate scales to enable us to measure respondents on each of them. Scale construction simply involved scoring respondents according to their responses to items identified as validly tapping the different dimensions. The more frequently a respondent gave a response in a particular mode, the higher was his or her scale score. Thus, for example, the highest score on the genetic scale was given to those who responded in the following way: (1) John Smith was successful because "black people as a group are somewhat down on the intelligence scale, but there are a few exceptions like John Smith"; (2) "Blacks come from a less able race and that explains why they are not as well off as white Americans"; and (3) "By nature, black people are less intelligent than white people." Respondents who denied a genetic reason for Smith's success, who disagreed strongly that blacks are less well off than whites for genetic reasons, and who chose a response to the IQ question other than the genetic one were assigned the lowest score on the scale. Respondents whose answers were mixed were given intermediate scale scores, depending upon how many genetic answers they gave. The supernatural scale was constructed in parallel fashion.

The construction of the other two scales followed a slightly different path. To score high on the individualist-radical scale, a respondent had to acknowledge radical explanations of racial differences and to deny individualistic ones. To score low, he or she had to deny radical explanations and to acknowledge individualistic ones. The individualist-environmental scale was constructed in a parallel way. Thus, on these two scales, a low score signifies identification with an individualistic understanding of racial differences, a high score signifies a disposition to environmental or radical explanations. Intermediate scores represented a rejection of both kinds of explanations in the two cases. (A detailed discussion of the construction and validation of these scales is included in Appendix B.)

The next step was to build an explanatory-mode typology based on respondents' joint scores on the four scales. For this purpose, we established cutting points for each scale, following criteria discussed in Appendix B. In effect, these criteria divided respondents into geneticists and nongeneticists based on their responses to the genetic scale, and supernaturalists or nonsupernaturalists based on their responses to the supernatural scale. Based on the joint distribution of the other two scales, respondents were classified as individualists, radicals, environmentalists, both radical and environmentalist, and neutral or intermediate on both of these dimensions. We then determined whether the persons falling into each of these classifications scored high or low on the genetic and supernatural scales. The results of this procedure produced the eleven distinct mode types depicted in Table 13. (A more detailed description is given in Appendix B.)

As table 13 shows, about half the respondents in the

sample were classified into "pure" types; they were found to explain racial differences in uni-causal terms. With 17 percent of the sample, the individualist is the most common of the pure modes. The environmental is next, with 12 percent. The other three pure modes each contain about 6 percent of the sample.

Another 30 percent of the sample's respondents were

Table 13 **Assignment of Respondents to Mode Type**

EXPLANATORY MODE	SCORED ON			N	%
	Genetic Scale as	*Supernatural Scale as*	*Individualist-Social Scales as*		
Uni-Causal (Pure) Modes					
Individualist	$\overline{G}$	$\overline{S}$	I	(87)	17.4
Geneticist	G	$\overline{S}$	N	(30)	6.0
Supernaturalist	$\overline{G}$	S	N	(29)	5.8
Environmental	$\overline{G}$	$\overline{S}$	E	(59)	11.7
Radical	$\overline{G}$	$\overline{S}$	R	(31)	6.1
Subtotal of uni-causal assignments				(236)	47.0
Multi-Causal (Mixed) Modes					
Individualist-geneticist	G	$\overline{S}$	I	(35)	6.9
Individualist-supernaturalist	$\overline{G}$	S	I	(55)	10.9
Geneticist-supernaturalist	G	S	N	(11)	2.1
Individualist-geneticist-supernaturalist	G	S	I	(19)	3.8
Radical-environmentalist	$\overline{G}$	$\overline{S}$	ER	(29)	5.8
Subtotal of multi-causal assignments				(149)	29.5
Non-Causal Mode					
Transitional	$\overline{G}$	$\overline{S}$	N	(103)	20.5
Not assigned				(15)	3.0
				(504)	100.0

G = genetic; $\overline{G}$ = not genetic; S = supernatural; $\overline{S}$ = not supernatural; I = individualist; E = environmentalist; R = radical; N = neutral.

classified into "mixed" modes; their explanatory style was multi-causal. The individualist/supernaturalist is the most common multi-causal mode (11 percent); the second most common is the individualist/geneticist (7 percent), followed by the radical/environmental (6 percent).

What we called a *transitional* type accounts for 20 percent of the cases. These respondents scored low on the genetic and supernatural scales and intermediate on both the individualist-environmental and the individualist-radical scales. In effect, they do not identify with any single mode or combination of modes. It would seem that we failed to account for all the variety in our conceptual scheme. As we proceeded, we would be especially watchful of this mode to gain better insight into its character. This transitional type also contains those few cases in which an individualist, supernatural, or genetic explanation was combined with an environmental or radical one.[4]

The Validity of the Mode Assignments

The next major step in our research was to assess the validity and reliability of the explanatory-mode concept and of the means adopted to make it operational. The major test of validity would come when the relationships among the modes and the other two elements in the conceptual scheme—perceptions and prescriptions—were examined. Reliability would be assessed when data collected from the same subjects at two points in time were scrutinized. At this juncture, however, it was appropriate to ask

4. Of the 103 respondents classified as transitional in their explanatory mode, the vast majority—95—scored low on the genetic and supernatural scales and intermediate on the individualist-environmental and individualist-radical scales. The remaining 8 cases combined an individualist, supernatural, or genetic explanation with an environmental or radical one. For present purposes, we have combined the two types into the transitional category. Given a larger sample, separate analyses of the two types would be called for.

some initial and crucial questions about validity. Was the assignment of respondents into mode categories valid? Did occupants of each mode belong there? Did their mode assignment correctly reflect their understanding of racial differences?

We obtained a partial answer to these questions by examining whether the mode assignments "predicted" responses to the individual items. We expected a high correspondence between mode types and item responses, of course. The correspondence did not have to be perfect, however, since it was not required, in our scale building, that respondents give *only*, for example, supernatural responses to be scored as a supernaturalist or deny all individualist items and accept all environmental ones to be scored as environmental. In other words, in building the scales and in making mode assignments, we employed relative rather than absolute criteria. For example, respondents scored as pure individualists might occasionally be found to answer an item in other than an individualistic way. Nevertheless, a minimum test of the validity of a mode assignment is that its occupants choose items that depict their mode more frequently than do occupants of other modes. In turn, items that are inconsistent with a mode should be chosen less frequently by occupants of that mode.

We found that the modes met this minimum test very well. We have relegated the details to Appendix B so as not to encumber the text unduly. The gist of the results is that respondents classified into particular modes generally chose items that were consistent with the mode and rejected those that were out of harmony. This was true both for the pure and the mixed modes. In the case of the mixed modes—for example, the individualist/supernatural—their occupants over-selected items from both their categories—in our example, over-selecting both individualist and supernatural and rejecting, relatively, genetic, environmental, and radical items. Those in the transitional type, as would be expected by the nature of their mode assignment, under-select all items. Given the manner in which the scales were built and the mode assignments made, it was not surprising that this minimum test was met. Still, it was necessary to make sure before we proceeded.

A further validity test made at this point in the analysis involved finding out how well the modes predicted responses to explanatory-mode items that were not included in the scales used to assign modes. These tests also support the validity of the mode typology.

It should be acknowledged that not all mode assignments were made accurately, simply because some respondents were inconsistent in their answers. We did not expect that a "perfect" measure could be produced at the first try even if we had proven that the conceptualization itself was impeccable. Because of the imperfections, the standard we adopted in further evaluating the mode typology was not that the results be error-free, but rather that they not reasonably be attributable to chance. This is no more, it is recognized, than usual social science procedure, since measurement of social variables is never perfectly accurate. It seems useful, nevertheless, to offer this reminder of what was fitting to demand of the typology at this exploratory stage.

Summing Up

This chapter has reported on the character of the follow-up study, the questions used therein to make the explanatory-mode concept operational, and the steps taken to build a mode typology. The mode typology passed an initial test of validity. In the next chapter, we examine the ability of the modes to predict responses to the problem of racial inequality.

Chapter 5   *The Relations between Explanatory Modes and Prescriptions for Racial Policy*

In Chapters 2 and 3, we explored in a preliminary fashion the idea that how whites explain social differences between blacks and whites is crucial to how they respond to racial inequality. At that stage of our work, however, the specification of explanatory modes included only six "pure" mode types. As described in Chapter 4, we then elaborated and refined the specification to take into account the existence of multi-causal explanations. There were then eleven mode types whose relationships to prescriptions needed to be examined.

In making the examination, our purpose was to determine whether or not modes make a statistically and substantively significant difference in the courses of action respondents subscribe to as means for bringing about greater racial equality. We framed the prescriptive questions with the ultimate goal in mind of monitoring the incidence of "racial prejudice" in the national white population. Therefore, survey questions had to be salient to whites, whose opportunities for personal contacts with blacks could range from no or virtually no personal contact, as would be the case in some parts of the country, to daily contact of varying frequency and intensity.

It was presumed that the principal way all white Americans are obliged to confront racial inequality in the society is in responding to public policies and legislation formulated to deal with racial discrimination. Many of the prescriptive questions, consequently, were directed at measuring respondents' attitudes toward various governmental strategies designed to end discrimination in education, housing, and employment. The prescriptive questions were also intended to measure the amount of personal affinity respondents felt for blacks. Such questions took the form of asking people what they thought they would do if they were confronted with a decision involving race—for example, how they would respond to their child marrying a black person. On the assumption that modes might also influence a person's definition of what constitutes prejudice and his or her ability to recognize the existence of institutional discrimination, questions were also included on these two themes.

In constructing the so-called prescriptive questions, we tried to provide response categories that would discriminate among the principal mode types. Thus, the answer category for the individualists, for example, said that the government should do nothing to break down discrimination, but that the problem should be left to individuals to resolve. Answer categories also allowed for support of reformist policies that environmentalists especially were expected to favor and for a more drastic measure which, if explanatory modes are decisive, would appeal particularly to those in the radical mode. The questionnaire, as noted earlier, has been reproduced in Appendix D. The section on prescriptions runs from questions 36 to 57; questions 11 and 68 are directed at learning how respondents define prejudice and at determining their sensitivity to racial discrimination.

The Descriptive Results

The white residents of the San Francisco Bay Area are probably more liberal than the national population concerning such matters as deciding what ought to be done about discrimination and what they are personally willing to do to bring about greater racial equality. It also seems probable that Bay Area residents are more sophisticated, on the average, than the national population in their ability to recognize prejudice and institutional discrimination. At the same time, judging from their responses, people in the Bay Area are very far from agreeing on these issues. There are those who remain highly tolerant of past and present discriminatory practices, and others whose opposition to discrimination extends to strong support for compensatory programs and, indeed, reverse discrimination to make up for perceived transgressions of the past. The modal response, however, usually falls somewhere between these two extremes. Something ought to be done, respondents appear to be saying, but not so much that the present generation of whites is made to sacrifice greatly to bring about full equality. This is essentially the message conveyed by the responses to question after question. Consequently, while we will not burden the text with a complete report of the results, some concrete information on how responses were distributed to a sample of questions affords a useful introduction to the more analytic treatment of the data. Hence, a brief account of the descriptive results follows.

One question asked respondents how much "they think the government should press business to have a fair proportion of blacks in all kinds of jobs"; it elicited answers fairly typical of those received to questions asking what policies government, business, and labor ought to follow to help bring about greater racial equality. Twenty-seven percent of the white respondents replied in a highly individualistic way, saying that "the government shouldn't do anything. This is a matter which should be left to business to decide for itself." Another 40 percent took a more moderate individualistic position by replying, "Government should make it clear that it favors such a policy but leave it up to individual businesses to decide how to follow the policy." Twenty-four percent took a considerably stronger position in support of the government taking action to reduce discrimination in employment. They said that the government should "refuse to give government contracts where companies are not following such policies." Finally, only 10 percent went even further to answer, "We've reached the stage where laws should be passed to allow levying fines on businesses which do not follow such policy."

A response category for some other questions described "compensations" of some kind to blacks to make up for past discrimination, but such options gained relatively little support. For example, when asked how they felt about a proposal that "employers ought to favor black over white applicants for jobs in order to make up for the past when whites were favored over blacks," only 4 percent said, "I favor such a policy until the employment rate for blacks is as high as it is for whites." Another 11 percent said, "I favor such a policy, but only if blacks are preferred when they are as well or better qualified as whites." The modal response, given by 74 percent of the respondents, was "The color of a man's skin shouldn't count; people should be hired only on the basis of how qualified they are on the job." Eleven percent supported an even more conservative position: "The decision should be up to the employer; if black employers want to be able to hire only blacks, they should be able to do so; similarly, white employers should be able to hire whom they please."

The strong resistance to compensatory efforts of any kind is also illustrated in responses to a question asking respondents how they would have a school board act if it were faced with the following situation:

Half of the children attending public schools in a town are black and half are white. However, out of 100 teachers in the school only ten are black. Black parents ask the school board to hire only black teachers until half of the teachers are black.

Less than 1 percent said that the board should "do what the black parents want even if this means hiring some teachers who aren't fully qualified." An additional 6 percent said, "Make every effort to try to get more black applicants and then hire qualified black teachers even if they may be less qualified than white applicants." The modal response, however, was "Make every effort to try to get black applicants but hire only on the basis of qualification." Two-thirds of the respondents gave this answer. Finally, the remaining 27 percent said, "Stick to the present policy of hiring the best teachers from among those who apply."

When respondents were asked more personal questions about what they would be inclined to do in situations where they had the option to support or to oppose discrimination, opinions were once again divided, but in these cases a larger proportion of respondents chose a discriminatory response than in the case of the more abstract policy questions. In one question, for example, respondents were confronted with the following situation:

> Frank and Lucille Jones live in an all-white community and own their own home. Frank's company transferred him to a job in another city. The Jones put their house up for sale and decide to sell it to a middle-class black family who want to buy it and are willing to pay the price asked. The Jones' neighbors hear about this and find a white family who are willing to buy the house and even pay $1,000 more than the Jones would get from the black family. What do you think you would do if you were in the Jones' situation?

Forty-two percent of the sample said that they would sell to the black family; 39 percent said they would sell to the white family. However, an additional 19 percent thought "it would depend on whether I was a close friend of my neighbors."

When we asked respondents abstractly about intermarriage between whites and blacks—as in the question, "Which of the following statements comes closest to expressing your personal feelings about marriage between blacks and whites?—46 percent of the respondents favored intermarriage. They replied that "people should marry anyone they choose regardless of race." Thirty-three percent chose the response, "It's not a good idea for blacks and whites to marry because their children will suffer." The other 22 percent said that "blacks and whites should marry their own kind."

When asked immediately thereafter to suppose that they had a child who wanted to marry a black person with a good education and a good job, 33 percent said they would object, 16 percent said they would disapprove but keep silent, 27 percent didn't know, 5 percent said they would not care either way, and only 20 percent said they would approve. This last figure is considerably smaller than the 46 percent who a moment earlier had affirmed that "people should marry anyone they choose regardless of race."

The amount of personal sacrifice called for in adopting a particular policy proved to be an important element in determining the policy's acceptability. This is evident in the decline of support for intermarriage when the question was asked in a personal rather than an abstract manner. It is also evident in the responses to a series of three questions asked about school integration. The first question was as follows:

> Suppose it were found that integrated schools didn't make any educational difference for either black or white children but that integrated schools did make for better relations between black and white youngsters. If this were found, how then would you feel about school integration?

In response, 87 percent (67 percent strongly and 20 percent mildly) expressed approval of integration.

The second question in the series omitted any reference to better race relations but did postulate some advantage for blacks only:

> Now, suppose it were found that integrated schools improved the education of black students but made no difference in the education of white students. If this were found, how would you then feel about school integration?

In response to this statement, 80 percent (50 percent strongly and 30 percent mildly) expressed approval of integration.

Finally, the third question in the series postulated some cost for whites:

> Now, suppose it were found that integrated schools improved the education of black students but that white students tend to do better in all white schools. If this were found, how would you feel about school integration?

Presented with this last situation, the percentage approving of integration dropped to 55 percent (21 strongly and 34 mildly).

It is evident from these results that cost influences how whites respond to the black situation in America. We shall later report on just how cost is related to the understanding of racial differences, especially when one's understanding suggests a course of action that involves a personal sacrifice.

The questions designed to elicit how people define prejudice and how much they accept or reject the practice of discrimination took two forms.[1] In one version, a group of

1. In formulating the questions on prejudice, the concept was made operational through items making negative ascriptions of minority groups. The prejudice of subjects was then judged on the basis of their degree of acceptance of such items. In the present discussion, consequently, the term *prejudice* is utilized in the conventional sense—that is, prejudice is indicated by an individual's holding of negative beliefs about out-groups.

statements purporting to describe incidents in American life were set forth and respondents were asked to report whether or not they felt such incidents were all right. The events described were instances of prejudice or discrimination as, for example, "The biggest country club in town refuses to let any blacks have membership in the club." The second approach called for respondents to read through a series of statements and to rank each statement as an indication of prejudice: definitely, possibly, probably not, or definitely not. In formulating the statements, we made an effort to represent examples of prejudice and discrimination as well as so-called reverse discrimination.

Variation was considerable in responses to different prejudice items and to different items focused on discrimination. For example, among items on prejudice, the statement "suppose someone believes that blacks are generally inferior to whites" was thought definitely to constitute prejudice by 63 percent; another 29 percent considered this statement possibly to indicate prejudice. The statement, "A white gambler rubbing a black person's hair to bring himself luck," generated considerably less agreement: 31 percent said that the statement definitely indicated prejudice; 26 percent, probably.

Among items describing discrimination, social club discrimination against blacks was judged to be "not all right" by 75 percent of the sample. Considerably fewer respondents—49 percent—saw anything wrong when told that "all of the women who clean floors for a large bank are black." "Having a police force that is 98 percent white in a community that is 30 percent black" was thought definitely to signal prejudice by 19 percent, with another 51 percent agreeing that such a condition might possibly be discriminatory.

The few questions asked about reverse discrimination produced condemnatory responses from a majority. Sixty-five percent would judge a contractor who only hired black labor to be acting in a prejudiced way. Eighty-three percent would consider as definitely or possibly prejudiced a black social club excluding whites from membership.

Having introduced in general terms the types of prescriptive questions included in our survey, and some examples of respondents' answers to these questions, we turn now to a major concern of our study—an analysis of the relation between how people explain racial differences and how they respond to prejudice and discrimination.

Explanations and Prescriptions

Reporting on the relations between explanations and prescriptions is made cumbersome by the large number of mode types whose responses are to be compared. In an effort to overcome, or at least to reduce, the built-in difficulties of communication, we first present a vignette of what we learned about the prescriptive positions of each mode. For the vignettes, we mainly rely on responses to individual prescriptive questions rather than on scales and indices built to summarize responses; this allows us to draw finer distinctions among the modes. Summary measures are used when it is time to compare the modes with one another in a more systematic and efficient fashion.

Before beginning, we emphasize that we did not expect that each explanatory style would always produce distinctive responses to the prescriptive items. We speculated that it was possible, and sometimes even likely, that different explanatory modes may generate quite similar responses to questions about what ought to be done about racial inequality. Where that happens, however, analyses—presented in later chapters—led us to believe it is the result of different thought processes leading to the same conclusion. At the same time, as the following vignettes show, occupants of each mode exhibit certain distinctive characteristics in their response to racial inequality that mark them off from occupants of other modes.

We begin the vignettes by considering the responses of occupants of the pure explanatory modes, since they can serve as an anchoring point for later comparison with the responses of the mixed types.

The Pure Modes

The explanatory modes labeled "pure" are those whose occupants consistently account for social differences between blacks and whites in a uni-causal way. Six pure modes were specified in our original conception. The so-called cultural mode, however, was abandoned when it became clear, in an early analysis of the follow-up data, that it did not constitute a distinct type. Thus, the pure types include the individualists, the geneticists, the supernaturalists, the environmentalists, and the radicals.

The Individualists

The pure individualists believe that racial differences are the result of choices made by individuals. Unlike the occupants of such mixed modes as the individualist-supernaturalist and the individualist-geneticist, the pure individualists refuse to acknowledge that racial differences may be, in the final analysis, innate. Also, the pure individualists resist the social explanations of racial differences that underlie the environmental and radical modes. Their understanding is that blacks, on the average, are down on the social scale because, as individuals, they choose to be there. In effect, human beings are endowed naturally to exercise control over their own destinies, and where they end up in this world is a direct result of how they decide to exercise that control.

Equipped with this explanatory perspective, the individualists, when faced with questions asking them what the government, business, or labor ought to do to combat racial discrimination and to bring about greater racial equality, respond that they should do nothing. Of the pure types, the individualists are consistently the most likely to over-subscribe to response categories advocating that the problem of racial inequality is for individuals to resolve. Compared with the average white respondent, for example, the individualists are 1.7 times more likely to say that the "government should be doing nothing at all to help blacks; it should be left up to individuals"; 1.5 times more likely to be against laws making it illegal for an employer to hire a person for an available job because of that person's race and to favor employers being free to hire whom they choose; and 1.9 times more likely to feel that the government should not interfere in the hiring policies that labor unions adopt, even if they include not admitting blacks to membership.

This disposition to individualistic responses is matched by especially strong resistance to proposals of a compensatory kind to bring about greater racial equality. Whenever a response to a question proposes temporary reverse discrimination to make up for past inequities, it is soundly rejected by the individualists. Thus, there is not a single individualist in the sample favoring laws to allow levying of fines on businesses that do not have a fair proportion of blacks in all kinds of jobs. Similarly, no individualists support a proposal that schools work hard to get more black applicants and then hire qualified black teachers, even if they may be less qualified than white applicants. Moreover, individualists are consistently the most likely of all the pure types to reject such proposals as offering special classes to black parents to teach them how they can help their children do better in school, setting up black studies programs exclusively for blacks, and hiring blacks until the employment rate for them is as great as for whites.

On matters of a more personal nature, such as favoring selling a house to a black family, opposing laws against miscegenation, and approving of a child of theirs wanting to marry a black person who had a good education and a good job, the individualists show less hostility. Both the geneticists and the supernaturalists show more. The modal responses of the individualists, however, are conservative.

The individualists, by virtue of their tendency to blame blacks for their own misfortunes are, next to the geneticists, the least likely of the pure types to recognize the prejudice that exists in the society, and are the least sensitive to institutional discrimination. Thirty percent of all respondents express the view that they see no sign of discrimination in having a police force that is 98 percent white in a community that is 30 percent black; 51 percent of the individualists feel this way.

The individualist explanatory mode affords those who harbor it a rationale for an outlook on racial relations that many would judge as prejudiced, bigoted, and probably racist. The individualists, we suspect, do not see themselves as prejudiced or bigoted. From their viewpoint, black people in America are deprived relative to whites by their own choice, not because of anything white people have done. Moreover, it is beyond the power of white people to set things straight. Black people have to do that for themselves.

Rather than pass judgment on the individualists, we simply wish to observe that by virtue of their numbers they have had and continue to have an important influence in shaping the tone of race relations in the country. While the San Francisco Bay Area is not representative of the country as a whole, it is likely that if the individualist mode of thinking about race relations is predominant in that area, it is likely to be the predominant mode in the country at large.

The Geneticists
The geneticists account for racial differences as arising from black genetic inferiority. The general effect of being

armed with this vision, judging from the data, is to assume that nothing can be done to change the status quo and, consequently, that there is no use in trying. Unlike the individualists, the geneticists do not believe that blacks are in a position to change their relative deprivation through their own efforts. Consequently, the tendency is smaller among geneticists than among individualists to choose, when offered, options that advocate leaving problems of racial inequality up to individuals to resolve. In their responses to the prescriptive questions, the geneticists consistently over-select responses averring that nothing can be done, too much has been done already, or, at best, what now is being done is enough. When asked how they feel about laws that prohibit an employer from refusing to hire a person for an available job solely because of the applicant's race, the geneticists over-select the answers that they are against such laws or that the government has gone too far in enforcing them.

The geneticists are opposed to programs of a compensatory nature that would help to make up for past discrimination. Indeed, on nine questions in which support for such programs is an option, the geneticists show more opposition than the individualists on seven. These results are in accord with the geneticists' view that since nothing can be done to bring about greater racial equality, there is no gain from making the effort. From the individualists' perspective, the trouble with such programs is not so much that they will fail as that they will derail blacks from helping themselves.

It is to be remembered, in reflecting on these findings concerning the geneticists' and individualists' responses to compensatory programs, that the findings are relative, not absolute. Individualists and geneticists are more likely than the average respondent to disapprove of such programs, but the average respondent, as previously discussed, is not very supportive either.

As has already been mentioned, the geneticists are the

least likely of the pure types to show sensitivity to the existence of prejudice as a social problem and, next to the individualists, are the least likely of the pure types to recognize institutional discrimination when it is practiced. Neither mode conceives of blacks as victims of white hostility or repression, and this may account for their relative insensitivity.

The geneticist view is not a popular way of explaining racial differences, at least not in the Bay Area, where only 6 percent of white respondents in our sample are classified in this mode. When the mixed modes are taken into account, about 19 percent of the sample turns out to subscribe to a genetic explanation in whole or in part. Given that there is probably social pressure against acknowledging a belief that blacks are genetically inferior, this figure possibly underestimates the actual frequency. The size of the figure will also depend upon the classification criteria. On this score, obviously, neither we nor social science generally can claim to be exact in such matters.

Relatively, however, the main opposition today to liberal racial policies appears to be based more often on individualistic arguments than on genetic ones. If the mode assignments are correct, there are about three times as many individualists as geneticists in the Bay Area.

The Supernaturalists

It is not as self-evident for the supernaturalists as for the individualists and geneticists how they will respond to the prescriptive questions. Conceiving of God as having made the races different may mean that the supernaturalists judge such differences to be innate. If so, this might lead them to share the geneticists' view that there is nothing to be done to bring about greater racial equality. The view that God is all-powerful may also be conducive to a conservative stance on the grounds that there is not very much that human beings can do if everything is in God's hands. At the same time, since God is seen generally as a benevolent figure, it could follow that the adherents of a supernaturalist explanation of racial differences feel that they have some responsibility to be sympathetic to black people and to try to do something to help them.

Of the pure types, the supernaturalists are the most likely to say "don't know," "can't say," or "no opinion" to the prescriptive questions. As will be reported on later, this is partly a function of their being less educated than the average respondent. Even when education is controlled for, however, supernaturalists continue to be the most disposed of the pure types to an inability to answer questions.

Among supernaturalists who do have opinions, however, their mode of explanation appears to pattern their reactions to racial differences. Since they believe God to have created the races different, supernaturalists are not disposed to undo God's handiwork. They are the most strongly opposed of the pure types to black-white intermarriage, both generally and in their own families. When it comes to government, business, and labor doing more to help blacks, however, the supernaturalists are always less conservative than the geneticists and individualists. Indeed, on some of the issues we asked about, such as school integration, the supernaturalists are the most supportive of all the pure types. Moreover, the supernaturalists are consistently more disposed to compensatory programs than are individualists or geneticists. They also show a greater tendency than the occupants of these other two modes to be sensitive and sympathetic to the problem of prejudice in the society, although they appear no more able than the geneticists to recognize the existence of institutional discrimination.

In sum, the supernaturalists adopt the enigmatic posture, relative to the two types already discussed, of being the most strongly opposed to breaking down racial barriers but of being relatively sympathetic to efforts by institutions of the society to help reduce racial imbalance. However, this sympathy does not lead to advocacy of radical proposals for change. The supernaturalists' modal posture is best described as moderately reformist.

The Environmentalists

The environmentalists, by virtue of their understanding that differences between whites and blacks are a result of historical and social forces, are freed from some of the impediments to supporting social change that characterize the modes just discussed. Unlike the individualists, the environmentalists do not blame blacks for their relative deprivation. Consequently, the environmentalists are open to considering strategies other than "blacks pulling themselves up by their own bootstraps." Unlike the respondents who believe that social differences are due to innate biological determinants, the environmentalists think that, as the ways social forces operate come to be understood, they can be made subject to human control. And, unlike the supernaturalists, the environmentalists do not have to contend with the conception that it is God who has made the races different. While not restricted in these ways, the environmental construction of reality has its own inhibiting component, namely, an aversion to assigning responsibility for the present state of affairs. While environmentalists recognize that the existing situation is unfair, they do not see themselves, or whites in general living today, as responsible for the black condition. Consequently, even though their perspective leaves them open to change the status quo, environmentalists are not led thereby to pursue it actively.

The prescriptive questions reveal the environmentalists to be essentially reformist in their response to racial inequality. Their modal position is that the institutions of society can and should do more than they are doing now to combat racial discrimination. At the same time, they are not especially disposed to tolerate, much less advocate, reverse discrimination or compensatory programs to correct for racial inequities. Compared with the average respondent, for example, the environmentalists are 1.7 times more likely to affirm that new and tougher laws against discrimination should be passed and strictly enforced. They are only 1.04 times more likely than the average respondent to believe that "the government needs to do more than fight discrimination; it should use tax money to insure better jobs, housing and education for black people even if this means discrimination in reverse." Similarly, when asked how they feel about the proposal that "employers ought to favor black over white applicants for jobs in order to make up for the past when whites were favored over blacks," the environmentalists are 1.3 times more likely than the average respondent to favor such a policy until "the employment rate for blacks is as high as it is for whites." They are 1.8 times more likely than the average respondent to say that they favor such a policy but "only if blacks are as well or better qualified than whites." The environmentalists consistently under-select the positions that, as described earlier, are over-selected by the individualists and the geneticists. And, on virtually all issues of social policy, they are equally or more open to reform than the supernaturalists. As a group, however, the environmentalists balk at drastically changing existing social arrangements to accommodate blacks in the social order.

Nevertheless, the environmentalists are strong civil rights supporters and on a personal level are much less open than geneticists, individualists, and supernaturalists to practicing discrimination. They exhibit considerably more openness to black-white intermarriage both in principle and in regard to their own children than do the individualists, geneticists, or supernaturalists. They are also more sensitive to the presence of both prejudice and discrimination in the society.

The environmentalists constitute 12 percent of the white respondents in our sample; the only pure mode to which more people are assigned is the individualistic, with 17 percent. The environmentalists clearly have an important influence upon the character of race relations in the society. We will say more on this topic in the concluding chapter when we consider the policy implications of the findings. We turn now to the last of the pure types, the radicals.

The Radicals

Central to the response of those in the radical mode to the prescriptive questions is their belief that whites are responsible for the relative deprivations suffered by blacks in American society. This belief produces an openness to changing, sometimes even to overturning, existing social arrangements to correct for past and present white injustice to blacks. Of the pure types, the radicals are by far the most supportive of compensatory programs and reverse discrimination. Compared with the average respondent, for example, they are 2.3 times more likely to favor the "government using tax money to insure better jobs, housing, and education for black people even if this means discrimination in reverse"; 3.7 times more likely to support "employers favoring black over white applicants for jobs in order to make up for the past when whites were favored over blacks"; and 3.5 times more likely to advocate that schools in mixed racial areas "make every effort to try to appoint more black teachers, even if black applicants may be less qualified than white applicants."

The radicals show an even stronger tendency to support civil liberties than the environmentalists. The latter, for example, are 1.6 times more likely than the average respondent to favor in principle white-black intermarriage, and twice as likely to say they would approve if a child of theirs wanted to "marry a black person who had a good education and a good job." Comparatively, the radicals were 1.8 times more likely to support the first proposal, and 3 times more likely to approve the second.

The radicals are the most likely of the pure types to be sensitive to the racial prejudice that exists in the society and to maintain that American institutions are racist. In the latter regard, they are more than 8 times more likely than the average respondent to think that the federal and state governments in America are racist. They are 2.8 times more likely to conceive the possibility that a "bank which requires a very good credit rating before making a loan" might be practicing discrimination.

Constituting 6 percent of the sample, the radicals number only half as many as the environmentalists; in fact, their number compares with that of the pure geneticists. In spite of their small numbers, however, they were undoubtedly a force in the civil rights movements of the 1950s and 1960s, although they did not succeed in accomplishing the more drastic changes in social policy that they advocated.

All in all, the portraits of the pure types that emerge from the analysis of the follow-up data are consistent with those derived from the BAS data, where, it will be recalled, the analysis was based on what people defined as the most important reason for racial differences but did not take into account the fact that some respondents were entertaining more than one reason for such differences. Because it was possible to weed out those disposed to multi-causal explanation in the follow-up analysis, the modes are more clearly identified there than in the earlier analysis.

The Mixed Modes

The responses of the individuals in the pure modes led us to expect that respondents who mix environmental and radical explanations of racial differences would hold more liberal attitudes on the prescriptive questions than the mixed modes that, in some combination, support individualistic, genetic, and supernatural explanations. Beyond that, however, we did not know what to expect of those who account for racial differences in multi-causal terms. In reflecting on the matter, we considered four possibilities. One possibility was that one element in a mixed mode might inform respondents' attitudes more than another element; for example, the responses of the individualist-supernaturalists might resemble those of the pure supernaturalists more than those of the pure individualists or vice versa. A second possibility was that the effects of the several components might be found to average out; for example, respondents who share radical and environmental explanations of racial differences might end up, in their responses, falling somewhere between the answers of the pure radicals and the pure environmentalists. At least for some combinations, an "additive effect" also seemed possible; for example, the individualist-geneticists might give more conservative responses to the prescriptive questions than either the pure individualists or the pure geneticists. The fourth possibility, of course, was that there would be no consistent pattern in how the mixed modes responded to prescriptive issues.

The data confirm the expectation that the radical-environmentalists would prove more liberal than the other mixed modes. As to the other four possibilities, it turns out that there is some support for each of them, but that the additive effect is most common.

Radical-Environmentalists

The radical-environmentalists, as we shall call them, are persons who say, in effect, that social inequality between the races has its roots and its sustenance in historical and social forces that are not entirely free of human manipulation. Throughout American history, whites have been engaged in manipulating such forces to white advantage and to black disadvantage. Unlike the environmentalists, then, the radical-environmentalists blame whites for blacks' social condition. And, compared with the pure radicals, they give more recognition to the effects of social forces in producing racial inequality.

In their responses to the prescriptive questions, the radical-environmentalists are never less liberal than the pure environmentalists; however, they are sometimes less and sometimes more liberal than the radicals. The variation is not patterned in an entirely consistent fashion, although certain tendencies warrant mention. To begin with, those in this mixed mode are less disposed to judge the government as racist than those in the radical mode. In all other respects, however, they are the most responsive of all the pure and mixed types to government, business, and labor doing considerably more than they are now doing to end racial discrimination. They are slightly more likely than the radicals to show sensitivity to the existence of prejudice and discrimination in the society. On the intermarriage questions, their responses resemble those of the radicals.

In summary, occupants of the radical-environmental mode resemble the pure radicals more than they do the pure environmentalists. Compared with that of the radicals, however, the radical-environmentalists' response to the black condition appears more intellectual and less emotional, more focused on social structure and less on conspiracy.

The Other Mixed Modes
The other four mixed modes are the individualist-geneticists, the individualist-supernaturalists, the geneticist-supernaturalists, and the individualist-supernaturalist-geneticists. We encountered the first two in the exploratory in-depth interviews, where their initial re-

sponse to questions about how they account for racial differences was individualistic—"Racial differences are the
result of blacks not trying hard enough." When pressed by
interviewers to account for why "blacks as a group do not
try as hard as whites," some respondents acknowledged
the root cause in their judgment to be genetic or supernatural. Occupants of the latter two mixed modes are considerably fewer in number, which may account for their not
emerging as types in any of the exploratory interviews.

Generally speaking, occupants of all four mixed modes
are more conservative than the occupants of any pure
mode. This conservatism is manifest in the responses to
questions asking what government, business, and labor
might do to further racial equality. It is also reflected in the
responses to more personal questions bearing on feelings
of personal affinity to blacks. Moreover, the mixed modes
are all less likely than the pure types to recognize and
acknowledge prejudice and discrimination in society. This
means that these mixed modes respond even more harshly
to black demands and desires than do the pure individualists and pure geneticists, who, as was discovered earlier,
are themselves quite conservative, if not reactionary.

Among these four mixed modes, no single one emerges
as consistently the least or most conservative. The mixed
modes having a supernatural component do not exhibit
the pure supernaturalists' somewhat sympathetic response
to the plight of black people. There is some tendency for
the mixed modes having an individualistic component to
affirm individualistic policies where they are offered the
option to choose them. And those in the individualist-
geneticist-supernatural mode, while not always giving the
most conservative answers, do so more often than any
other mixed type. The general effect of being in one of
these traditional mixed modes is to compound the conser-
vatizing effects of the pure individualistic and pure geneticist modes, and to mute the pure supernaturalists' disposi-

tion to support some institutional effort to improve the black condition in America.

Given the absence of sharp and consistent differences among these mixed types, we first thought that it might be appropriate to combine them in further analysis. It turned out, however, that while the occupants do not differ consistently in their prescriptions, they do differ in other respects that are of some substantive and theoretical importance. Consequently we continued to analyze them separately.

The Transitionals

The so-called transitionals, it will be recalled, are mostly respondents who scored low on the supernatural and genetic scales and in the middle on the individualist-environmentalist and individualist-radical scales. In effect, these are people who do not fit into our explanatory-mode framework. Whether or not they harbor an explanation of racial differences other than any that our instruments have tapped is unfortunately not a question that can be answered with the present data. The best we can do is to try to gain some insight into the character of the transitionals by comparing their responses with those of the other mode types.

The transitionals' responses to the prescriptive questions are consistently in between those of the individualist, supernaturalist, and genetic modes and those of the radical and environmentalist modes. In effect, if we characterize the former modes as traditional and the latter two as modern, the transitionals are in the middle. It is possible that respondents in this mode are in transition from a traditional view to a more modern one, but this possibility cannot be established with any degree of certainty with the data at hand.

Summary Measures

To summarize our findings on the relation between explanations and prescriptions, we constructed two scales to tap the two principal themes addressed in the prescriptive questions. The first scale, which we labeled the institutional intervention scale, is addressed to measuring the extent to which respondents support institutional policies designed to combat discrimination. In order to score high on the institutional intervention scale, a respondent had to

- favor government pressure on business to have a fair proportion of blacks in all kinds of jobs;

- favor schools hiring more qualified black teachers even if this means not hiring some more qualified white teachers;

- oppose the idea that employers should be left free by government to hire anyone they choose, even if they exclude blacks;

- disagree that property owners should have the right to sell, or refuse to sell, to whomever they choose.

The institutional intervention scale, by virtue of being a continuous rather than a typological variable, does not capture all the nuances in policy alternatives discussed in the vignettes. For present purposes, however, it is a useful tool for comparing the degree to which the different modes are liberal or conservative in their attitudes toward the role that society's institutions should play in combating racial discrimination.

The second scale is designed to measure how much personal affinity these white respondents feel for blacks, personal affinity being measured in terms of wanting traditional racial barriers to be broken down. To score high on the personal affinity scale, a respondent had to approve of interracial marriage between blacks and whites both as a general principle *and* in regard to his or her own child. The respondent also had to favor open housing laws, which make it illegal for anyone who puts their property up for sale to refuse to sell to a person on the basis of that person's race. A low score on the personal affinity scale indicates that the respondent takes the opposite view on these questions. (The details of the construction of these scales and their validation are reported in Appendix B.)

Table 14 compares the different modes in terms of how much their average scores on the two scales deviate from the score of the average respondent. A deviation of 10.0 corresponds to one standard deviation above or below the mean.

The results presented in Table 14, while they do not address all the fine points covered in the vignettes, never-

Table 14 **Institutional Interventionism and Personal Affinity by Explanatory Mode (in deviations from Mean Scores)[a]**

EXPLANATORY MODE	INSTITUTIONAL INTERVENTION	PERSONAL AFFINITY
Mixed Traditional		
Individualist-genetic	−7.3	−6.9
Individualist-supernatural	−6.5	−6.9
Genetic-supernatural	−6.6	−8.6
Individualist-genetic-supernatural	−8.3	−8.3
Pure Traditional		
Individualist	−4.4	1.8
Genetic	−3.8	−2.1
Supernatural	.6	−3.8
Transitional	2.4	1.7
Modern		
Environmentalist	6.8	7.0
Radical	10.0	9.9
Radical-environmentalist	12.9	9.2
Eta	.62	.56
N	(484)	(471)

[a] Standard deviation = 10

theless document the central thrust of their findings. We discover that the modern modes—comprising the environmentalists, the radicals, and the radical-environmentalists—show the most support for institutions engaging in efforts to combat discrimination and also express the greatest personal affinity for blacks. At the opposite extreme, the modes that mix two or three of the traditional ways of accounting for racial differences show the most opposition to institutional intervention and feel the least personal affinity. The three pure traditional modes are all less conservative in outlook than any of the mixed traditional modes but considerably more conservative than the modern modes. The transitionals fall exactly between the traditional and the modern modes in their average scale scores.

Among the three modes constituting the modern set, the environmentalists are the least liberal on both scales. The radical-environmentalists more closely resemble the radicals than the environmentalists. They score as more liberal than the radicals on the institutional intervention scale and slightly less liberal on the personal affinity scale.

The response pattern of the three pure traditional modes is different on the two scales, confirming what was reported in the vignettes. The individualists are the most strongly opposed to institutional intervention but, of the three modes, show the most personal affinity for blacks. In turn, the supernaturalists, while the most open to institutional activity to combat discrimination, are the least likely of the three modes to want traditional racial barriers to be broken down.

The results also reveal some variation in the responses of the mixed traditional modes. These modes' responses to the individual questions, however, did not show consistent differences, except that as a group they were always more conservative than any of the other modes.

The differences in responses among the three major mode groups—the mixed traditionals, the pure traditionals, and the moderns—are all significant statistically.[2] The differences between the scores of the environmentalists and the other two modern groups are also statistically significant. Finally, the score of the pure supernaturalists on institutional intervention is significantly different from the scores of the individualists and the geneticists on this scale. Most other differences are not statistically significant.

Summing Up

The basic postulate of these inquiries is that how whites explain racial differences will influence how they respond to the relative deprivation of blacks in the society. It does not follow from this postulate that each mode of explanation must generate a different response; for example, the geneticists and individualists may respond to racial inequality in statistically similar ways. For the postulate to be valid, however, it is required that where similar responses are produced between modes, they are arrived at by a different cognitive process.

This does not mean that we would have persisted in arguing for the importance of explanatory modes if all the differences had proven statistically insignificant. Clearly, on theoretical grounds, we anticipated statistically significant differences in some instances as, for example, between the responses of the individualists and the environmentalists and radicals. At the same time, no theory is upset because the differences in the scale scores of the geneticists and the individualists are statistically insignificant. At this stage of our research we had not demonstrated that the modes are the source of the similarities and dissimilarities in responses that we had found. The possi-

2. That is to say, there is 1 chance in 20 or less that differences in responses could have occurred by chance.

bility of the relationships being spurious had still to be addressed.

The matter of spuriousness aside, reservations could also be expressed that the correspondence between explanations and prescriptions was not great enough to justify our claims that the modes are crucial to determining how whites respond to racial inequality. Although the relationship we found between explanations and prescriptions is moderately high by social science standards (eta-squares of .39 and .31), we recognized that we needed to return to the question of whether the modes were crucial to prescription when more analytical work was completed. This need is discussed in the concluding chapter.

For now, having demonstrated that explanations and prescriptions are related, we want to return to our investigation of where perception fits into the picture. In the next chapter we examine the relationship between perceptions and explanations, and in the following one we investigate their joint relation to prescriptions.

Chapter 6 **Perceiving and Explaining Racial Differences**

The idea that perception-based measures of "prejudice" are inadequate, used alone, for social indicator purposes is fundamental to our approach. As previously discussed, perception-based measures equate racial prejudice with the acceptance of negative stereotypes of blacks. In part, the inadequacy of such measures lies in their classifying as prejudiced some perceptions that have a basis in fact. For example, the perception that "during their lifetimes, blacks are more likely than whites to get in trouble with the police" may cast blacks in a negative light, but it is scarcely an accurate indicator of prejudice that someone affirms what is, in fact, true.

Measures of racial prejudice based solely on perceptions have an even more serious limitation. Whether negative or positive, perceptions of racial differences can be accounted for in different ways, some of which may produce or signify a favorable attitude toward blacks and others an unfavorable response. Consequently, a perception alone will not indicate how the perceiver responds to blacks. Thus, to judge whether harboring the belief that "blacks are more likely to get in trouble with the police" constitutes a hostile or friendly stereotype, one must also know whether that perception is explained as the result of an inherent defect in black character, of discrimination against blacks by police departments, or of something else.

Despite these limitations, perception-based measures have been widely used in studies of prejudice and, seemingly, to good effect. Scores on such measures have been found to be associated with the expression of social distance toward blacks and feelings of hostility toward them as well as with resistance to efforts to reduce racial inequality.[1] In the language we have been using, perception-based measures appear to be predictive of prescription, without mode of explanation being taken into account.

Perhaps our contention is wrong that it is necessary to know how a perception is accounted for in order to be able to predict the related prescription. It is also possible that perception-based measures "work" because there is a strong association between the racial differences people perceive and the way they explain these differences. Thus, while such stereotypes as "blacks are less intelligent than whites," "blacks are less likely to work hard than whites," or "blacks are less moral than whites" could be explained within the framework of any of the explanatory modes we have identified, they are usually explained, when they are believed, predominantly from one or several explanatory modes that, in turn, are associated with negative prescriptions.

However, even if one demonstrated that this was the case, one would still be unjustified in ignoring explanatory modes in measuring white racial attitudes. For one thing, unless the association between perception and explanation is perfect, perception-based measures are subject to some error. For example, if it should turn out that a majority who perceive "blacks as working less hard than whites" account for this as genetically produced but a minority hold to an environmental explanation of such differ-

---

1. See Robin M. Williams, Jr., *Strangers Next Door, Ethnic Relations in American Communities* (Englewood Cliffs, N.J.: Prentice-Hall, 1964); and Hubert M. Blalock, Jr., *Toward a Theory of Minority-Group Relations* (New York: John Wiley, 1967).

ences—"after being discriminated against for so many generations, it is no wonder that blacks don't have the initiative whites do"—the perception is, at best, only an imperfect indicator of "prejudice" or how the perceiver feels about blacks.

Another important reason for including explanation is that it is the component linking perceptions and prescriptions. Why should particular perceptions be associated with particular prescriptions? Where the association is imperfect, how is it to be accounted for? These questions cannot be answered unless the explanatory component is incorporated into our model.

These problems raise the question of how the relationship between perceptions and explanations develops. It seems logical that in the socialization process, perceptions occur first and then explanations of them are formulated. If blacks are not seen as different from whites, there is nothing to be explained. At the same time, as we have remarked earlier, once a mode of explanation has been internalized, it is likely to influence additional perceptions. While our cross-sectional data afford no means to determine the time order of perceptions and explanations, they do permit exploration of how much and in what ways perceptions are associated with explanations.

In thinking about how perceptions and explanations might be related, we anticipated, on the basis of some preliminary evidence from the in-depth interviews, that the relationship would depend on whether the perceived racial differences were thought to be related to character or social structure. Characterological differences include perceptions to the effect that blacks differ from whites in personality, values, living habits, customs, and the like. Examples would be that, compared with whites, blacks are more or less hard-working, intelligent, sloppy, ambitious, concerned about their children's education, and so on. Social structural differences, in turn, consist of perceptions about status and class differences between the races, both actual differences and differences in opportunity. Examples would be that, compared with whites, blacks actually have better or poorer educations, jobs, or housing, and that blacks have greater or lesser *opportunities* for well-paying jobs, to live where they please, to get good medical service, and so on. Different modes of explaining racial differences, we anticipated, would be associated, first of all, with whether characterological and/or social structural differences are perceived and, if so, with whether the perception is more favorable to blacks or to whites.

Tapping Perceptions

In formulating the follow-up questionnaire, we included questions to assess respondents' perceptions in both the characterological and social structural realms. Among the questions relative to character was one that listed a number of traits—e.g., hard-working, intelligent, ambitious, sloppy, honest—and instructed respondents to indicate whether they thought each trait was more characteristic of blacks or whites, or whether there was no difference. A second question was identical except that it asked respondents now to reply as they anticipated most Americans would answer the question. A group of questions about character traits listed a set of values—e.g., owning their own homes, earning a lot of money, seeing that their children went to college, having a good time—and asked respondents to say whether they believed such things were more important to whites or blacks living in America today, or if there was no difference.

To measure the component relating to social structure, we asked questions about the relative opportunity afforded blacks and whites for such things as having a good job, getting a good education, living in satisfactory housing, and getting adequate medical care. We also asked respondents what they perceived the actual situation of blacks to be relative to whites in these and other areas of life. Additional questions asked respondents to report their perceptions of how much discrimination blacks experience in such realms of life as living where they please, being treated fairly by white storekeepers, being given fair treatment by police, and the like. For the reader interested in the full text of the perception questions, they are questions 16 to 31 in the questionnaire reproduced in Appendix D.

The Descriptive Results

Generally speaking, the white population of the Bay Area is inclined to deny assertions that the character traits of blacks differ from those of whites. As shown in the top half of Table 15, when asked whether particular traits are more characteristic of whites than blacks, the modal answer for each trait is that there is no difference. On the average, about 25 percent do perceive differences, and they tend to see whites as having the "positive" traits and blacks as having the "negative" ones, with the exception that blacks are more likely than whites to be perceived as religious, as athletic, and as having a good sense of humor.

When asked how they think most white Americans would answer this question, respondents see, as is indicated in the bottom half of Table 15, much more negative stereotyping in the culture than they see in themselves. For every trait except being religious and good at sports, a majority thinks that most white Americans have positive images of themselves and negative images of blacks. Indeed, on such traits as working hard, being intelligent, and ambitious, more than 70 percent of respondents say that most white Americans believe these to be white traits.

"No difference" is also the modal response to most items in the question asking whether certain values are more important to the average black or to the average white family. The results are reported in Table 16.

Table 15 **Acceptance of Racial Stereotypes (in percent)**

| DESCRIPTION | A. RESPONDENT *personally* THINKS DESCRIPTION APPLIES MORE TO: | | | | |
	Blacks	Whites	No Dif-ference	Can't Say; No Answer	Total
Good at sports	43%	1	50	6	100%
Religious	25%	5	57	13	100%
Likely to cheat or steal	24%	1	58	17	100%
Sloppy	15%	5	62	18	100%
Good sense of humor	15%	5	67	13	100%
Likely to commit sex crimes	14%	3	62	21	100%
Warm and friendly	9%	14	64	13	100%
Oversexed	6%	1	60	33	100%
Willing to work hard	3%	35	52	10	100%
Honest	2%	12	69	17	100%
Ambitious	2%	40	47	11	100%
Intelligent	a	29	56	15	100%

| DESCRIPTION | B. RESPONDENT THINKS THAT *most Americans* THINK DESCRIPTION APPLIES MORE TO: | | | | |
	Blacks	Whites	No Dif-ference	Can't Say; No Answer	Total
Likely to cheat or steal	70%	1	18	11	100%
Good at sports	63%	6	23	8	100%
Likely to commit sex crimes	60%	2	25	13	100%
Sloppy	58%	5	25	12	100%
Oversexed	52%	2	23	23	100%
Religious	29%	21	34	16	100%
Good sense of humor	19%	29	38	14	100%
Warm and friendly	7%	49	30	14	100%
Willing to work hard	2%	76	13	9	100%
Intelligent	1%	75	14	10	100%
Ambitious	1%	76	14	9	100%
Honest	1%	65	23	11	100%

N = 504 both sets
a Less than 0.5%.

Among respondents who attribute values as more important to one race or the other, the values most often associated with blacks are owning a big car, participating in sports, going to church, and having a good time today. Values of a more economic nature, commonly associated with being successful in America, are attributed much more frequently to whites, such as taking very good care of one's home, owning a summer home on a lake, being involved in community activities, and being concerned about having good police protection in their communities.

In response to questions designed to measure perceptions of differences relating to social structure, very few respondents see blacks as more privileged than whites. Answers divide primarily between no differences being perceived or whites being judged as more advantaged;

Table 16 **Perception of Racial Differences in Values**

| VALUE | RESPONDENT JUDGES VALUE MORE IMPORTANT TO: | | | | |
	Black Family	White Family	No Difference	Can't Say; No Answer	Total
Owning a big car	58%	4	37	1	100%
Participating in sports	27%	4	68	1	100%
Going to church	25%	5	68	2	100%
Having a good time today	23%	2	73	2	100%
Owning their own business	16%	27	55	2	100%
Seeing that children go to college	12%	38	48	2	100%
Having an exciting sex life	10%	2	86	2	100%
Earning a lot of money	10%	19	70	1	100%
Having good police protection	7%	29	62	2	100%
Involvement in community activities	6%	41	51	2	100%
Own summer house on a lake	6%	48	43	3	100%
Take good care of one's home	1%	41	57	1	100%

N = 504

there is considerable variation depending upon the subject under question.

This variation can be seen, by way of a first example, in Table 17, which reports the responses to the question of whether whites or blacks have the greater opportunity to do the listed things.

Table 17   **Perception of Opportunities Available to Whites and Blacks**

| TYPE OF OPPORTUNITY | GREATER CHANCE FOR: | | | | |
	Whites	*Blacks*	*No Dif-ference*	*Can't Say; No Answer*	*Total*
Live where one pleases	78%	2	16	4	100%
Well-paid job	64%	5	26	5	100%
Financial help when in need	47%	16	25	12	100%
Treated fairly by police	46%	3	33	18	100%
Good education	42%	3	53	2	100%
Treated fairly by store-keepers	38%	2	47	13	100%
Good medical services	32%	4	56	8	100%

N = 504

The most agreement is found with respect to whites having greater opportunities than blacks to live where they please and to get well-paid jobs. In other realms, such as getting a good education, getting financial help when in need, being fairly treated by police, and getting good medical services, the consensus is not so great. Indeed, on the last three items, more people believe that whites and blacks have equal opportunities than believe that whites have an advantage.

After being told that there is sometimes a discrepancy between having the opportunity to do something and actually doing it, respondents were asked to compare the average black and the average white person with respect to their actually having a good job, a good education, good housing, and good medical care. The responses to this question are reported in Table 18.

Table 18   **Perceptions of Possession of Social Goods by Whites and Blacks**

| TYPE OF SOCIAL GOOD | GROUP MORE LIKELY TO POSSESS A SOCIAL GOOD: | | | | |
	Whites	Blacks	No Difference	Can't Say; No Answer	Total
Good job	78%	2	18	2	100%
Good housing	76%	2	20	2	100%
Good education	66%	3	29	2	100%
Good medical care	48%	4	47	1	100%

N = 504

A substantial majority of respondents believe whites to be better off than blacks in all areas save medical care, where the sample is divided about equally between those saying no difference and those saying whites get better medical care. Once again, only a handful of respondents say that blacks are privileged relative to whites.

Comparatively, however, substantially more respondents perceive opportunities to be available to blacks than perceive that blacks take advantage of them. Recall from Table 17 that 26 percent replied that blacks have as much opportunity as whites to get a well-paid job. Table 18 tells us, however, that only 18 percent believe that blacks are doing as well job-wise as whites. Parallel figures for getting a good education are 53 and 29 percent and for getting good medical care, 56 and 47 percent.

The responses to other questions designed to discover prevailing white perceptions of what it means to be black in the United States are similar to those just reported. By and large, there is little tendency to see blacks as superior to whites either in terms of character or social structure. Mostly respondents divide between perceiving whites in

more favorable terms or perceiving no differences between the two races.

Perceptions and Explanations:
Expected Relationships

We have already mentioned our general expectation
that the different explanatory modes would be found related to whether or not racial differences are perceived at all
and, if so, to whether the differences perceived are characterological and/or social structural in kind. Before presenting the results, we want to specify our expectations in
these respects for each explanatory mode and to set forth
our reasons for holding them.

Turning to the pure modes first, it might seem that we
should have expected the individualists, relatively, to deny
any characterological or social structural differences between the races. At least this appeared the logical conclusion to draw from the individualists' denial that there are
such things as group differences, and their assertion that
all differences are at their root individual. It is to be remembered, however, that the ideological make-up of individualists includes the belief that if "only they would try,
blacks could be as successful as whites." Implicit in such a
belief, it appeared, is an acknowledgment of group differences of both a characterological and social structural kind:
"Blacks don't work as hard as whites and they are less
successful than whites." What characterizes the individualists, however, is that they see such differences as resulting from individual choice rather than from the characteristics of the group. Thus, at the same time as group
differences are perceived, they are, by virtue of the individualists' explanation of them, effectively denied.

While all of this created ambiguity about the individualists' probable responses to the perception questions, we
still anticipated that the individualist would be distin-

guished from the other modes in being the most disposed to deny *both* characterological and social structural differences.

In contrast to the individualists, the geneticists were expected to affirm racial differences that stem both from social structure and character. By virtue of their belief that racial differences are innate, the geneticists were likely to find confirming "evidence" most directly in perceived characterological differences. Once these were acknowledged, a logical accompaniment, from the geneticists' perspective, would be social structural differences.

The supernaturalists, once again, were difficult to predict. Given their acknowledgment that God made the races different, it would seem to follow that they would acknowledge differences—especially character-related ones. As discussed earlier, however, conceiving of God as the controlling agent may convey other instructions to the supernaturalists, among which might be a call to avoid being judgmental. This dictum could result in the supernaturalists acknowledging only racial differences that do not reflect negatively on either race. In effect, we had no firm theoretical ground for predicting the perceptions for the supernaturalists as we had for the individualists and geneticists or, for that matter, the environmentalists and the radicals.

With regard to the occupants of the latter two modes, we expected that relative to the other modes they would be disposed to deny the existence of characterological differences and to acknowledge the social structural ones. It should be noted that the occupants of the environmental and radical modes of explaining racial differences might acknowledge character-based differences, even differences that involve seemingly negative descriptions of blacks. For example, the perception that "blacks are less hard working than whites" can be attributed as readily to generations being denied access to the larger rewards of the society as to genetic differences. We suspected, however, based on the evidence presented in the last chapter, that, given their basic sympathy for blacks, those in the environmental and radical modes would not be disposed to acknowledge characterological differences between the races that others might ascribe to prejudice. To acknowledge social structural differences, on the other hand, conforms with both modes' explanatory styles and to the sympathetic posture toward blacks with which both modes are associated.

Since the occupants of the radical mode appear more emotional in their response to the black condition, it was conceivable that they would be found more often to deny characterological and to affirm social structural differences than the occupants of the environmental mode. The perceptions of both modes, however, were likely to differ considerably less from each other than from the perceptions of the other three pure modes.

With the exception of the radical-environmentalists, whom we anticipated would be found to perceive racial differences in ways akin to the environmentalists and radicals, the mixed modes were more difficult to predict. The difficulty stemmed from the fact that all the other mixed modes either contain elements that, in their pure form, were expected to have different perceptual consequences or contain a supernatural element about which we had no firm prediction. We simply had to wait and to see whether one element in a combination had more, less, or equal power than the other element(s) in generating an effect.

Perceptions and Explanations:
Findings

In order to convey the main substance of the findings, we shall, as in the preceding chapter, first summarize them in narrative form and then introduce supportive statistical material.

The Pure Modes

Of the pure modes, the geneticists, as expected, are the most likely to affirm characterological differences between the races and to do so in ways that conform to their belief in black inferiority. Of the pure types, they are the most likely to say that whites work harder than blacks, are more intelligent, more ambitious, and more likely to be honest. In turn they are the most likely to say that blacks tend more than whites to cheat and steal, to commit sex crimes, to be sloppy, and to be oversexed. The geneticists are also the most disposed of the pure types to attribute to whites such values as believing it important to own their own business, to earn a lot of money, to see that their children go to college, to have good police protection in their neighborhoods, to be involved in community action, and to take good care of their homes. Interestingly enough, the geneticists are also the most likely of the pure types to affirm that blacks are more prone than whites to be religious, to be good at sports, to believe it important to own a big car, and to have a good time. In sum, the geneticists, in their perceptions of character-based racial differences, conform to the traditional image of the prejudiced person.

The occupants of the environmental and radical modes are the most disposed of the pure modes to deny characterological differences between the races. Compared with the average respondent, and with the geneticists in particular, both modern modes are found consistently less likely to attribute positive traits to whites and negative ones to blacks. In turn, they are more likely to say there are no differences or to attribute middle-class values to blacks and less likely to attribute them only to whites. Comparing the two modes, we found no statistically significant or consistent differences between them.

While very different from each other in their perception of characterological differences, the two pure modern modes and the genetic are all inclined, compared with the average respondent, to acknowledge social structural differences. This is true whether comparisons are based on perceptions of the opportunities available to blacks and whites in the society or on the perceived reality of the respective social positions of the two races. Thus, for example, all three modes report that whites have a greater opportunity than blacks to get a good job or a good education in America and also that whites on the average do have better jobs and are better educated.

These tendencies to affirm social structural differences, while manifest in all three modes when compared with the average respondent, are nevertheless stronger for the environmentalists and the radicals than for the geneticists, especially concerning the relative opportunities that whites and blacks enjoy in the society. The three modes are closer together in their perceptions that whites are, in fact, more privileged than blacks. The geneticists appear to be saying it is not so much that the opportunities are not there as that blacks are not capable of taking advantage of them that accounts for their deprived status. The two modern modes, on the other hand, take the position that it is the absence of opportunities, not any characterological defects, that accounts for blacks being relatively deprived. In their perceptions of social structural differences, the two modern modes are similar, with some slight tendency for the radicals to affirm such differences more frequently than the environmentalists.

Concerning the individualists, we had tentatively predicted that they would be found, relatively, to deny both characterological and social structural differences. Compared with the average respondent, they are in fact the most disposed of the pure modes to deny differences relative to social structure. Once again, the individualists display their relative inability to perceive that social structure may act as a constraint on human behavior.

While more disposed than the average respondent to

deny characterological differences, the individualists are somewhat less inclined to do so than the occupants of the two pure modern modes. That the two modern modes should be more apt to deny characterological differences than the individualists is in accord with these modes' explanatory styles.

The supernaturalists show a tendency, relative to the average respondent, to deny social structural differences, although they are less likely to do this than the individualists. They are also more likely than the average respondent to deny characterological differences, at about the same level as the individualists. The thought processes underlying the supernaturalists' responses are not self-evident. The best we could do at this juncture was to repeat the speculation, expressed earlier, that the supernaturalists are inhibited from being judgmental by their conception of God. While this speculation would help to explain their resistance to ascribing negative characteristics to blacks, it does not shed light on their relative inclination to deny social structural differences. Perhaps a clearer picture would emerge later when we examined the background from which the supernaturalists come.

To summarize these results statistically, we created two scales to represent the variation in respondents' perceptions of characterological and social structural differences. The social structural scale sought to assess the extent to which respondents acknowledge that whites are more privileged than blacks in American society. Three items were used to build the scale—are whites or blacks in America more likely to have a good job, more likely to have good housing, and more likely to have good medical care? To score high on this scale, respondents had to reply that whites were more likely than blacks to have these things. To score low a respondent had to deny that whites were favored in these respects.

The characterological scale was designed to assess the

degree to which blacks are viewed as possessing certain middle-class values. Respondents scored high on this scale if they believed that the term *sloppy* is more applicable to black than to white people in America, that taking good care of their home is more characteristic of white than black families, and that white parents consider it more important to see that their children get to college than black parents do. To score low on this scale, respondents had to assert that blacks are no different than whites in these respects. (See Appendix B for more detailed descriptions of these scales.)

Based on these two scales, Figure 1 portrays the relative tendency of the five pure modes compared with the sample as a whole to affirm or deny social structural and characterological differences between the races. The vertical axis represents the degree of affirmation or denial of social structural differences, scored in terms of the deviations from the mean score on the social structural scale. The horizontal axis, in turn, represents the degree of affirmation or denial of characterological differences, scored in terms of the deviations from the mean score on the characterological scale. Scores above zero signify a tendency to perceive differences more frequently than the average respondent; scores below zero, a tendency to perceive differences less frequently than the average respondent. Ten points correspond to one standard deviation above or below the mean. Each of the pure types is located on the graph in terms of its scores on the two scales. Thus, the graph reveals for each type its relative disposition to affirm or deny characterological and social structural differences between the races compared to the sample as a whole.

The environmental and radical modes are located in the upper left quadrant of Figure 1, signifying their tendency to deny characterological differences and to affirm social structural ones. Note that the two modes are about equally likely to deny characterological differences; the radicals, however, are somewhat more disposed to affirm social structural differences.

The fact that the geneticists are alone in the upper right quadrant of the graph signals their disposition to affirm both kinds of differences. Their tendency to affirm characterological differences more often than social structural ones is indicated by their position in the quadrant; they are located closer to the X than to the Y axis.

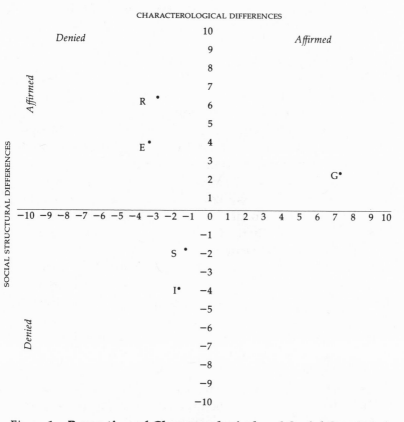

Figure 1   **Perception of Characterological and Social Structural Differences by Occupants of the Pure Modes (Scores Are Deviation From Mean; Standard Deviation = 10)**

The supernaturalists and the individualists are located in the lower left quadrant of the graph, signifying their disposition to deny both characterological and social structural differences. Relatively, the individualists are more disposed to deny social structural differences.

Using other measures of the two kinds of differences, we find some slight variation with respect to the relative position of the modes within quadrants. The variation does not change the conclusions drawn from Figure 1. Whatever measure we use, each type falls into the same quadrant as it does in Figure 1.

The Mixed Types

Figure 2 replicates Figure 1 except that the location of the mixed types has also been graphed.

Of the mixed types, we only ventured a prediction about the radical-environmentalists. As can be seen in Figure 2, our expectation is confirmed: the radical-environmentalists fall into the same quadrant of the graph as the pure modern modes. Relatively, the radical-environmentalists are slightly less likely than the environmentalists and the radicals to deny characterological differences. They are more likely than both of the pure modern modes to perceive social structural differences.

Of the mixed traditional modes, the two that include both an individualistic and genetic component fall into the previously unoccupied lower right quadrant of the graph, signifying their disposition, relative to the total sample, to deny social structural differences and to affirm characterological ones. It is to be noted that both of the mixed types in this quadrant share a genetic component *and* the geneticists' tendency to affirm characterological differences. In their denial of social structural differences, these mixed types are not like the geneticists but rather resemble the individualistic component of their mix.

The individualist-supernaturalists fall into the same

quadrant as the pure individualists and the pure supernaturalists. The three modes are alike in the degree to which they deny characterological differences. The individualist-supernaturalists, however, are considerably more likely than the pure modes to deny social structural differences. The geneticist-supernaturalists, as can be seen, resemble the pure geneticists more than the pure supernaturalists in their perceptions; their relative tendency is to affirm both

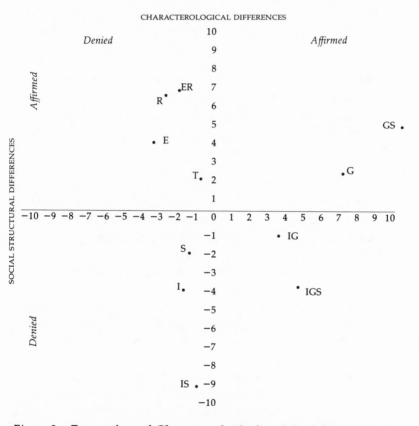

Figure 2   **Perception of Characterological and Social Structural Differences by Occupants of All Modes (Scores Are Deviation From Mean; Standard Deviation = 10)**

characterological and social structural differences.

There is one mode—the transitionals—still to be considered. On the characterological scale, their score is virtually equivalent to that of the average respondent. On the other scale, the transitionals show a slight tendency to affirm social structural differences. It is possible that the relatively neutral perceptions of the transitionals reflect their ambivalence about choosing any explanation of racial differences as paramount.

So far, we have not remarked about the statistical significance of the results. The groups that are relatively distinct statistically are (G and GS), (IG and IGS), (I and S), (IS), (T), and (E, R, RE). Within each of the sets of parentheses, the differences are not significant. The results are about equivalent statistically when other measures of characterological and social structural differences are substituted for those employed here.

Summing Up

We expected to find that how people perceive racial differences is related to how they account for them. By and large, the analysis confirmed this expectation. Whether racial differences are perceived and, if so, the nature of the perceived differences are both related significantly to explanatory mode.

We have written Chapter 6 as if perceptions were a result of explanations rather than the other way around. This was purely a literary device to help cope with the complexity of the material. It is our conviction, as has been reported earlier, that, except possibly among young children, perceptions and explanations of racial differences are in interaction with one another, the one influencing and being influenced by the other. Thus, the correspondence we have just witnessed between perceptions and explanations is more probably the result of an interaction than of explanation always following upon perception.

Still to be demonstrated is our contention that explanations afford an interpretation of the relationship between perceptions and prescriptions. We address this topic in Chapter 7, where we also consider what prescriptions are likely to be advocated where perceptions and explanations are not in agreement.

The Joint Relations of Perceptions and Explanations to Prescriptions

Thus far in our research we had discovered that how racial differences are explained is related to the policies prescribed as means to bring about greater racial equality. We also learned that perceptions of racial differences are associated with explanations of them. Our next step was to examine the relation between explanation and prescription when perception is also taken into account.

Our aim was to test the proposition that among people with similar perceptions of racial differences, their mode of explaining these differences is importantly related to how they respond to the social inequality experienced by blacks in America. Confirmation of this proposition would afford even more decisive evidence of the need to include the explanatory component when monitoring changes in racial attitudes over time. It would also help to explain why the perception-based measures of prejudice in past research have been only weak predictors of how whites respond to blacks at the levels of social policy and private actions.

Perceptions and Prescriptions

To pursue these larger goals, it was first necessary to examine the bivariate relation between perceptions and prescriptions. We were assuming all along, of course, that the two are related, in part because this relationship was shown in past research. Moreover, our own findings that explanations and prescriptions are related, and that perceptions and explanations also are related, suggested strongly that there would also be an association between perceptions and prescriptions.

In past research, perception-based measures of prejudice have usually been restricted to items designed to find out whether characterological differences are affirmed or denied. The perception of social structural differences has not been a part of such measures. Indeed, to our knowledge, the relation between the perception of social structural differences and prescriptions has not been explored previously. This omission is plausible, given the conceptual and theoretical assumptions of past research. If holding negative characterological stereotypes is equated with being prejudiced, researchers would expect those endorsing such stereotypes to be found less sympathetic to the cause of racial equality than those rejecting such stereotypes. The same logic would not apply as easily to the holding of social structural perceptions that cast blacks in an underprivileged position relative to whites since, in matter of fact, blacks are less privileged in many ways relative to whites. It should be noted that in some instances research is to be faulted for not considering the possible truth of some negative characterological stereotypes, but for present purposes, that need not concern us.

In examining the relation between the perception of characterological differences and prescriptions, we utilized the characterological measure described in the previous chapter. This measure, it will be recalled, distinguishes respondents according to whether or not they state that the term *sloppy* is more applicable to black than to white people in America, that taking good care of their homes is more a characteristic of white than black families, and that white parents consider it more important to see that their children get to college than black parents do. Respondents scoring high on this scale affirmed all three differences; those scoring at the low end of the scale denied them all.

To measure prescriptions, we relied on the institutional intervention and personal affinity scales introduced in Chapter 5. The former assesses the extent to which respondents support steps taken by the government and other institutions of society to bring about greater racial equality and to reduce racial discrimination; the latter measures the extent to which white persons feel personal affinity with blacks.

Table 19 reports scores on the two prescription scales according to the extent to which characterological differences between the races are affirmed. We constructed the table by first separating respondents according to their scores on the characterological scale. For each resulting group of respondents, we then computed average scores on the two prescription scales. We then subtracted these average scores from the mean scores of the entire sample on the two scales. Thus, the scores reported in the table are deviations from the mean scores of the entire sample.

With one exception, Table 19 confirms the expectation derived from past research that the more frequently re-

Table 19   **Scores on Institutional Intervention
and Personal Affinity by Perception
of Characterological Differences
(in deviations from mean scores)[a]**

SCORES ON:	CHARACTEROLOGICAL DIFFERENCES			
	None Perceived	One Perceived	Several Perceived	All Perceived
Institutional intervention	.8 (62)	1.9 (108)	−1.6 (94)	−2.5 (216)
Personal affinity	2.1 (59)	1.8 (111)	−2.3 (91)	−5.5 (206)

[a] Standard deviation = 10

spondents perceive character-based differences between the races, the less support they will give to institutional efforts to reduce discrimination. The exception occurs at the lower end of the characterological scale, where, as can be seen, those who acknowledge one difference are more supportive on the average than those who deny all differences. Without exception, however, the higher the score on the characterological scale, the fewer feelings a respondent has of personal affinity for blacks. Thus, these results generally conform to the findings of previous research. Perceiving characterological differences between the races that cast blacks in a negative light is associated with resistance to institutional and personal efforts to bring about greater racial equality.

As noted earlier, there is no past research on which to base a prediction about how those who acknowledge and those who deny social structural differences between the races will score on the two prescription scales. Common sense suggests that more support for institutional intervention will come from those who recognize a problem of racial inequality in America than from those who deny the existence of such a problem. Persons who do not perceive a problem, it would seem, can hardly be expected to advocate efforts to deal with it.

In the case of personal affinity, relying on common sense might lead one to expect those who deny social structural differences between the races to show more personal affinity than those who acknowledge such differences. It is fairly well established, after all, that people tend to feel closer to others whom they perceive to be like themselves. Given, however, that the individualists are inclined to deny social structural differences, and that the occupants of the modern modes are the most likely to affirm them, it is probable that the perception of social structural differences will be found to be associated with feelings of personal affinity with blacks.

To assess these speculations, we utilized once again the institutional intervention and personal affinity scales to measure prescriptions. For our measure of the perception of social structural differences, we employed the social structural scale described in Chapter 6. This scale scored respondents according to whether they affirmed or denied that whites are more likely than blacks to have good jobs, good housing, and good medical care. The higher the score, the greater the affirmation of social structural differences.

Table 20 compares the scores on the institutional intervention and personal affinity scales of those denying the existence of social structural differences, of those weakly affirming such differences, and of those consistently affirming these differences.

Table 20 **Scores on Institutional Intervention and Personal Affinity by Perception of Social Structural Differences (in deviations from mean scores)[a]**

SCORES ON:	SOCIAL STRUCTURAL DIFFERENCES		
	Denied	*Weakly Affirmed*	*Strongly Affirmed*
Institutional intervention	−6.1 (78)	−2.0 (176)	3.8 (222)
Personal affinity	−2.1 (71)	−3.0 (174)	3.4 (218)

[a] Standard deviation = 10

As can be seen in Table 20, the greater the perception of social structural differences, the higher are the scores on institutional intervention; that is, the perception of social structural differences strongly encourages the belief that something should be done to correct them. Strong affirmers also have the highest scores on personal affinity. However, those who deny show more resistance to interacting with blacks than those who weakly affirm.

Given these findings, we felt that a plausible next step was to consider the joint effects of the two measures of perception on prescription. To this end, we collapsed the characterological scale into two categories: those *denying* all or two out of the three characterological differences, and those *affirming* all or two out of three characterological differences. We could not similarly collapse the social structural scale without distorting the results. Consequently the trichotomized version of the scale was retained.

Table 21a reports the scores on the institutional intervention scale according to how respondents are classified on the two perception scales. Table 21b presents scores on the personal affinity scale.

Table 21 **Scores on Institutional Intervention and Personal Affinity by Perception of Characterological and Social Structural Differences Considered Jointly (in deviations from mean scores)**[a]

a. Scores on Institutional Intervention

	SOCIAL STRUCTURAL DIFFERENCES		
CHARACTEROLOGICAL DIFFERENCES	Denied	Weakly Affirmed	Strongly Affirmed
Affirmed	b	−4.8 (73)	.9 (84)
Denied	−6.4 (66)	.1 (103)	5.4 (138)

b. Scores on Personal Affinity

	SOCIAL STRUCTURAL DIFFERENCES		
CHARACTEROLOGICAL DIFFERENCES	Denied	Weakly Affirmed	Strongly Affirmed
Affirmed	b	−7.1 (74)	−.1 (83)
Denied	−1.8 (59)	0 (101)	5.4 (134)

[a] Standard deviation = 10
[b] Too few cases for stable score.

The strongest support for institutional intervention comes from respondents who strongly affirm social structural differences and who deny characterological differences. As can be seen in Table 21a, their score of 5.4 on the institutional intervention scale is considerably larger than that for any other perception group. The least support for institutional intervention comes from those who deny both characterological and social structural differences. Among those who affirm characterological differences, considerably more opposition to institutional intervention comes from those who weakly affirm social structural differences than from those who strongly affirm them. Comparatively, the denial of characterological differences is associated with support for institutional intervention whereas the denial of social structural differences is associated with opposition to institutional intervention.

With one exception, the results are the same for personal affinity and institutional intervention. The strongest supporters of institutional intervention—those who strongly affirm social structural and who deny characterological differences—also exhibit the greatest personal affinity. The personal affinity score of this perception group, as is shown in Table 21b, is 5.4. As with respect to institutional intervention scores, scores on personal affinity are negatively associated with the perception of characterological differences and positively associated with the perception of social structural differences. The major difference between the two tables is that most opposition to institutional intervention comes from those who deny both social structural and characterological differences, whereas the least personal affinity is exhibited by those who affirm characterological and weakly affirm social structural differences. (This result could very well be a consequence of individualists being predominant among those who deny both kinds of differences and geneticists being over-represented among those who affirm characterological and weakly affirm social structural differences.)

Overall, scores on the institutional intervention scale are more closely related to how social structural differences between the races are perceived than to whether or not characterological differences are acknowledged. Feelings of personal affinity, however, are more heavily influenced by the perception of characterological than social structural differences.

Perceptions, Explanations, and Prescriptions

At this point we turned to a central concern of our study: how much, if at all, will taking the explanatory component into account help us to understand the prescriptive consequences that follow from particular perceptions. Although perceptions and explanations are related, as we saw in the last chapter, the relationship is far from perfect. Thus, the same perceptions might be explained in different ways.

Our procedure was to ascertain, for respondents who share the same perceptions of racial differences, whether their mode of explaining these differences makes a significant difference, both statistically and substantively, in their scores on the institutional intervention and personal affinity scales. For this analysis, we categorized respondents' perceptions according to their scores on the characterological and social structural scales, as reported earlier in this chapter. Such categorization produced the six perception groups already utilized in Table 21.

As can be imagined, this procedure was a tedious one, involving a painstaking examination of the effect of explanatory mode on prescription for each of the six perception combinations. So as not to burden the text with the details, we have relegated them to Appendix C. All in all, the results provide consistent evidence that the prescriptions associated with a particular set of perceptions is strongly dependent on how the perception is accounted for.

Further evidence of the importance of explanations to prescriptions was provided when we compared the bivariate relation between modes and prescriptions with the relation between modes and prescriptions when perceptions are introduced as a control, using analysis of variance. Table 22 reports, in its first column, the deviations from the mean on the institutional intervention scale scored by each mode type without perceptions being controlled (these figures are equivalent to those reported earlier in Table 19). In the second column, the scores of each mode type on institutional intervention are reported with perceptions controlled.

The summarizing statistic, eta, tells us that the relation

Table 22   **Institutional Intervention by Explanatory Mode with and without Perceptions Controlled (in deviation from mean scores)**[a]

EXPLANATORY MODE	PERCEPTIONS NOT CONTROLLED	PERCEPTIONS CONTROLLED
Mixed Traditional		
Individualist-genetic	−7	−7
Individualist-supernatural	−6	−5
Genetic-supernatural	−6	−7
Individualist-genetic-supernatural	−8	−7
Pure Traditional		
Individualist	−5	−4
Genetic	−3	−3
Supernatural	+1	+1
Transitional	+3	+2
Modern		
Environmentalist	+7	+6
Radical	+10	+8
Radical-environmentalist	+13	+11
Eta	.61	.54

N = 472
[a] Standard deviation = 10

between modes and prescriptions is reduced only slightly when perceptions are taken into account, from .61 to .54. This result is confirmed by the figures in the body of the table. There is little or no reduction in scores on the institutional intervention scale when perceptions are controlled. The power of the modes to discriminate prescriptions remains.

We obtained substantially the same results when we substituted the personal affinity scale for the institutional intervention scale, as shown in Table 23. Once again, there is only a slight reduction in eta under the controlled condition, from .55 to .49, and the personal affinity scores by

Table 23 **Personal Affinity by Explanatory Mode with and without Perceptions Controlled (in deviation from mean scores)**[a]

EXPLANATORY MODE	PERCEPTIONS NOT CONTROLLED	PERCEPTIONS CONTROLLED
Mixed Traditional		
Individualist-genetic	−7	−7
Individualist-supernatural	−7	−6
Genetic-supernatural	−9	−8
Individualist-genetic-supernatural	−8	−6
Pure Traditional		
Individualist	−2	−2
Genetic	−2	−1
Supernatural	−4	−4
Transitional	+2	+2
Modern		
Environmentalist	+7	+6
Radical	+10	+8
Radical-environmentalist	+10	+8
Eta	.55	.49

N = 459
[a] Standard deviation = 10

mode remain the same or are only slightly reduced when perceptions are taken into account.

Of the two analytical procedures, the one whose results are reported in Appendix C is more useful than the analysis of variance because its results show more clearly that the same perception may have different prescriptive consequences depending on how the perception is explained. The results of both procedures, however, demonstrate a strong relation, which is independent of perception, between explanatory modes and prescriptions.

The Status of Perceptions

A related concern was the status of perceptions in our conceptual scheme. Once explanations are taken into account, do perceptions continue to affect prescriptions independently? Or is their influence on prescriptions wholly a function of their association with explanations?

To answer these questions, we first examined the relation between perceptions and prescriptions of respondents who subscribed to the same explanatory modes. It was not always possible to do this, given that there are only a few cases in some modes and that occupants of some modes share common perceptions. Although the sample was limited, the results indicate that the strength of the relation between modes and perceptions is substantially reduced when mode is taken into account. There remains, however, a slight independent effect of perceptions on prescriptions. (The details are reported in Appendix C.)

Utilizing analysis of variance to the same ends produces similar results. The eta for the bivariate relation between perceptions and scores on institutional intervention is reduced from .41 to .17 when mode is introduced as a control. The reduction is about the same when personal affinity is substituted for institutional intervention; the bivariate eta of .39 is reduced to .19 with the control.

Summing Up

Both from the results reported here and from the more technical analysis reported in Appendix C, the conclusion is warranted that how white people explain their perceptions of racial differences significantly influences what they are willing to support by way both of social policy and individual action to bring about greater racial equality in the society. In terms of developing social indicators, these results firmly establish the need to include the explanatory component when monitoring white racial attitudes over time. There is still considerable work ahead to perfect the measurement of explanatory modes. It is also necessary to continue the measurement of perceptions in further social indicator development. While the independent status of perceptions appears to be much smaller than previously assumed, there is no doubt that they play a significant role in the cognitive processes that determine white responses to the racial situation in America.

The next chapter summarizes our efforts to find out how people come to adopt particular modes of explaining racial differences.

Chapter 8 *Sources of Mode Recruitment*

At the outset of this discussion of how individuals come to adopt a particular mode of explaining racial differences, it should be noted that the follow-up study was designed at a time when the full range of explanatory modes had not been specified. We had a fairly clear idea of the pure modes that would emerge, but we had no clear expectations about the number and character of the mixed modes. This made it difficult to decide what data to collect for exploring the sources of mode recruitment.

Our procedure was to formulate hypotheses about the sources of recruitment to the pure modes. We hoped that the data collected to test these hypotheses might also prove useful in accounting for recruitment to the mixed modes.

In formulating hypotheses, we were informed to some extent by general sociological and social psychological theory. The historical and contemporary literature on race relations in the United States was also a source of inspiration. We found little in the literature, of course, that dealt explicitly with how individuals are recruited to the modes we have specified. A number of works, however, have dealt with matters closely related to our concerns.[1] Also contributing to hypothesis formulation and hence data collection were insights and hunches about the sources of

1. See subsequent footnotes to this chapter for citation of relevant literature.

mode recruitment we gained from conducting the in-depth interviews and from participating in the Bay Area Survey.

Because our data were cross-sectional, there was a limitation on how far the sources of mode recruitment could be pursued. We recognized the importance of historical processes whose operation could not be examined adequately with data collected at only one point in time. We nevertheless sought to specify some of these historical processes with the view that, in the future, they could be subjected to more rigorous examination through the use of longitudinal data.

Generation of Socialization

To begin with, we assumed that if longitudinal data were available on the distribution of the modes in the Bay Area or in the national population, they would reveal a decline in adherence to the modes we have labeled traditional—the individualistic, the genetic, the supernatural, and their various combinations—and an increase in identification with the modes labeled modern—the environmental, the radical, and the mix of these two. While there is no hard data to demonstrate such a shift, the history of race relations in the United States suggests that it has taken place. Changes in a number of indicators that have been found to be associated with explanatory modes, or for which such an association might be reasonably inferred, also point to a shift in the distribution of the modes.

That there has been a decline in genetic thinking about race is suggested strongly by the historical literature.[2]

2. Among historical works on race relations that give some attention to the ideas that have helped to sustain racial inequality at different points in American history are Lerone Bennett, Jr., *Before the Mayflower, A History of the Negro in America, 1619–1974* (Chicago: Johnson, 1962); Frederick Binder, *The Color Problem in Early National America as Viewed by John Adams, Jefferson, and Jackson* (The Hague: Mouton, 1968); George M. Frederickson, *The Black*

None of it is addressed explicitly to establishing just how many Americans were geneticists at different points in American history. However, ideas to the effect that blacks are innately inferior to whites are considerably more prevalent in earlier than in later historical writings.

Data from public opinion polls of the national population also suggest a decline in adherents to genetic explanations of racial differences. In 1963, 31 percent of white respondents to a national survey expressed acceptance of the stereotype that "blacks are inferior to white people." By 1971, the figure was 22 percent.[3] There are no earlier national surveys in which exactly the same question was asked. However, in 1942, 58 percent of white respondents to a national survey answered "no" (48 percent) or "don't know" (10 percent) when asked, "In general, do you think that Negroes are as intelligent as white people—that is, do they learn just as well given the same education and training?"[4] In part, this decline probably resulted from the fact that it was no longer as socially acceptable as it once was for a white American to admit openly that he or she believed that blacks are inferior. Also indicated, however, is a genuine decrease in the proportion of Americans who subscribed to a genetic explanation of racial differences.

No similar data exist to show that supernatural and indi-

Image in the White Mind (New York: Harper and Row, 1971), and *White Supremacy, A Comparative Study in American and South African History* (New York: Oxford University Press, 1980); Thomas Gossett, *Race, The History of an Idea in America* (Dallas: Southern Methodist University Press, 1968); Winthrop Jordan, *The White Man's Burden, Historical Origins of Racism in the U.S.* (New York: Oxford University Press, 1974); and William Stanton, *The Leopard's Spots, Scientific Attitudes toward Race in America, 1815–1859* (Chicago: University of Chicago Press, 1960).

3. National polls conducted by Louis Harris and Associates.

4. The 1942 survey was conducted by the National Opinion Research Center (NORC), as were additional polls asking this question in 1944, 1946, 1956, and 1963. The percentages answering "no" to the question were 48 in 1944, 40 in 1946, 20 in 1956, and 19 in 1963. See Herbert H. Hyman and Paul B. Sheatsley, "Attitudes toward Desegregation—Seven Years Later," *Scientific American* 211 (July 1964):16–23.

vidualistic explanations of racial differences also have fewer adherents than in the past. Certainly, no sharp decline has occurred in the proportion of the population who say they believe in God. This belief was held by more than 90 percent of the population in the 1930s, and the latest figures indicate that the proportion continues to exceed 90 percent.[5] But, of course, believing in God cannot be equated with accepting a supernatural explanation of racial differences. Among the occupants of all the modes are people who believe in God.

While belief in God has not declined, it seems unlikely that the story of Ham is used as much as in the past to support the contention that God intended second-class citizenship for blacks. Favorable references to such an interpretation can be found relatively frequently in respectable theological journals and church literature of earlier periods.[6] Except possibly in the publications of extremist groups, such a reference would not be acceptable today in theological circles. If the teaching of such doctrine has declined in seminaries, it seems likely that it has also declined in the pulpit.

As to individualistic explanations of racial differences, our own evidence demonstrates that they have far from disappeared. Still, there is good reason to believe that the individualistic explanatory style has given way, albeit slowly over the last decades, to environmental and radical explanations. A shift in racial attitudes may not have been sufficient to bring about the civil rights movement; we conceive of such a shift as necessary, however, to the gen-

5. American Institute of Public Opinion Surveys. See also the Gallup Opinion Index, *Religion in America*, (Princeton, N.J., American Institute of Public Opinion, 1976), and Jackson W. Carroll, Douglas Johnson, and Martin E. Marty, *Religion in America, 1950 to the Present* (San Francisco: Harper and Row, 1979).

6. H. Shelton Smith, *In His Image, But . . . : Racism in Southern Religion, 1780–1910* (Durham, N.C.: Duke University Press, 1972); and Kyle Haselden, *The Racial Problem in Christian Perspective* (New York: Harper and Row, 1959).

eration of both white and black support for the movement. Central to the genesis of the civil rights movement was what we have described as the radical explanation of racial differences. Important to its sustenance was the support provided by those who see racial differences as a product of the environment. Had these explanatory styles not been in the ascendency, the civil rights movement might not have occurred.

If there has been a trend in the direction postulated, our data should show that the subscribers to the modern modes are younger on the average than the subscribers to the traditional modes, with those in the transitional mode falling somewhere in between.

With regard to the traditional modes, we anticipated that the pure geneticists would be older on the average than the pure individualists. There are considerably more individualists than geneticists or supernaturalists in the sampled population, and from this result alone it seems reasonable to conclude that the individualistic mode has the greater survival power of the three modes. Moreover, it is probably still more socially acceptable to profess an individualistic understanding of racial differences than a genetic or supernatural one. By and large, we also expected that subscribers to the mixed traditional modes would be older on the average than those in the pure traditional modes. Older people in the sample would have grown up at a time when all three traditional ways of explaining racial differences were more in vogue than they are today. We entertained no firm predictions about the relative average ages of the subscribers to the mixed traditional modes.

Our prediction about the modern modes was that the radicals would be found to be the youngest on the average and the environmentalists the oldest, with those combining both explanations falling in between. Among those who favor social change, the young are usually the more drastic and insistent in their demands.

Table 24 reports the average age of the subscribers to each mode. Note that the average age of the sample as a whole is 45 years of age.

Table 24 **Average Age of Subscribers to the Different Explanatory Modes**

EXPLANATORY MODE	AVERAGE AGE
Mixed Traditional	
Individualist-genetic	54
Individualist-supernatural	51
Genetic-supernatural	60
Individualist-genetic-supernatural	52
Pure Traditional	
Individualist	43
Genetic	48
Supernatural	50
Transitional	42
Modern	
Environmentalist	41
Radical	34
Radical-environmentalist	38
Average Respondent	45

N = 489

The results confirm the expectations, by and large. The subscribers to all of the traditional modes are older on the average than the subscribers to any of the modern modes, with the transitionalists falling between in average age. In turn, those in the mixed traditional modes are older on the average than those in the pure traditional modes, with the oldest group being the geneticist-supernaturalists. Of the pure traditional modes, the individualists, who average 43 years of age, are the youngest. The supernaturalists and geneticists average out at about the same age, 50 and 48, respectively. At 34, the radicals, as expected, are the youngest of the modern modes, and the environmentalists, at 41, the oldest. The radical-environmentalists fall in between with an average age of 38.

By virtue of being based on cross-sectional data, these results do not warrant a conclusion that a generational shift in racial attitudes has taken place. It is possible that younger people in the sample, when they reach the age of older respondents, will achieve the same distribution of racial attitudes. Still, the results are not in conflict with a generational theory of change.

Education

If a generational shift in white racial attitudes is taking place, what is the source of the change? Presumably it is a result of alterations in socialization that could take several forms. The content of what agencies of socialization teach about race relations could have undergone a change, or while socialization agents are teaching the same things, there might have been a shift in their clientele. That is to say, relative to the past, agents that teach a more modern understanding of racial differences may be attracting a larger audience than agents still affording traditional interpretations. Another possibility, of course, is that both processes are at work simultaneously.

Nothing systematic is known about what has been and is being taught about race by the most crucial of socializing agents, the family, and because of the impossibility of doing so within the framework of our study design, we made no attempt to find out. The data do allow a tentative exploration of the impact of another socializing institution, namely, the school.

There is no way to compare what the nation's schools, colleges, and universities are teaching about race today with what was being taught a generation or two ago. Probably the subject is being addressed only minimally, if at all, in many of the nation's schools, and even at the college level many students may not be exposed to courses in which the subject of race is taken up. Insofar as racial differences are being addressed, it seems a fair assumption that, except possibly in isolated cases, schools today are not teaching a genetic theory that depicts blacks as innately inferior to whites. Such teachings may not have characterized the past either. However, it is reasonable to assume that genetic explanations of racial differences would be more seriously challenged in school settings today than in the past.

It also seems unlikely that a supernatural interpretation of racial differences is being widely taught, although there is no reason to believe that, at least in public school settings, such a theory was being taught in the past either. But children were more likely to be exposed to such explanations in Sunday schools in the past.

By emphasizing performance and merit and by conveying the impression that high achievement is something of which everyone is capable, schools, by implication, may be affording credence to an individualistic interpretation of racial differences. It is highly unlikely that such an interpretation is now being taught formally anywhere. Judging from textbooks, the idea that human beings are in full control of their own destinies was much more widely communicated in the past than it is today. Indirectly, as a consequence, the idea that black deprivation is a result of blacks not trying hard enough could readily have been communicated.

The chances are that a systematic study would find that the most widely taught explanation of racial differences comes closest to what we have labeled the environmentalist mode: an explanation that essentially denies that the races are different characterologically and that accounts for social structural differences as historically and socially caused.[7] Radical theories are probably being conveyed in

7. Studies have been done on the extent to which race relations is taught in American colleges and universities. See, for example, Helen E. Amerman, "Instruction in Race Relations in American Colleges and Universities,"

some educational settings, but more likely at the college level, and principally in courses in the social sciences. Environmental and radical explanations of racial differences are not entirely modern phenomena, of course. They were advanced from the time blacks first came to America. However, as the social sciences have developed, such interpretations have been more widely communicated and more cogently argued.[8] Also, with proportionately more Americans going to school and getting more education than ever before, the forum for these ideas has greatly expanded.

It should follow, if these observations are correct, that the more education people get, the more they will be exposed to and come to accept modern interpretations of racial differences. Moreover, given the same educational level, the more recently people have attended school, the greater will be the likelihood of their being socialized to a modern mode. Thus, if there is a shift in racial attitudes, it is, at least in part, because more people are getting more education than ever before and because the content of the education they are receiving is different than in the past.

Since it is not possible with cross-sectional data to test adequately the proposition that a shift in a distribution of racial attitudes is taking place, it follows that it is also not possible to use these data to test adequately additional

---

mimeographed (Chicago: The American Council on Race Relations, 1950); and Peter I. Rose, *The Subject Is Race, Traditional Ideologies and the Teaching of Race Relations* (New York, Oxford University Press, 1968). These and other studies, while they attend to course content, do not give explicit attention to how instruction seeks to account for racial inequality in America and the world.

8. Among a number of studies devoted to the treatment of the subject of race by social scientists are George Ward Stocking, Jr., *American Social Scientists and Race Theory, 1890–1915*, Ph.D. dissertation in American Civilization, University of Pennsylvania, 1960 (available from University Microfilms); John Rex, *Race Relations in Sociological Theory* (New York: Schocken Books, 1970); and Stanford M. Lyman, *The Black American in Sociological Thought, New Perspectives on Black America* (New York: Putnam, 1972).

propositions about the sources of such a possible shift. Longitudinal data, clearly, are necessary to establish whether the shift is taking place and, if so, whether the educational changes just outlined are a source of it.

Cross-sectional data about how much education subscribers to each mode have had is not entirely useless, however. On the one hand, if it should turn out that occupants of different modes are alike in their educational backgrounds, then it becomes highly dubious that amount of education is an important influence on the mode people come to adopt. Such a result would also make it more likely that the age effect found earlier is less a result of generational changes in racial attitudes than of people changing modes over the course of their lifetimes. On the other hand, while the existence of an association between level of education and explanatory mode would not confirm the proposition that education is a source of generational change in mode distribution, it would leave the possibility open. Furthermore, such an association would establish level of education as a source of mode variation in a static, if not a dynamic, way.

Let us examine the data first to determine the association between level of education and mode without taking age into account. Table 25 reports the mode distributions of respondents of different levels of education.

Table 25 **Mode Distribution by Level of Education**

MODE CLASS	LEVEL OF EDUCATION					
	Grammar School	*Some High School*	*High School*	*Some College*	*College Graduate*	*Total*
Mixed traditional	64%	31%	28%	18%	4%	27%
Pure traditional	36	38	37	20	19	21
Transitional	0	13	21	33	17	22
Modern	0	17	14	28	60	29
N =	(33)	(89)	(164)	(103)	(101)	(436)

The results provide strong confirmation of the expectations. The higher the level of education, the greater is the tendency to adopt a modern mode and the smaller the disposition to choose a traditional mode. The effect of education on subscribing to a mixed traditional mode is especially dramatic. Among respondents whose education ended at grammar school, 64 percent are in a mixed traditional mode. The corresponding figure for those who have completed college is 4 percent.

Table 26 addresses the question of whether education of the same level is more disposing to a modern mode if it has been acquired in the recent than in the distant past. The answer is yes; 55 percent of the college-educated young chose a modern mode, as compared with 40 percent of the college-educated middle-aged and 29 percent of older college attenders. When respondents received their education also makes a difference to the mode adoption of those who went no further than high school, with younger respondents (24 percent) the most disposed to a modern mode; the oldest (8 percent) the least.

Table 26   **Explanatory Mode by Level of Education and Age**

MODE	EDUCATION: AGE:	HIGH SCHOOL OR LESS			SOME COLLEGE OR MORE		
		15–29	*30–49*	*50+*	*15–29*	*30–49*	*50+*
Mixed traditional		17%	21%	53%	6%	11%	18%
Pure traditional		33	55	28	13	22	24
Transitional		25	15	11	26	28	29
Modern		24	9	8	55	40	29
N =		(87)	(80)	(116)	(62)	(65)	(76)

So far, in presenting the data on how education affects the explanatory modes people adopt, we have combined the explanatory-mode categories rather than keeping them distinct. We did this because there were grounds for formulating some general propositions about how education might affect the adoption of classes of explanatory mode. We would have had to know considerably more about the educational content to which respondents were exposed to predict the effect of education on recruitment patterns to particular modes within classes. Still, given the exploratory nature of this inquiry, there is something to be gained from a comparison of the educational backgrounds of the occupants of the different modes. This comparison is found in Table 27, which reports the proportion of the occupants of each mode who are college graduates.

Table 27 **Proportion of College Graduates among Occupants of Each Mode**

EXPLANATORY MODE	% COLLEGE GRADUATES
Mixed Traditional	
Individualist-genetic	8
Individualist-supernatural	2
Genetic-supernatural	2
Individualist-genetic-supernatural	0
Pure Traditional	
Individualist	11
Genetic	23
Supernatural	10
Transitional	22
Modern	
Environmentalist	37
Radical	31
Radical-environmentalist	51
Total Sample	21

N = 489

As can be seen, and as we learned earlier, the modern modes include among their members considerably more college graduates than the transitional or any of the traditional modes. Among the former, the radical-environmentalists have the highest proportion of college graduates. This is in line with the level of sophistication previously exhibited by the occupants of this mode. They are followed, in turn, by the environmentalists and the radicals. The lower figure for the radicals is, in part, a function of their being younger, since not all of them had had a chance to complete college. However, even when age differences are taken into account, the radicals remain the least likely of the modern modes to be college graduates.

There are more college graduates proportionately among the pure traditional modes than among the mixed traditional modes. The figures for the geneticists come as a surprise. While they are less likely to have graduated from college than the occupants of the modern modes, they match the transitionalists in this regard and are twice as likely to be college graduates as the individualists or supernaturalists. The college educated among the geneticists tend to be considerably older than the average respondent, suggesting that, in the past, a genetic explanation of racial differences enjoyed considerably more acceptance than it does today among the more highly educated.

To what extent are these results for education a result of the aforementioned age differences among the occupants of different modes? The answer is some. The eta for Table 27 is .49; when the table is redone using analysis of variance and controlling for age, the eta is reduced to .42. Education continues to have considerable effect on mode, independent of age. As already mentioned, with age controlled, the radicals remain the least well-educated of the modern modes while the geneticists continue to be the most highly educated of the pure traditional modes.

Recruitment to the Traditional Modes

So far, in exploring the sources of recruitment to the different modes, we did not try specifically to identify the social processes out of which traditional understandings of racial differences emerge. We did find that older people are more likely than young ones to hold traditional explanations, but had not yet discovered why. And, in accounting for the relative disposition of less educated respondents to favor the traditional modes, we suggested only that this is a result of their having less exposure to education in the modern modes, not of the individualistic, supernatural, and genetic explanations being actively promulgated in the nation's elementary and high schools. In sum, what we learned so far told us something about why the traditionalists are not modern but not why they are traditionalists.

Our speculations about this question led us to consider religion as a possible socializing agent to at least some traditional understandings of racial differences. The church seemed the most likely socializing agent to teach a supernatural explanation of racial differences. We expected, consequently, respondents with a religious affiliation to adopt the pure supernatural mode or a mixed mode with a supernatural component more often than those without such an affiliation. Among those who say, when asked about their religion, that they are Protestant, Catholic, Jewish, or religious in some other way, 28 percent are in a mode having a supernatural component as compared with 9 percent of the unaffiliated. In the case of the pure supernatural mode, however, this difference virtually disappears; 6 percent of the affiliated are in this mode as compared with 5 percent of the unaffiliated.

Not all churches, however, teach that God is the source of racial differences. Such teaching has not been present in Roman Catholicism nor is it a doctrine likely to be taught in liberal, mainline Protestant churches. It is certainly not present in Judaism. Insofar as it is taught at all, conservative or more fundamentalist denominations should be expected to be most likely to do so.

There are only nine Jews in the sample but not one of

them is in the pure supernatural or in a mixed traditional mode with a supernatural component. As between Protestants taken as a whole and Roman Catholics, Protestants show the greater proclivity for the supernatural mode. Thirty-three percent of Protestants are in a mode having a supernatural component as compared with 26 percent of Roman Catholics; the corresponding figures in the pure supernatural mode are 8 and 3 percent.

As expected, however, among Protestants denomination influences attitudes on race. Among denominations disposed to more fundamentalistic teachings, such as the Baptist, for example, 49 percent are in a mode having a supernatural component, and 22 percent are in the pure supernatural mode. Among members of sects such as the Assemblies of God and the Church of the Nazarene, 58 percent are in a mode with a supernatural component; 12 percent are in the pure supernatural mode. The figures for members of more theologically liberal churches are smaller than the Protestant average and considerably smaller than for the more fundamentalist churches. Only 13 percent of United Presbyterians are classified in a mode having a supernatural component. For Episcopalians, the figure is somewhat higher—23 percent—but still below the Protestant average of 33 percent. Members of churches falling in between the extremes on the theological spectrum, such as the Methodists and the Lutherans, also fall in between the extremes in their disposition to supernatural explanations of racial differences. Twenty-six percent of the Methodists and 27 percent of the Lutherans are in a mode with a supernatural component.

Theoretical considerations also led us to expect an association between religious affiliation and subscription to an individualistic interpretation of racial differences. It is not that we believe individualistic interpretations are being taught directly by the churches. We know of no doctrinal basis for their doing so. Churches may nonetheless contribute indirectly to the adoption of an individualistic mode by their parishioners through presenting a world view that conceives of individuals as controlling their own destinies. The theological idea that God has created human beings in his own image but then left them free to choose for or against him has been widely entertained in Christian, especially Protestant, thought. A logical extension of such thinking is to believe that human beings have extensive free will but, because their freedom is granted by God, are under constraint to use it responsibly. Such a general world view is consistent with the kind of interpretation of racial differences that we have labeled individualistic. Blacks, like everyone else, are in control of their own destinies. They may choose to exercise that control wisely or unwisely. If they do the latter they are to blame, but it is also in their power to set things straight.

The doctrine that human beings are in control and responsible for their destinies is not a theological tradition in all religions, and indeed may not be formulated in precisely this way in any religion. Max Weber, whose *Protestant Ethic and the Spirit of Capitalism* is the inspiration for this discussion, suggested that this doctrine came to be communicated, albeit sometimes indirectly, in Calvinism and in the ascetic branches of American Protestantism.[9] According to Weber, the doctrine of individual freedom was not an element in Lutheranism because of that faith's commitment to salvation by grace. Nor was the doctrine present in Roman Catholic tradition.

Weber's observations may no longer be valid. Moreover, there may be no validity to our assumption that the described theological ideas are conducive to an individualistic understanding of racial differences. We cannot, with these data, engage in a thorough test to find out, but we

9. Max Weber, *The Protestant Ethic and the Spirit of Capitalism*, trans. by Talcott Parsons (London: George Allyn and Unwin, 1930).

can determine whether members of those churches that Weber associated with individualism are more disposed than members of other churches to adopt the individualistic mode. Specifically, are Presbyterians, the inheritors of Calvinism, and the ascetic branches of American Protestantism—namely, the Methodists, the Congregationalists, and the Baptists—more disposed to the individualistic mode than Roman Catholics and Lutherans?

Too few Congregationalists are in the sample to allow them to be included in the comparisons. It is possible, however, to compare other denominations with respect to the proportion of their adherents who are individualists. We have also included in Table 28, where these proportions are displayed, the figures for respondents without a religious affiliation.

Table 28   **Proportion of Pure Individualists among Members of Selected Denominations**

| | DENOMINATION | | | | | |
MODE	Presbyterians	Methodists	Baptists	Lutherans	Roman Catholic	Unaffiliated
% Pure Individualists	42	48	19	13	22	12
N =	(28)	(27)	(37)	(30)	(104)	(151)

Except with respect to the Baptists, the results are in accord with expectations. Presbyterians and Methodists are about twice as likely as Roman Catholics to be in the individualist mode and more than three times as likely as Lutherans. The relatively lower figure for Baptists is partly the result of Southern Baptists avoiding this mode. Out of fifteen Southern Baptists in the sample, not a single one is a pure individualist. Among twenty-two other Baptists, the proportion who are individualists is 31 percent, which is still short of the figures for Presbyterians and Methodists, although it is higher than the scores for Lutherans and Roman Catholics. (Baptists, it will be recalled, were the most disposed of the various denominations to supernatural interpretations of racial differences.) The religiously unaffiliated show a smaller disposition to the individualist mode than any denominational group.

As to the remaining pure traditional mode, the genetic, we are not aware of any historical evidence that churches have ever promulgated a genetic explanation of racial differences.[10] Consequently, we did not expect to find the religiously affiliated to be any more inclined to this mode than the unaffiliated. On the contrary, because those with religious convictions are strongly attracted to individualistic and supernatural explanations of racial differences, there are fewer among them than among the unaffiliated for whom a genetic explanation is an option.

Few pure geneticists are found in the sample—only 6 percent; therefore, we could only compare in a tentative way the members of different religious faiths with respect to their disposition to this mode. That comparison reveals Protestants to be pure geneticists considerably less often than the religiously unaffiliated. However, Roman Catholics turn out to be slightly more inclined to the genetic mode. The figure for Protestants is 1 percent; for the religiously unaffiliated it is 7 percent, just slightly above the figure for the sample as a whole; and for Roman Catholics it is 10 percent. We are not aware of a possible reason for the Roman Catholic figure, and the differences between that figure and those for other groups may well be too slight to be stable. Still, this finding perhaps warrants further exploration in future investigations.

No such ambiguity attends the results for the modern

10. Smith; Haselden.

modes. Here, as can be seen in Table 29, the religiously unaffiliated are considerably more likely to be in one of the modern modes than the Protestants, Catholics, or respondents who describe their religious affiliation in other ways. As between the religious subgroups, those affiliated with other religions are the most likely to be in a modern mode, while Catholics and Protestants fall somewhat behind, with roughly equal proportions of each adopting one of the modern modes.

Table 29   **Proportion of Respondents in a Modern Mode by Religious Affiliation**

	RELIGIOUS AFFILIATION			
	Protestant	Catholic	Other Religious	Non-Religious
% in a Modern Mode	13	14	20	40
N =	(194)	(104)	(50)	(151)

While it appears from the above analysis that individuals' religious convictions influence the mode they adopt, it should be recognized that our interpretation of how that influence is exercised is based on inference rather than on hard evidence. While it is theoretically plausible to say, for example, that Methodists are more inclined than Lutherans to favor individualistic explanations of racial differences because of doctrinal differences between the two faiths, no evidence has been presented that doctrinal differences are, in fact, the source of the denominational differences. There are obviously other ways that the relations between religious affiliation and explanatory mode may have come about. With our limited data, we cannot test the doctrinal interpretation or introduce enough controls to assure even that the basic relations are not spurious. (Controlling for age and education, the basic differences remain.) Even though no firm conclusions can be drawn, the results warrant that the religious factor be included in further exploration of mode recruitment.

Other Social Factors

In addition to the schools and the churches, the mass media also are likely to play a role in shaping racial attitudes. Over the past few decades, dramatic changes have occurred in the ways that blacks have been depicted on the screen, over the air waves, and in publications. Such changes probably result as much from the media responding to cultural changes as instigating them. Nevertheless, if adequate data were available, investigators would probably find that exposure to the mass media exerts some influence on the formation of racial attitudes in the United States, probably in the direction of fostering the modern explanatory modes, and especially the environmental one. A cross-sectional study is not an effective instrument for studying mass media effects, however, and we made no effort to do so even in a superficial way.

Moreover, as already mentioned, we made no effort to measure the effects of parents' racial attitudes in shaping the racial attitudes of our respondents. Nor did we look into the influence of peer groups. It isn't that such agents are unlikely to be influential; we strongly suspect that they are. However, it was not feasible to ask about parental and peer group racial attitudes in the detail necessary to allow us to classify them by explanatory mode. Clearly, such a task might be better studied longitudinally, by means of a design that would permit investigators to obtain data from parents and peer group members directly.

A cross-sectional study is also an unsuitable instrument for studying the effects of interracial contacts on racial attitudes, since it allows no way to establish the sequence of the variables. We did ask white respondents, however, to report on the extent and character of their contacts with

blacks, on the assumption that, even though we were unable to establish causal ordering, it would be instructive to
learn how, if at all, subscribers to the different modes
differed in interracial interaction. We expected to find the
occupants of the modern modes to have more contact with
blacks than those in the traditional modes, given the
former's greater sympathies to the deprivations suffered
by blacks in the society. On the same ground, we anticipated that we would find the occupants of the pure traditional modes to have more contact with blacks than those in
the mixed traditional modes. Within classes of mode, it
seemed likely that the radicals would show the greatest
proclivity among the modern modes toward interracial
contact. This assumption is based on the relatively greater
empathy for blacks shown by the radicals in the early
examination of modes and prescriptions. For the same reason, it was predicted that of the pure types, the supernaturalists would show the most interracial contact. As between the mixed traditional modes, we had no firm
expectations as to their relative responses.

Table 30 reports the proportion of subscribers to each
mode who report both that they have one or more close
black friends *and* that they have been entertained in the
home of a black.

As predicted, the general tendency is for the modern
modes to have the greatest contact, followed first by those
in the pure traditional modes and then by those in the
mixed traditional modes. There are some exceptions, however, most notably the supernaturalists, who not only
score higher on racial contact than any of the other traditional modes, but also score higher than the environmentalists. Also out of harmony with expectations is the finding that the occupants of a mixed traditional mode—the
individualist-geneticist—have more interracial contact
than two of the pure traditional modes—the individualists
and the geneticists. The radicals, as expected, have more

interracial contacts on the average than the other two modern modes.

It is regrettable that the data do not allow more in-depth examination of the interplay between racial contact and the ideas people form about why the races are different. This topic, however, is most suitably pursued in longitudinal study.

In further exploring the social processes that govern mode adoption, we attempted to determine whether any of the other background variables on which data were collected were related to choice of mode in substantively and/or statistically significant ways. Included among these

Table 30   **Proportion of Subscribers to Each Mode Who Report Both That They Have One or More Close Black Friends and That They Have Been Entertained in the Home of a Black**

EXPLANATORY MODE	% WITH BLACK FRIEND AND ENTERTAINED BY BLACK
Mixed Traditional	
Individualist-genetic	31
Individualist-supernatural	11
Genetic-supernatural	8
Individualist-genetic-supernatural	5
Pure Traditional	
Individualist	20
Genetic	16
Supernatural	34
Transitional	25
Modern	
Environmentalist	28
Radical	49
Radical-environmentalist	35
Total Sample	24

N = 489

variables were sex, marital and family status, region of the country in which raised, and employment status. This exploration did not lead to many productive new insights. In most instances, it confirmed our hunches about the social sources from which different modes would be recruited. We limit our report here to the speculations that proved correct rather than to comment on all of the findings in tedious and unenlightening detail.

Sex. We anticipated that women would be relatively more attracted to the supernatural mode than men simply because, generally speaking, in America women are more inclined than men to be religious. In fact, men and women are about equally likely to choose a mode having a supernatural component. Twenty-two percent of the women do so as compared with 23 percent of the men. And, surprisingly, men (8 percent) are considerably more likely to choose the supernatural mode in its pure form as compared with 3 percent of women respondents. Our expectation that men would be more disposed to the individualistic and genetic modes than women also is not confirmed. By a slight margin, men are more likely to choose a mode with a genetic component than women—21 percent as compared with 17 percent. Women, however, show a slightly greater inclination than men to select modes with an individualistic component—40 percent as compared with 37 percent. The differences, for the most part, are slight. At least in this sample, sex does not appear to be a significant influence on mode choice.

Marital and Family Status. Differences in the marital and family status of the occupants of the different modes are attributable largely to age differences. We found no independent effect of any significance.

Geographic Origins. Had national data been available, we would have expected some variation in mode

distribution by region of the country, with respondents in
the East and West being more disposed to modern explanatory styles than those residing in the South and Midwest.
We would also have expected the supernaturalist mode to
be more prevalent in the South and Midwest. Since all our
respondents live in the Bay Area, they cannot be considered representative of the present population of the re-
gions in which they were raised. Nevertheless, we find
that 31 percent of respondents who had been raised in the
East are occupants of a modern mode as compared with 26
percent of those raised in the West, 21 percent for those
raised in the Midwest, and 19 percent for those raised in
the South. Those raised in the South and the Midwest
over-subscribe to the supernatural mode in both its pure
and mixed forms compared with the sample as a whole.
Six percent of the total sample are pure supernaturalists as
compared with 20 percent of respondents raised in the
South and 13 percent of those raised in the Midwest.
Twenty-five percent of the sample as a whole chose a
mode with a supernatural component compared with 57
percent of Southern and 40 percent of Midwestern respondents. There is a corresponding under-selection of modes
with a supernatural component by those raised in the East
and West.

Occupation. The relation between occupational status
and mode is about what we expected, given the earlier
findings on the association between education and mode.
The greater the average amount of education of the incum-
bents for an occupation, the greater is the tendency of the
members of that occupation to choose a modern mode.
Thus, respondents who are attending college are the most
likely to adopt one of the modern modes—42 percent do
so—followed by 36 percent of those professionally employed, 29 percent of those in a white collar job, and 21
percent of those in blue collar occupations. Twenty percent of housewives choose a modern mode. The effect of

age as well as average education is reflected in the figure for the retired. Eight percent of the retired are in a modern mode.

Concerning respondents who choose a traditional mode, the mixed traditional modes are especially favored by blue collar and retired respondents and by housewives. Among respondents choosing a pure traditional mode, the white collar worker is most strongly attracted to the individualistic mode—74 percent choose it—followed by 59 percent of the professionals. Among the handful of students who choose a pure traditional mode, 4 out of 6 individuals choose the individualistic mode.

The supernaturalists are recruited especially from blue collar workers and from the retired. The pure genetic mode over-attracts professionals and housewives.

Among respondents who choose a modern mode, occupation does not seem to determine which mode is selected, except that blue collar workers show a marked tendency to adopt the radical mode.

These results partly reflect age and educational differences among different occupational groups. Controlling for age and education, insofar as this is feasible given the small sample sizes, indicates a residual occupational effect but not as strong as in the bivariate relations. It will require a longitudinal study and a larger sample to sort out the effects of occupation with precision.

Psychological Factors

Thus far, our exploration of the sources of recruitment to the modes was based on the assumption that a person's understanding of racial differences is largely a product of socialization; that is, what determines one's mode are the social influences to which one has been exposed. The evidence presented makes it clear that mode is at least partly a result of socialization.

We needed also to consider the possibility of psychological factors working in mode adoption. Personality, for example, might be a force in determining the range of ideas about race to which people allow themselves to be exposed and the mode of understanding racial differences they ultimately adopt. Unfortunately, the present data set is not ideally suited to explore the effect of personality on mode adoption. At the time we were developing the research instrument, we had not formulated a theory about how personality may influence mode choice. Including items to allow measurement of tendencies toward authoritarianism and anomie seemed a good idea, given the evidence from past research that these personality traits are related to prejudice. No other effort, however, was made to examine the possible psychological element in mode adoption.[11]

Past research had found both authoritarianism and anomie to be associated with racial stereotyping and with adopting conservative positions on racial policy. The association between such personality traits and explanatory mode had not been examined previously. However, since racial stereotyping and conservative responses to prescriptive questions were found in our data to be related more to the adoption of traditional than modern modes, we anticipated an association between authoritarianism and anomie and the adoption of traditional modes. Moreover, since those in the mixed traditional modes are found more disposed to racial stereotyping and to conservative prescription than those in the pure traditional modes, we also expected that the former would be found more inclined to authoritarianism and anomie than the latter. We held no firm expectations about the differences we might find among the subtypes.

11. A useful summary of psychological theories bearing on race relations is contained in Richard D. Ashmore and Frances K. Del Boca, "Psychological Approaches to Understanding Group Conflicts," in Phyllis A. Katz, ed., *Towards the Elimination of Racism* (New York: Pergamon Press, 1976).

Table 31 reports the mean scores of subscribers to each mode on a scale of authoritarianism constructed by combining responses to questionnaire items taken from the F scale as developed in *The Authoritarian Personality*.[12] The higher the scale score, the greater is the authoritarianism. Scale scores can range from 0 to 10. Details of scale construction are reported in Appendix B.

Table 31 **Mean Scores on a Scale of Authoritarianism by Mode**

EXPLANATORY MODE	MEAN SCORES ON AUTHORITARIANISM
Mixed Traditional	
Individualist-genetic	7.5
Individualist-supernatural	5.5
Genetic-supernatural	6.5
Individualist-genetic-supernatural	6.0
Pure Traditional	
Individualist	3.4
Genetic	3.0
Supernatural	3.7
Transitional	2.6
Modern	
Environmentalist	1.2
Radical	2.5
Radical-environmentalist	1.8
Total Sample	3.5

N = 382

All occupants of the mixed traditional modes score higher on authoritarianism than occupants of the pure traditional modes. In turn, the pure traditionalists score higher than the transitionalists and those in the modern modes.

12. T. W. Adorno, Else Frenkel-Brunswik, D. J. Levinson, and R. N. Sanford, *The Authoritarian Personality* (New York: Harper and Row, 1950).

The scores of the modern modes are the lowest. Looked at in this way, the results confirm the inferences drawn from the results of previous research.

Within mode classes, the differences, for the most part, are not great enough to warrant speculation about their meaning. Most worthy of note, perhaps, is the fact that the authoritarianism score of the radicals is higher than that of the environmentalists. This result could be a function of the radicals being less well-educated than the environmentalists. It is also possible that the radicals' score reflects the general tendency, observed elsewhere, for those who take extreme positions, whether on the right or left, to be more authoritarian than their more moderate counterparts. Also to be noted in Table 31 is that among the pure traditionalists the supernaturalists have the highest authoritarian score and the geneticists the lowest. Again, this finding could be a function of educational differences between the modes; the geneticists are better educated on the average than the supernaturalists, it will be recalled. It could be significant, however, that the occupants of the mode for which an authority figure is most in evidence are themselves the most disposed to be authoritarian.

Before speculating further on these results, it seemed wise to see how much, if at all, they are a result of the modes being different in age and educational background. Given the controversy about whether the F scale is a measure of personality or of cognitive sophistication, it was especially important that education be controlled. Analysis of variance controlling for age and education and then for both in combination produces etas that are only slightly lower than for the bivariate relation; authoritarianism continues to show a statistically significant effect. With education controlled, for example, the eta is reduced from .49 to .42. With age controlled, the reduction is from .49 to .47, and with age and education taken into account, it is from

.49 to .39. Moreover, as can be seen on Table 32, the mean scores on authoritarianism for the different modes, with age and education controlled, reveal a pattern that is weaker but nevertheless quite similar to that obtained without the controls, as shown in Table 31. Once again, the mixed traditional modes score as most authoritarian, followed by the pure traditionalists, the transitionalists, and finally the modernists. Moreover, the radicals continue to score higher on authoritarianism than the environmentalists. In turn, the supernaturalists score higher than the occupants of the other pure traditional modes. Note, however, that the differences between the individualists and the geneticists, observed in Table 31, have now disappeared.

The results for anomie are considerably weaker and not

Table 32   **Mean Scores on a Scale of Authoritarianism by Mode with Age and Education Controlled**

EXPLANATORY MODE	MEAN SCORES ON AUTHORITARIANISM
Mixed Traditional	
Individualist-genetic	7.2
Individualist-supernatural	4.8
Genetic-supernatural	6.4
Individualist-genetic-supernatural	5.8
Pure Traditional	
Individualist	3.2
Genetic	3.1
Supernatural	3.8
Transitional	2.7
Modern	
Environmentalist	1.7
Radical	2.8
Radical-environmentalist	2.3
Total Sample	3.5

N = 382

nearly as consistent with expectations as those obtained for authoritarianism. To measure anomie, we used items from the well-known Srole scale; the construction of the scale is described in Appendix B. Scores can range from 0 to 10; the higher the score, the greater is the anomie.

The eta for the bivariate association between anomie and mode is .25; for authoritarianism it was .49. The eta is largely sustained when age and education are controlled; it drops to .22 from .25. However, when the full results are examined, as they are in Table 33, which reports the mean scale scores for each mode with age and education controlled, there is considerable variation from the pattern found for authoritarianism and mode. The mixed traditionalists are not consistently the most anomic nor, in turn, are the pure traditionalists always more anomic than the modernists. The principal similarity between the results for authoritarianism and for anomie is that, in both instances, the supernaturalists and the radicals score higher than other members of their mode class.

It could be argued that this finding makes good sense. Among occupants of the pure traditional modes, the supernaturalists are the only ones who conceive an authority figure as responsible for black-white differences. It also seems reasonable that of the three pure traditional modes, the supernaturalists are most likely to be recruited from persons who believe that this world has no meaning. Among the modern modes, that the radicals are the most authoritarian, as we have noted, is consistent with what has been generally observed about persons who take more extreme positions. In turn, their anomie seems to reflect their discomfiture with the way things are, especially as regards race relations in the society.

The problem with such ad hoc speculation, of course, is that it is not grounded in any larger theory that would account for the full array of results including, to us, inexplicable differences among the mixed traditional types. It seems wisest to conclude that the results for anomie and mode leave open the possibility that the mode one adopts is influenced by how meaningful one finds life to be. However, just what the connections are, how they come about, and whether they are significant cannot be answered with these data.

The results for authoritarianism are more definitive and, since they are more in keeping with what previous research has found, more persuasive. Still, even if we had no reason to doubt the empirical findings, we would still need to establish the process by which persons with or without an authoritarian disposition come to adopt their mode styles. Unfortunately, we are unable to attempt, much less accomplish, this task with the present data set.

Returning to the more general question of the role psy-

Table 33   **Mean Scores on a Scale of Anomie by Mode with Age and Level of Education Controlled**

EXPLANATORY MODE	MEAN SCORES ON ANOMIE
Mixed Traditional	
Individualist-genetic	6.0
Individualist-supernatural	4.0
Genetic-supernatural	4.0
Individualist-genetic-supernatural	5.5
Pure Traditional	
Individualist	4.0
Genetic	3.0
Supernatural	5.5
Transitional	3.5
Modern	
Environmentalist	3.5
Radical	4.5
Radical-environmentalist	3.0
Total Sample	4.0

N = 432

chological factors may play in mode adoption, we recognize that we have not given the topic adequate treatment in our inquiry. This was probably inevitable given the exploratory nature of our endeavors. If the explanatory-mode concept is to be advanced and its dynamics more thoroughly understood, these results at least make evident that the psychological factor cannot be ignored.

Summing Up

Our explorations of the sources of mode recruitment bore some fruit. They demonstrated, once again, that the modes are distinctive entities rather than simply variations along a single dimension. They identified education and religion as important social influences on mode choice. The explorations did not establish that a generational shift in racial attitudes has taken place, but the analysis by age and education suggested that the possibility of such a shift having occurred is strong. Albeit somewhat tentatively, the chapter also indicated that along with social factors, personality is influential in determining what modes people adopt; however, we were unable to determine the process by which that influence is effected.

That we did not learn more is a result, in part, of the impossibility of adequately establishing the causal order of variables in cross-sectional studies. It is also the case, as we earlier remarked, that we could hardly have addressed satisfactorily the question of mode recruitment without prior knowledge of what mode typology would emerge. But perhaps the most fundamental obstacle to identifying more fully the sources of mode recruitment was our relative lack of historical knowledge of the cultural roots of the different modes, of their distribution in the population at earlier periods of time, and of the societal forces that nourished and sustained them in America's past.

Such historical research may be thought premature

until the mode concept has been more highly refined than was possible in this initial effort. Sooner or later, however, the historical questions will have to be answered if mode recruitment and change is to be examined effectively. We shall comment further on additional work to be done to advance the explanatory-mode concept in the final chapter. For now, we must consider the matter of spuriousness. It could still turn out that the modes are not as important in determining how whites respond to blacks as the findings so far suggest. This is the subject of the next chapter.

Chapter 9 *Testing for Spuriousness*

It remained to be demonstrated that the relationships between modes and prescriptions, reported upon in Chapters 5 and 7, are not spurious. It was conceivable that what people say they are willing to do personally and to support by way of social policy to bring about greater racial equality in the society are *not* a consequence of the way they understand racial differences to come about. Rather, the associations found between explanations and prescriptions may result from their sharing a common cause. Thus, for example, the conclusion that a genetic explanation leads to a relatively hard line against proposals to break down racial barriers may be false. It could be that something else, as yet unspecified, leads *both* to the adoption of the genetic mode and to resistance to efforts to reduce racial imbalance. Thus, while a statistical association exists between explanations and prescriptions, the interpretation that the explanations are the source of the prescriptions may be in error.[1]

As is well known, survey data affords no way to prove that a relation is causal. The best that we could do was to suggest and to test hypotheses to the effect that explanations and prescriptions have a common cause and are not,

1. For discussions of causal analysis of survey data, see Herbert Hyman, *Survey Design and Analysis* (New York: The Free Press, 1955); and Morris Rosenberg, *The Logic of Survey Analysis* (New York: Basic Books, 1968).

consequently, themselves causally related. Even if we continued to find modes related to prescriptions when taking into account presumed common causes, we would still not have demonstrated conclusively that explanations were the source of prescriptions. There would always be the possibility that a common cause existed that, if identified and introduced into analysis, would demonstrate that the statistical association between explanations and prescriptions was spurious, and that the substantive interpretation that modes are a source of prescriptions was wrong.

Investigators who are committed to a proposition, as we are, are probably not the best ones to demonstrate that the thesis is wrong. Still, it behooved us to play the devil's advocate and to try our best to establish that explanations and prescriptions are *not* causally related.

Age, Education, Religion, and Personality as Test Factors

The procedure we followed to try to prove ourselves wrong was to consider first the possibility that the factors identified in Chapter 8 as sources of recruitment to the different modes may also be sources of recruitment to different prescriptions. That is, the same factors that influence people to adopt a particular mode may also lead them to adopt particular prescriptive positions.

The principal factors found to be associated with mode recruitment, it will be recalled, are age, level of education, religious affiliation, and disposition to authoritarianism. A plausible case can be made for each factor as a possible source of prescriptive postures as well. If, as we have surmised, older people are more likely to have been socialized to traditional modes because such modes were more prevalent in America's culture in the past than today, it also seems possible that older people would be socialized to the prescriptions we found to be associated with the traditional modes because such prescriptions were more prevalent in America's past. Similarly, if it is true that the more education people get, the more likely they are to be exposed to and to identify with modern modes of explaining racial differences, it also seems plausible that education might expose people more to the prescriptions that have been found associated with the modern modes. In effect, a possible reason why modes and prescriptions go together is that they are taught together. If one learns one, one learns the other. This, of course, would constitute a different process from one in which prescriptions are derived from modes.

Religion might also influence modes and prescriptions simultaneously by virtue of being taught together in religious instruction. If one learns, for example, a supernatural explanation of racial differences in church, it seems plausible that one might also learn there the somewhat distinctive prescriptive posture we have found associated with the supernatural mode. Once again, if the two are learned together, we can hardly conclude that modes lead to prescriptions.

As regards personality being a possible common cause of both modes and prescriptions, we were not sure of the process by which a tendency towards authoritarianism and the adoption of particular modes comes about. However, if it seems reasonable to surmise that authoritarian tendencies lead to explanations of racial differences that place the blame for racial differences outside the white community, it also seems plausible that authoritarians would not take prescriptive positions that put the burden of correcting things on the white community.

To test these speculations, we performed analysis of variance, first for the bivariate relation between modes and prescriptions and then introducing age, education, religion, and scores on the authoritarianism scale as controls, singly and in combination. Comparing the etas summarizing these analyses of variance afforded a means to assess the effect of the controls on the discriminatory power of the modes. If under the condition of a single control or combination of controls, the etas fall to zero or close to it, the conclusion to be drawn is that the bivariate relation between mode and prescriptions is indeed spurious in its suggestion that modes lead to prescriptions. If the etas, under all control conditions, approximate the eta for the bivariate relation, this would constitute evidence that the association between mode and prescriptions is not caused by age, education, religion, and/or authoritarianism. The third possibility, of course, is that the etas under one or all control conditions are substantially reduced but not close to zero. This would signify what might be termed a partial explanation of the bivariate relation. That is, the bivariate relation comes about, in part, because the two have a common cause or common causes. However, a residual effect remains, meaning that the modes continue to have some influence on prescriptions, independent of these other factors.

We undertook analyses of variance of the kinds just described using, first, the institutional intervention scale as a prescription measure; we then repeated the analyses, substituting the personal affinity measure. The etas produced using the institutional intervention scale are reported in the first column of Table 34; the etas using the personal affinity scale are in column 2.[2]

Looking first at what happens to the association between modes and institutional intervention under different control conditions, we see in column 1 that the answer is "not very much." There is a slight reduction in the size of the etas under all control conditions but even when age, education, religion, and authoritarianism score are con-

2. In these analyses age, education, and authoritarianism were used as linear covariates; religion was a nominal variable with four categories—Protestant, Catholic, other religions, non-religious.

trolled simultaneously the reduction in etas is only from
.65 to .54. Clearly, modes exert a considerable influence on
prescriptions, independently of these other factors.

The reduction in the association between modes and
personal affinity is somewhat greater under most conditions of control, but once again, as the figures in column 2
show, the controls do not reduce the bivariate eta of .57
below a still substantial .43. Based on this evidence, the
null hypothesis is denied effectively; the relation between
modes and prescriptions does not come about because age,
education, religion, and/or authoritarianism are common
causes of both of them.

Statistics such as eta, while affording a useful means to
summarize a complex set of relationships, may also, on
occasion, serve to obfuscate what is actually taking place.

Table 34 **Measures of Association (Etas) between Modes
and Scores on the Institutional Intervention and
Personal Affinity Scales without Controls and
with Age, Level of Education, Religious
Affiliation, and Authoritarianism Scale Scores
Controlled Singly and in Combination**

	ETAS BETWEEN MODE AND:	
CONTROLS	*Institutional Intervention*	*Personal Affinity*
None	.65	.57
Age	.63	.50
Education	.58	.58
Age and education	.56	.50
Authoritarianism scale score	.61	.52
Authoritarianism scale score, age, education	.55	.47
Religion	.64	.53
Religion, age, and education	.56	.46
Religion and authoritarianism scale score	.60	.47
All four controls	.54	.43
N =	(380)	(370)

In the present instances, for example, etas could remain high even if the discriminating power of particular modes were sharply reduced or enlarged when controls were introduced. While it is not expedient to present tables to show the power of each mode to discriminate on the prescriptive measure for each and every control condition, a presentation of some of this data is called for.

For this purpose, the most reasonable procedure, in our judgment, is to compare the discriminatory power of modes on prescriptions where there are no controls with that power under maximum control conditions. Table 35 makes these comparisons by reporting how much the scores of each mode differ from the average score of the total sample on the two prescription scales.

By comparing the figures in rows 1 and 2, which report, respectively, scores on the institutional intervention scale without and with controls, we find that, while the discriminatory power of the modes is reduced slightly when the controls are introduced, the reduction is relatively uniform in all mode categories. In both rows, the modern modes achieve the highest scores on the institutional intervention scale followed, in turn, by the transitionalists, those in the pure traditional modes, and finally those in the mixed traditional modes. The supernaturalists score higher than the individualists and geneticists, and among the modern modes, the environmental radicals score slightly higher than the radicals and environmentalists.

Making the comparison substituting the personal affinity scale, we find pretty much the same results: scores are reduced slightly but relatively uniformly when controls are introduced. In sum, in both comparisons, the modes' discriminatory power is retained substantially and uniformly when the controls are introduced.

Table 35 *Deviations from Average Scores of the Total Sample on the Institutional Intervention and Personal Affinity Scales by Mode under Controlled and Uncontrolled Conditions*

EXPLANATORY MODE	INSTITUTIONAL INTERVENTION		PERSONAL AFFINITY	
	Without Controls	*With Controls[a]*	*Without Controls*	*With Controls[a]*
Mixed Traditional				
Individualist-genetic	−8	−6	−8	−5
Individualist-supernatural	−7	−5	−6	−5
Genetic-supernatural	−10	−9	−9	−4
Individualist-genetic-supernatural	−7	−5	−9	−7
Pure Traditional				
Individualist	−5	−4	−2	−2
Genetic	−4	−5	−4	−4
Supernatural	1	1	2	1
Transitional	2	2	1	1
Modern				
Environmentalist	7	5	8	6
Radical	10	9	9	7
Radical-environmentalist	12	11	8	6
N =	(380)	(380)	(370)	(370)

[a] Age, education, religion, and authoritarianism score

Other Controls

In addition to age, education, religion, and authoritarianism, other variables whose relation to mode was examined in Chapter 8 included sex, marital status, region of the country in which raised, occupation, and anomie. None of these was found to be strongly related to mode adoption. However, for present purposes, we tried analyses of variance, routinely introducing these variables as controls singly and in different combinations to assess how much, if at all, they attenuated the bivariate relation between mode and the two prescriptive measures. The answer is not very much. In the case of institutional intervention, the bivariate eta of .62 is never reduced below .58. The bivariate eta for mode and personal affinity also is only slightly reduced from .57 to .48. Examination of the results in all their detail shows no basic change in the relative discriminatory power of the modes when these controls are introduced.

Political Orientation

This is about as far as we found it possible to pursue the matter of spuriousness with the data at hand. We considered the possibility that modes and prescriptions might be the joint product of general political orientation. However, the time order of political orientation relative to the other two variables is ambiguous and cannot be inferred reasonably, much less established, with only cross-sectional data. Despite this ambiguity, we did examine the relation between mode and the two prescription scales with political orientation controlled. In turn, we looked at the association between political orientation and prescriptions with mode controlled. The etas are reported in Table 36.[3]

3. See question 113 in Appendix D for the measure of political orientation. It was used in these analyses as a nominal variable with five categories—radical, liberal, middle of the road, conservative, strong conservative.

Political orientation reduces somewhat the association between modes and prescriptions; the etas on institutional intervention are reduced from .62 to .58 and on personal affinity from .57 to .48. If political orientation is presumed the antecedent variable, then the results suggest that a small part of the association between modes and prescriptions is a result of both being influenced by political orientation. It is equally reasonable to assume that mode is antecedent to political orientation, in which case the reduction in eta would signify that part of the mode's influence on prescriptions is processed through political orientation.

Looking at the etas for political orientation and prescriptions with and without mode being controlled, we see that for both dependent variables there is a substantial reduction in the size of the association when the control is introduced. This could mean, if political orientation was considered the antecedent variable, that the influence of political orientation on prescriptions is exercised primarily through the modes. Or, if political orientation is viewed as inter-

Table 36   **Measures of Association (Etas) between Modes and Prescriptions and between Political Orientation and Prescriptions with and without Controls**

	ETAS BETWEEN:	
CONTROLS	*Modes and Institutional Intervention*	*Modes and Personal Affinity*
None	.62	.57
Political orientation	.58	.48
CONTROLS	*Political Orientation and Institutional Intervention*	*Political Orientation and Personal Affinity*
None	.36	.43
Modes	.12	.25
N =	(440)	(426)

vening and mode as antecedent, the results would signify that the association between political orientation and prescriptions is largely spurious. Clearly, modes and prescriptions are related to political orientation. To sort out the interconnections in a precise way would require longitudinal data. For now, the most that can be said is that it remains ambiguous whether modes are a function of general political orientation or the opposite.

Summing Up

The fact that the relation between modes and prescriptions has not been found spurious in any of the tests reported in this brief chapter does not warrant a conclusion that prescriptions are derived from modes. As we have already remarked, there is no way to establish conclusively that a relation is not spurious. The possibility remains that modes and prescriptions have a common cause but that we have not succeeded in identifying that cause. This ambiguity is inherent to survey analysis, of course, and not unique to the present situation. Living with the ambiguity means both remaining open to the possibility of spuriousness, and—as if the possibility of spuriousness had been resolved—working to refine the explanatory-mode concept and its measurement. How both these objectives might be accomplished is addressed in the concluding chapter. First, however, a penultimate chapter ties up some loose ends that have accumulated along the way.

Chapter 10 *Extensions of the Explanatory-Mode Concept*

There remained a number of unanswered questions about the explanatory-mode concept and its measurement that we explored with the data and that are taken up, in the style of a potpourri, in this chapter. The first question concerned the reliability of the indicators used to classify respondents into mode categories. So far, reliability was assumed, but its existence remained to be demonstrated. The second question focused on the behavioral validity of the assertion that modes generate prescriptions. How people account for racial differences was shown to be related to the attitudes they express about what should be done to bring about greater racial equality. Would the same results occur if behavioral indicators were substituted for the attitudinal ones? Moreover, how would the costs or benefits of acting in accord with their ideology affect individuals' behavior? How racial differences are accounted for by black Americans was the third question explored. Finally, we took up the question of the generality of the modes. Are the modes issue-specific or are they used by people to account for most kinds of life experiences that call for an explanation?

The data allowed us to explore these questions, not achieve final answers to them. We judge the explorations to cast enough additional light on the explanatory-mode concept to warrant this report.

Reliability

In reporting on the steps taken to classify respondents into mode categories, we considered the extent to which our indicators produced consistent classifications. We had yet to consider whether the explanatory-mode questions produced stable responses when asked of the same respondents at more than one point in time.

Of course, stability of response in repeated measurement is not an absolute criterion for judging reliability. Stability would not be expected, for example, where there has been a genuine change in attitude or behavior. We have no evidence to establish whether the ways that individuals understand racial differences are fixed or variable. While we suspect that they are most likely to be fixed, at least among adults, this suspicion is based simply on widespread evidence that basic attitudes tend to be slow to change. Attitudes on race relations could be an exception to the general tendency. Given the changing status of blacks in the society and changes in the way the media and other institutions portray black persons and black lifestyles, intergenerational change in racial understanding could be widespread. Still, such changes are unlikely to be rapid and we should not expect an overwhelming amount of change over the short run if our measures are reliable.

The data at hand to measure stability of response were limited to the response of 109 white subjects who were interviewed in the Bay Area Survey and who filled out a questionnaire in the follow-up survey.[1] The two surveys were conducted about twelve months apart. Two explanatory-mode questions—one asking respondents how they account for socio-economic differences between the races and the other asking them to explain racial differences in performance on IQ tests—were asked in substantially

1. See the discussion in Appendix A of the design of the follow-up study. See also Apostle.

equivalent fashion in the two surveys. By comparing respondents' answers to these two questions in the Bay Area Survey with their answers to them in the follow-up study, we can assess stability of response.

It will be recalled that the socio-economic question was asked in two parts. Respondents were first presented with a series of statements intended to portray each explanatory mode and were asked how much they agreed or disagreed with each statement. Then they were asked to choose from the series of explanations the one they judged to be the most important reason for differences in the socio-economic status of blacks and whites.

Table 37 reports the extent to which responses to the first part of the socio-economic question were in agreement at the two time periods. The first row of the table shows the proportion of respondents who gave exactly the same responses to each of the subparts of the question; i.e., they answered strongly agree, moderately agree, moderately disagree, or strongly disagree in both the Bay Area and the follow-up studies. The second row reports the proportion of respondents who were consistent in direction but not in degree; they answered agree or disagree both times but strongly in one instance and moderately in the other. The third row notes the proportion of respondents who were consistent, at least in direction, both times. The fourth and fifth rows then report the amount of disagreement: row 4, respondents expressing moderate agreement in one instance and moderate disagreement in the other; row 5, respondents who were two or three scale points apart in their responses to the two questions.

If we judge stability to have been achieved only when answers at the two time periods are precisely the same, the proportion of responses that are stable ranges from 41 percent for the radical mode to 66 percent for the genetic mode. The average for all modes is 55 percent. Using consistency in direction, but not necessarily in degree, as the

Table 37 **Stability of Responses in the Bay Area and the Follow-Up Surveys to the Question Asking Respondents to Account for Socio-Economic Status Differences between the Races**

CONSISTENCY	RESPONSES IN:					AVERAGE FOR ALL MODES
	Individualist Mode	Genetic Mode	Supernatural Mode	Environmental Mode	Radical Mode	
Wholly consistent	54%	66%	52%	58%	41%	55%
Consistent in direction	23	17	23	28	25	13
Subtotal	77	83	75	86	66	78
Slightly inconsistent	14	6	2	5	23	11
Strongly inconsistent	9	11	22	9	11	11
N =	(100)	(100)	(86)	(106)	(95)	(97)

criterion of stability, we find a marked increase in the proportion of stable respondents, the range now being from 66 percent for the radical mode to 86 percent for the environmental one, with an average overall of 78 percent.

Before interpreting what these figures imply about reliability, it is useful to examine the amount of response stability generated by the other two explanatory-mode questions, and then to compare stability scores for the explanatory-mode questions with the stability achieved by other questions asked equivalently in both surveys.

Table 38 reports the correspondence in responses to the questions asking subjects to choose the most important reason for socio-economic differences between the races and the most important reason for whites doing better on intelligence tests than blacks.

Table 38 **Stability of Responses in the Bay Area and Follow-Up Surveys to Questions Asking Respondents to State the Most Important Reason for Racial Differences in Socio-Economic Status and in Performance on IQ Tests**

CONSISTENCY	SOCIO-ECONOMIC QUESTION	IQ QUESTION
Wholly consistent	62%	75%
Answered both times in a traditional Mode	9	7
Answered both times in a modern Mode	7	3
Not consistent at all	22	16
N =	(74)[a]	(69)[a]

[a] Respondents who answered in cultural mode one or both times are omitted.

The majority of respondents—62 percent on the socio-economic question and 75 percent on the IQ question—gave exactly the same responses on the two questions.

Seventy-eight percent of respondents answered in the same mode class both times on the socio-economic question; 84 percent did so on the IQ question.

By and large, the amount of stability generated by the explanatory-mode questions was about as great and sometimes greater than that achieved by other questions in the two surveys, although strict comparison is not possible given variation in the number of answer categories for different questions. The question on institutional intervention, which offered respondents a choice of seven categories in which to answer, produced entirely consistent answers from 51 percent of respondents, with an additional 37 percent deviating by only one point on the scale of responses. The question on black-white intermarriage, with three answer categories, produced 71 percent concordance. Seventy-four percent answered the question about attitudes toward a child marrying a black person in the same way both times.

In addition, responses to the questions about explanatory modes were as stable as the answers to two standard questions in survey research. Fifty-six percent of the subjects answered a question asking how they would rate their social class in the same way in both surveys. A question asking respondents to report their political position produced 64 percent concordant responses.

All in all, the results suggest that the questions designed to tap explanatory modes produced responses as stable, if not more so, than other attitudinal questions. Although some measurement problems relating to the explanatory-mode questions have not been resolved, as discussed earlier, these figures on reliability demonstrate that explanatory modes are phenomena about which people, to a considerable extent, have stable commitments.

Costs and Benefits

A reservation that may be expressed about our inquiry, although no more so perhaps than about any investigation based on attitudinal data, is that while we have demonstrated that how people explain racial differences is related to what they *say* they might do or support to bring about greater racial equality, we have not shown that respondents' modes have anything to do with actual behavior. In our original proposals, we outlined plans for a series of experiments designed to assess the behavioral consequences of subscribing to different modes. These experimental plans called for bringing respondents, who had been assigned to a mode based on their responses to the survey instrument, into a laboratory setting in various combinations. These subjects would then have been put into situations designed to parallel in behavioral terms the options offered them in the survey's prescriptive questions. In effect, would mode, judged on the basis of attitudes, predict what their occupants would actually do when faced with varying opportunities to help reduce racial tensions and generate greater racial equality? Unfortunately, the experimental component of our proposal was not funded, in part we believe because the sponsors wished to be assured that the explanatory-mode concept was viable at the level of attitudes before agreeing also to support a test of its behavioral consequences.

While we have not engaged in any behavioral testing of explanatory modes, we have reflected upon this subject almost from the onset of our investigations. The possibility has not escaped us that when people are in a situation where they are obliged to choose between behaving in a way to support the principle of racial equality or not doing so, their choice may be more heavily influenced by what they perceive to be the costs or benefits of the alternatives than by what their understanding of racial differences tells them they ought to do. Ideology, as a guide to behavior, might be especially vulnerable to self-interest when considerable personal sacrifice is required to act to support racial equality as, for example, continuing to send your child to an integrated school in which there is a good deal of open and sometimes violent racial conflict.

Our plans for the laboratory experiments included an effort to determine at what point costs or benefits might derail people from acting out of ideology in concrete situations. It occurred to us, while we planned the follow-up study, that we might be able to simulate a situation, although not a substitute for a test undertaken under controlled laboratory conditions, in which costs and benefits would become a variable intervening between explanatory mode and support or opposition to a policy designed to reduce racial inequality.

In our simulation, respondents were told to assume three different consequences following from school integration and were then asked how much they would approve or disapprove of school integration in each of the three cases. One of the consequences set forth was that whites and blacks would both benefit from school integration because it produces better human relations. A second was that blacks would benefit educationally from integration while whites, however, would experience no educational benefit or cost. The third consequence was that black children would be helped educationally but white children would be harmed.

It was anticipated that respondents would more strongly approve school integration under the first of these circumstances than under the second, and that they would support integration least under the third. The results are as expected. School integration gained the most support—67 percent strongly supported it—when its effects were described as improving human relations with no academic benefit or harm to either black or white students. It gained the least support—24 percent strongly approved—when it was proposed that black students would be benefited educationally but white students hurt. Support for school integration was intermediate between, but closer to the first of these extremes, where its effects were described as neutral for white children and beneficial for black ones. In this instance, 57 percent expressed strong approval.

A more crucial question we wanted to address with these data was what happens to the association between modes and attitudes toward school integration when the above described costs and benefits are taken into account. Several outcomes were possible. It could have been that when modes and attitudes toward school integration were in conflict, people act out of self-interest, however much doing so may go against their understanding of racial differences. A second possibility was that mode influences behavior regardless of cost or benefit. A third possibility was that while costs and benefits are a consideration in determining action, mode continues to exert an independent effect.

The data afforded most support for the third of these possibilities. Among the occupants of each mode, the smaller the benefits, and the greater the costs, the smaller was the support for school integration. This finding can be seen in Table 39, which reports the proportion of the occupants of each mode who strongly supported school integration under the conditions of benefits and costs described immediately above.

At the same time, under each benefit and cost condition, mode does influence the amount of support that school integration receives and in a pattern quite similar to that revealed in earlier tables where the bivariate relation between mode and prescriptions was examined. Greatest support comes from the modern modes, followed by the transitionalists, the pure traditional types, and finally the mixed traditional types. Among the pure traditionalists, also as observed before, the supernaturalists are revealed to be more sympathetic to steps to reduce racial discrimination than are the individualists and geneticists. The geneticists are harsher than the individualists by a slight margin. These results, then, are not in conflict with the thesis that explanatory modes are a central component of racial attitudes.

Explanatory Modes among Blacks

Understandably, given the assignment to develop social indicators of racial prejudice, our research has focused on white racial attitudes. Once racial attitudes are examined from the perspective of explanatory modes, however, it

Table 39 **Support for School Integration by Explanatory Mode under Different Conditions of Cost and Benefit (in percent strongly supportive)**

EXPLANATORY MODE	CONDITIONS		
	Benefits Blacks and Whites	*Benefits Blacks Only*	*Harms Whites, Benefits Blacks*
Mixed Traditional (combined)[a]	40	35	10
Pure Traditional			
Individualist	59	51	15
Genetic	45	40	12
Supernatural	74	68	26
Transitional	75	68	17
Modern			
Environmentalist	91	87	33
Radical	78	73	40
Radical-environmentalist	88	85	49
Total Sample	66	59	21
N =	(488)	(488)	(488)

[a] Mixed traditional modes have been combined since they do not differ significantly in responses.

becomes as germane to inquire about how black members of the society account for perceived racial differences as it does to ask how whites do so.[2] Given their relative socio-economic deprivation relative to whites in American society, blacks can be expected to harbor some explanations as to how their poorer status came about. What their explanations are and how they are distributed in the black population undoubtedly affect the state of race relations in this country. Studying blacks' explanations is important both for social indicator and political purposes.

While we recognized early on in our inquiries that blacks' understanding of racial differences might be an important topic to pursue, it was not practical for us to do so given our primary commitment to study white attitudes and a lack of resources to conduct equivalent studies in both communities. It happens, however, that there were black respondents to the two surveys and, with some slight modification, they were asked the same explanatory-mode questions as white respondents. Consequently, responses of the two groups can be compared. More extensive analysis of black respondents is precluded by their numbers; there were only sixty in the follow-up survey. Still, while the comparison must be tentative, it nevertheless illustrates the ways in which the two groups confront the phenomenon of racial differences.

Table 40 presents both black and white responses to the question asking respondents how much they agree or disagree with six statements purporting to explain differences in the average socio-economic status of the two races. In the version of the questionnaire distributed to black re-

2. For a report on the attitudes of black Americans on the general subject of race relations, see Howard Schuman and Shirley Hatchett, *Black Racial Attitudes, Trends and Comparisons* (Ann Arbor, Mich.: Survey Research Center, Institute of Social Research, University of Michigan, 1974). While this study does not deal with how blacks account for racial inequality, it does provide information on black perceptions of their social conditions and on what they believe to be necessary to bring about greater racial equality.

spondents, a genetic explanation was not included among possible responses. Hence, there is no figure in the genetic cell for blacks.

Black respondents show some support for each of the explanatory modes they were asked about. Understandably, however, the relative support given to different modes is not the same for blacks and whites. Blacks, as might be expected, are considerably more disposed than whites to the radical mode, and considerably less in agreement that racial differences are caused by individuals. Otherwise, whites show a slightly greater disposition to environmental explanations, whereas blacks slightly favor supernatural ones. Adding up the figures across the rows of Table 40 shows that blacks, like whites, are given to multi-causal explanations, but because the sample is small, it is not possible to sort out blacks whose mode is uni-causal from those who hold to multi-causal explanations.

We can compare responses of blacks and whites to the second part of the socio-economic question, in which, it will be recalled, respondents were asked to choose the most important reason for black-white differences. This comparison, reported in Table 41, yields results roughly comparable with those in Table 40. Once again, the radical mode gains considerably more support from blacks than it does from whites. Whites lean more heavily to the environmentalist and individualist modes. Blacks are found to be slightly more inclined to the supernaturalist and cultural modes than whites. No one explanation gains the support of a majority of blacks, although the two modern modes taken together constitute a bare majority, 58 percent. Fully 30 percent of blacks, however, favor the two traditional modes asked about, namely, the supernatural or individualistic.

These results suggest that a fuller inquiry into black interpretations of racial differences might be useful. Were such an inquiry to be pursued, however, it would seem

Table 40 **Proportion of White and Black Respondents Agreeing Strongly or Moderately with Different Explanations of Socio-Economic Differences between the Races**

			MODE			
	Genetic	Supernatural	Individualist	Environmental	Radical	Cultural
Whites	21% (469)[a]	32% (478)	50% (472)	81% (483)	47% (458)	45% (441)
Blacks	Not asked	37% (47)	34% (53)	73% (56)	85% (55)	33% (51)

[a] Ns represent number of respondents who answered question asked about each mode.

Table 41 **Proportion of Black and White Respondents Citing Different Explanatory Modes as Most Important Reason for Socio-Economic Differences between the Races**

			MODE				
	Genetic	Supernatural	Individualist	Environmental	Radical	Cultural	(N)
Whites	3%	9	22	49	8	9	(470)
Blacks	Not asked	13%	17	33	25	13	(50)

wise to start with qualitative interviews, as we did for our study of white attitudes, and to plan the explanatory-mode questions so that they are in tune with black experience. It would also be desirable, if our entire model were to be replicated, to reframe the questions on perceptions and prescriptions. Some exploratory examination of the interplay between perceptions, explanations, and prescriptions using the data from black respondents proved unsuccessful, partly because of the small sample size but also because the questions had not been worded in a suitable fashion. Black responses to the prescriptive questions, for example, showed very little variation since few blacks said that nothing should be done to help them.

The Generality of the Modes

In Chapter 3, when analyzing the Bay Area Survey data, we briefly explored the idea that the modes constitute means that people adopt to account, not only for racial differences, but for a wider range of phenomena. We found some correspondence between respondents' answers to questions about how they account for racial differences and to questions asking them to explain poverty and to account for the fact that people vary in how long they live. The correspondence was not high, although it was greater than that attributable to chance. Only 23 percent answered the race and the longevity question in a concordant way, and the correspondence was only slightly larger between the race and poverty questions. These figures suggested that most people are not committed rigidly to a single mode of structuring reality.

In planning the follow-up study, we decided to explore further the interplay between understandings of racial differences and other phenomena and, to this end, included a considerably wider range of questions asking respondents to account for different life experiences than had been asked in BAS. In addition to questions about racial differences, we also asked respondents to say what they considered to be the major reason for suffering in the world (question 1 in the questionnaire); how they would account for a situation in which twin brothers grow up, one to become a successful lawyer and the other to become a criminal who would spend most of his life in jail (question 2); how they explain unexpected tragedies in life, when through no fault of their own people are suddenly killed, as in an airplane accident (question 3); and what they believe to be at fault when people become alcoholics (question 5). We also asked respondents what forces have most influenced their own lives (question 75), and repeated two questions already asked in BAS—the one asking respondents how they account for poverty in America (question 9) and the other asking them to explain why some people die young while others live to a ripe old age (question 5).

An examination of Appendix D shows that we sought, insofar as possible, to include in the answer categories to each question the same range of explanations as for the race questions. Thus, for example, in the question asking about what has most influenced respondents' lives, we included "the way you were brought up" to portray the environmental mode; God or some other supernatural force (supernatural); the characteristics you were born with (genetic); what people in power decide (radical); and will power (individualist). This range of explanations was not relevant to all the described life situations. It did not make sense, for example, to depict an individualistic explanation of why someone dies in a commercial airline accident. Thus, not every question included the same set of explanations, although most did. We added luck and fate as additional possible explanatory modes where they seemed appropriate.

Our analysis of these data was directed at finding the degree of correspondence between respondents' mode of accounting for racial differences and their modes of accounting for other experiences. We were interested in determining both how much general correspondence exists and whether the correspondence is greater for some life situations than for others.

To pursue these questions, we were obliged to follow a moderately complex procedure. We sorted out respondents first according to the mode they chose to explain the nonracial life situations. For each group of respondents, we then calculated the correspondence between their explanatory mode, based on their responses to the racial questions, and their mode of explaining the nonracial situation. This procedure affords a serviceable although somewhat incomplete means for assessing the generality of the modes. We say incomplete because we omitted respondents who answered luck or fate or who wrote in answers to the nonracial questions.

Table 42 presents the results of these efforts. The total column shows the proportion of respondents whose answers to the questions about each of the life situations are consistent with their mode of explaining racial differences. The total row reports, for each mode of accounting for the life situations, the average proportion whose answers to such questions correspond with their mode assignment on the racial questions.[3]

The correspondence between the modes of explaining racial differences and modes of accounting for other life situations is considerably greater than chance. If answers were completely random, only 17 percent of the respondents on the average would give consistent responses as compared with the average of 46 percent actually achieved.

The average figures, however, mask considerable varia-

3. The figures in Table 42 should be read as follows: for example, of the sixty-four respondents who said that airplane accidents are supernaturally caused *and* who were assignable into a mode of accounting for racial differences, 63 percent accounted for racial differences in the supernatural mode or in a mode having a supernatural component.

Table 42 **Correspondence between Mode of Explaining Racial Differences and Mode of Accounting for Other Life Situations (in percentage consistent)**

LIFE SITUATIONS	MODE OF EXPLAINING DIFFERENCES					
	Individualist	Genetic	Supernatural	Environmental	Radical	Total Average
Airplane accident	a	a	63% (64)	29% (146)	a	40% (210)
Dying young	60% (163)	31% (39)	58 (98)	30 (10)	65% (20)	55 (330)
Twins growing up different	73 (120)	29 (21)	71 (21)	33 (146)	a	53 (308)
Poverty	75 (56)	45 (11)	70 (60)	45 (128)	34 (44)	54 (299)
Alcoholism	63 (122)	27 (89)	54 (22)	29 (63)	a	44 (296)
Suffering	69 (54)	17 (35)	a	20 (83)	43 (37)	36 (209)
Self	51 (79)	22 (67)	48 (67)	24 (140)	25 (4)	38 (357)
Average	64	26	60	31	43	46

[a] No provision was made in life situation questions for answers in these cells.

tion for both the different modes and the different life situations. As can be seen from the average figures reported in the total row, those who gave supernatural and individualistic answers to the life-situation questions are considerably more likely to have given consistent answers on the race questions than respondents whose responses to the life-situation questions were genetic, environmental, or radical. The smallest concordance—26 percent—is scored by the geneticists. This suggests that genetic explanations are more likely to be issue-specific than supernatural and individualistic ones. On this score, environmental and radical explanations fall somewhere in between.

The amount of correspondence is also affected by the type of life situation being explained. Here it is to be recognized that, because of empty cells, the figures are not strictly comparable. If we restrict comparisons to the three life situations where there are no empty cells—dying early, poverty, and personal life—explanations of poverty are the most likely to coincide with explanations of racial differences for all modes except the radical one. The smallest correspondence, in all comparisons, is between explanations of racial differences and what individuals conceive to be the major influence controlling their own lives.

Overall, it would appear that some people conceive of a single control agent as being central to a wide range of their life experiences. Other people, probably many more, vary in the explanatory style they adopt to account for different things. Are the modes generalizable then? For some people, apparently they are; for others, they are not.

The possibilities of further exploration of the data to specify the variation in more detail, to sort out the uni- from the multi-causalists, and to examine the sources of different explanatory styles are being pursued in a companion project to the present one.[4] The results of that in-

4. Charles Y. Glock and Thomas Piazza, "Exploring Reality Structures," in Thomas Robbins and Dick Anthony, *In Gods We Trust: New Patterns of Religious Pluralism in America* (New Brunswick, N.J.: Transaction Books, 1980).

quiry may have implications for the future study of the generality of explanatory modes, but from what we have learned so far, they seem unlikely to affect our more narrow concern with social indicators of racial attitudes.

Summing Up

This chapter was intended to test further the explanatory-mode concept and to open up new avenues of inquiry utilizing the concept. By and large, the concept emerges from these tests relatively unscathed. In this regard, the major contribution of the chapter was to identify costs and benefits as additional factors to be taken into account in measuring racial attitudes. The potential for undertaking studies along similar lines in the black community was a further outcome of the chapter. It appears that the explanatory-mode concept may be as relevant to understanding black racial attitudes as it is to understanding white attitudes. The chapter also suggested that the explanatory-mode concept may be applicable to phenomena other than racial differences, which, if demonstrated, would open new lines of inquiry extending beyond those pursued here.

Chapter 11 **Summary and Implications**

In this final chapter, we present a brief summary of the central findings of the research. We provide an assessment of the project with respect to its aspirations to contribute to social indicator development. We consider the project's implications for future research on racial attitudes and, more generally, on attitude research. And we discuss how the findings illuminate the black condition in America and what they suggest about the prospects for improving it.

What Was Learned?

An understanding of the explanatory component in white racial attitudes was the principal outcome of our inquiries. This is not to say that we were the first to specify the existence of the component. At least two earlier investigators have suggested that how racial differences are explained probably constitutes an important element in racial attitudes.[1]

Our contributions have been to elaborate the explanatory-mode concept, to make it operational, and to demonstrate it to be a crucial component of white racial attitudes. In the end, a typology of eleven different modes of explaining racial differences was produced. Five of these

1. This point was made in footnote 23, Chapter 1.

modes attribute racial differences to a single cause—to God, to genes, to individual blacks, to environment, and to white racism. Five additional modes are multi-causal. Their occupants subscribe to two or more reasons as to why racial differences exist. Multi-causal or mixed modes, as we came to call them, comprise two types: those made up of a combination of the traditional modes—supernatural, genetic, and individualistic explanations—and those composed of the modern modes—environmental and radical explanations. Virtually no one was found who subscribed to modes in both sets. The eleventh category, labeled the transitional, is made up predominantly of people who could not be classified on the basis of the available data.

To categorize people according to their explanatory mode, it will be recalled, we built four scales—a supernatural scale, a genetic scale, an individualist-environmental scale, and an individualist-radical scale. We then made mode assignments on the basis of subjects' scores on these scales.

Beyond building the explanatory-mode typology, our major efforts were devoted to assessing the significance of explanatory modes for the way people respond to racial inequality in America—that is, whether or not they countenance anything being done to bring about greater racial equality and, if so, what. We engaged first in an examination of the bivariate relation between the modes people subscribe to and their willingness (1) to engage personally in activities designed to break down racial discrimination and (2) to support institutional efforts to this end. By and large, modes and prescriptions were found to be related in ways that supported our theoretical expectations.

Our next step was to investigate the relation between how racial differences are perceived and how they are explained. Although we took this step primarily to prepare for later examination of the joint effects of perceptions and modes on prescriptions, the results assumed some importance in their own right. In our analysis, we made a distinction between perceptions of racial differences relating to character and those associated with social structure. The former compares blacks and whites with regard to traits such as intelligence, ambition, cleanliness, and the like. The latter concerns the relative social status of the two races and the opportunities available to them to improve their social position. The mode of explanation with which a person identifies was found to be related significantly to whether he or she perceives one, both, or neither of these two kinds of racial differences—and in ways that made theoretical as well as common sense. Relative to the average respondent, the environmentalists and radicals are disposed to deny characterological but to affirm social structural differences. In effect, through their perceptions, environmentalists and radicals affirm their belief that racial differences are not innate. In turn, the geneticists, through their perceptions, demonstrate their belief that racial differences are innate. We found that geneticists perceive characterological differences and also, since the geneticists presume them to follow, social structural differences. But the individualists and the supernaturalists tend to deny both kinds of differences. The perceptions of the occupants of the mixed modes also follow distinct patterns.

Given that our data were cross-sectional, we could not determine the order in which perceptions and explanations of racial differences occur. It seemed likely, however, that once a mode of explaining racial differences is internalized, it functions as a lens through which additional perceptions are processed.

Previous research has found a zero-order relation to exist between perceptions and prescriptions. This has mainly meant that negative perceptions of characterological differences are associated with tolerance of discrimination and little disposition to do very much to break down racial barriers. Our inquiries are supportive generally of earlier research in this regard. The more strongly whites affirm characterological differences, the less they support institutional efforts to combat discrimination and the less personal affinity they feel for blacks. The perception of social structural differences has the opposite effect; the more whites affirm these differences, the greater is their personal affinity and support for institutional intervention.

A possible problem, we discovered, with examining the relation between perceptions and prescriptions without taking explanations into account is that the same perception may be accounted for in quite different ways and, therefore, may lead to quite different prescriptive consequences. In such circumstances, it is the explanation, much more than the perception, that governs the prescriptive outcome.

The environmentalists and the radicals are inclined to have perceptions that encourage them to be intolerant of discrimination, and their modes of explanation reinforce and extend this tendency. In those instances where there is a disparity—where environmentalists and radicals acknowledge characterological differences and/or deny social structural differences—their modes rather than their perceptions inform their prescriptive attitudes. The geneticists, while relatively somewhat disposed to acknowledge social structural differences, are not led thereby to support institutional efforts to reduce discrimination or to feel a personal affinity for blacks. Their mode rather than their perception informs their prescriptive responses. Similarly, the relative tendency of individualists to deny characterological differences does not result in their being prescriptively supportive. Once again, it is their mode rather than their perceptions that is determinative. The same is true for the supernaturalists and the mixed modes.

We recognized that these results could be spurious, a

result of some additional variable or set of variables—not yet introduced into the analysis—being the source both of explanatory modes and prescriptions. As a step toward identifying variables that might have this effect, we investigated a variety of possible sources of mode recruitment. This analysis identified age and education as having a significant effect on whether the mode adopted is of a mixed traditional, pure traditional, or modern variety. Generally speaking, older and less well-educated persons are especially attracted to the mixed traditional modes and, to a lesser extent, the pure traditional modes, while more highly educated, young persons favor the modern modes. By and large, age and education are not especially influential in determining which mode within a set is adopted, with the exceptions that the genetic mode appeals relatively more to older college-educated respondents and the radical mode to both less well-educated and more highly educated respondents.

Religious affiliation is also a force in mode recruitment. The supernaturalists, as expected, tend to be members of more fundamentalist denominations. Branches of Protestantism, such as the Presbyterian and the Methodist, which have been associated historically with an individualistic theology, are the source of considerably more individualists than would be expected to be caused by chance. Geneticists, on the other hand, tend either to have no present religious affiliation or to be Roman Catholic. The modern modes all have a disproportionate number of occupants who are religiously unaffiliated.

An association was found between the amount of racial contact and explanatory mode. Occupants of modern modes exhibit more interracial contact than do those in the pure traditional modes, which, in turn, have more interracial relationships than those in the mixed traditional modes. This finding could be a result of persons being educated, through racial contact, to adopt a modern mode;

or mode might influence racial contact. It is not possible to make a definitive judgment on this point with cross-sectional data.

The only other important relation uncovered in the analysis of mode recruitment was that the modern modes are less likely than the pure and mixed traditional modes to recruit persons with authoritarian tendencies. While demonstrating that authoritarianism and mode adoption are related, the data did not allow the exploration necessary to establish how the relation had come about.

Following this analysis, tests for spuriousness were made, introducing the variables found to be significant in mode recruitment as controls. Under all test conditions, modes continued to have a strong independent relation to prescriptions. The results, in sum, lend strong support to a conclusion that how racial differences are explained is crucial to how whites respond to the black condition in America and what they are willing to do to improve it.

Social Indicators Development

Our investigation was motivated, it will be recalled, by a concern to develop model social indicators of racial prejudice. The end in view was a research instrument that, when administered periodically to a national sample of white Americans, would afford a measure of the extent of racial prejudice over time and also provide a vehicle for testing theory about attitude change in that subject area. It behooves us now to consider whether these goals have been achieved and, more generally, to assess the possible contributions of our work for social indicator development.

To begin with, it is self-evident that we have not succeeded in developing model social indicators of racial prejudice. In retrospect, we should have known better than to use the term *racial prejudice* in our research proposal. At the time, however, we had not anticipated the difficulties of working objectively with a pejorative concept. Moreover, we had not thought through the implications of what our focus on explanatory modes might imply for the label we adopted to characterize our endeavors. Once we began to grasp the ramifications of our explorations, it became apparent that we were dealing with something different from what has been historically conceived of as racial prejudice. We could have tried, perhaps, to incorporate explanatory modes into a definition of prejudice by designating some modes as prejudiced and others as unprejudiced, but this would have meant becoming judgmental, a position we were trying to avoid. Moreover, such a classification did not strike us as appropriate. Under the circumstances, it seemed the wisest course to find a substitute term that would more accurately and less pejoratively describe what our inquiries were about.

This substitution did not involve a major reformulation of the project's principal goal. We still hoped to make a contribution to social indicators, but through developing a research instrument for studying white racial attitudes, rather than racial prejudice, over time. Strictly speaking, we have not accomplished that goal. The most highly developed research instrument we have produced, the one reproduced in Appendix D, is not set up for administration to a national sample; and further data collection, for which we do not have the resources, would be required in order to put it in an appropriate form.

Clearly, before an instrument suitable for national use can be produced, some refinement in the specification of the modes is needed, especially the mixed traditional and the transitional modes. It will be recalled that while we were able to specify how the traditional mixed modes differ from one another in their perceptions of racial differences, we were not able to do so with respect either to their prescriptions or their social origins. This inability was largely a result of the small number of cases representing these modes in our inquiries. There is also an obvious need to identify more clearly the transitional mode. The causal analysis suggested that in their understanding of racial issues the occupants of this mode are in transition from being traditional to being modern. The means used to classify these respondents, however, suggest the alternative possibility that the transitionalists may have an explanation of racial differences other than the ones our inquiries uncovered. The conceptualization of the pure modes and of the mixed modern mode appear to us less in need of refinement, although they should be subject, of course, to additional tests before being accepted as we have formulated them.

As a preliminary step, some further work on measurement is also required. The scales used to develop the explanatory-mode typology could be strengthened if more items were available to build them. Also, for a national effort it would be desirable to strengthen the measures of prescriptions and perceptions through the use of additional items. These additions and modifications could be based on what our analysis revealed about the strengths and weaknesses of the items used in the follow-up study. However, before administering any revised instrument to a national sample, researchers should make at least one test run to ensure that the revisions work properly and allow the construction of summary measures that are more discriminating than those we were able to produce.

Some further work to assess the behavioral validity of the prescriptive measures is also required. We reported earlier on our aborted plans for this purpose. To ascertain that explanatory modes affect behavior as well as attitudes, some effort to test behavioral validity should probably still be on the agenda. Perhaps, however, such a test might be made in conjunction with a national study rather than prior to it.

While it did not fulfill its ultimate goal, the project has nevertheless made a contribution to social indicator development, we believe, in conceptualization, in measurement, and in providing a model suitable for application—once additional preliminary work is completed—in repeated national studies of white racial attitudes.

The principal conceptual contributions are specifying the explanatory component of white racial attitudes and, to a lesser extent, distinguishing between characterological and social structural perceptions. Of course, these conceptual contributions are subject to confirmation. However, if they are confirmed, with or without modifications, any effort to generate social indicators of white racial attitudes will be obliged to take these innovations into account.

We believe that our project's most significant contribution to measurement in regard to social indicator development has to do with the explanatory-mode variable being typological rather than continuous. Our construction of the mode typology and the related analysis illustrate the possibly greater rewards to be achieved through adopting a more complex classification of social phenomena than is ordinarily attempted. In this respect, we admit to being iconoclastic about what we consider an undue commitment in the social indicator movement to ordinal and interval measurement. We recognize that such measurement has been long favored by social scientists and the applied statisticians who serve them.

Our reservations concern the rarely tested assumption of such measures that distinctions in degree are usually adequate for ordering variation in social phenomena. The impression we have gained from many years of social inquiry, in addition to our present experience, is that such variation is often more accurately captured by distinctions in kind. Certainly, in the present instance, we see no way that the insights gained about explanatory modes could have been achieved by the use of one or more ordinal or interval measures.

Most importantly, the project has contributed, albeit in a form with some rough edges, a model for the development of social indicators of white racial attitudes. The model is one that specifies which data are to be collected, how variables are to be built, and how analysis may be pursued. The model also includes a set of theoretical ideas about the sources of white racial attitudes that may be tested should the model be applied in a repeated way. Whether or not the model is successfully applied on a national scale, our experience in testing it will have been instructive to others engaged in social indicator development. Moreover, if success is achieved, we shall have gained a unique and cumulative body of data on racial attitudes, a topic of crucial importance to society and to the social sciences.

Implications for Further Inquiry

The model that has been developed for studying white racial attitudes may be useful for studying other social phenomena as well. We see several possibilities. First, the model would seem appropriate for studying how groups other than whites respond to the black condition in America. The most likely group would be American blacks themselves. It will be recalled that some limited exploration of black attitudes was described in Chapter 10. Blacks, like whites, perceive racial differences, they have explanations of them, and they have opinions about what should be done to bring about greater racial equality. The distribution of perceptions, explanations, and prescriptions differs in the black and the white communities. However, as far as we were able to determine, based on a small number of cases, the model appears to be as applicable to studying black racial attitudes as to studying white attitudes. The model also seems useful for studying the racial attitudes of other subgroups in American society, for example, Native Americans and Chicanos.

An additional possibility is that the model could also be

used in the study of attitudes toward other racial, ethnic, and religious groups, and possibly toward other kinds of groups. We did try one question in the follow-up study to see what kind of distribution we would get if, instead of being asked to explain racial differences, respondents were asked to account for the notion that Jews in American society seem to be better off than other Americans. Respondents were given the option of replying that they did not think that Jews are better off than non-Jews, but only 6.5 percent chose it. The other choices allowed them to answer in the supernatural, the individualistic, the environmental, the radical, and the genetic modes. We also added a cultural explanation.[2]

As might be expected, respondents tend to choose different reasons to explain Jewish privilege than black deprivation. However, all respondents chose an explanation from the alternatives presented to them, rather than selecting the option that none of the reasons offered expressed what they believed. This would seem to suggest that the explanatory component is as much a part of attitudes toward Jews as it is of attitudes toward blacks. For lack of room on the questionnaire, we did not try to test the applicability of the full model for studying attitudes toward Jews. The responses to the explanatory-mode question, however, suggest that the full model would be applicable. If so—although a full test would be necessary to make sure—it seems likely that the model would be applicable for studying attitudes toward out-groups generally, at least in a literate society such as the United States.

As reported above, we have engaged in some exploration of the possibility that the explanatory-mode concept, though not necessarily the full model, could be applied to studying attitudes toward social phenomena other than intergroup relations. The control agents invoked to ex-

2. See question 7 in Appendix D.

plain other social phenomena are not always the same as those referred to when racial differences are to be accounted for. However, there is a greater tendency than might be attributed to chance for people to account for other social phenomena in the same manner as they account for racial differences.

Among questions about the more general applicability of the explanatory-mode concept that we have not explored, or have explored only tentatively, are the following:

1. To what kinds of social phenomena is the explanatory-mode concept applicable? It appears that explanatory modes are invoked when there are differences to be accounted for—e.g., some people suffering, others not; some people being poor, others not; some people becoming alcoholics, others not. But is the concept equally applicable to all social differences? Are there some social differences for which modes of explanation are not invoked?

2. What is the full range of control agents that people invoke to explain social differences? Our explorations of racial and other social differences have dealt with the following control agents: God, the self, genes, environment, culture, fate, luck, and people in power. Is this the full range or are there still other agents of control to which people refer when explaining social phenomena? Are different control agents invoked in other cultures?

3. Given answers to these questions, to what extent are explanatory modes generic and to what extent issue-specific? Or, to put it another way, do people vary with respect to the type or number of control agents they call upon to explain different phenomena? Our preliminary explorations suggest that some people refer to the same control agent to account for them all, while other people's mode of explanation varies depending upon the social difference they are asked to explain. With the limited data available to us, we were not able to discover how multi-

causal explanation is patterned, although it is clearly not completely random.

4. If it is true that explanatory modes come into play only when there are social differences to be accounted for, then it is quite possible that our full model, not just its explanatory component, might be applicable to studying such phenomena. Differences have to be perceived. Once differences are perceived, their existence opens up the possibility of something being done about them. Thus, just as it was relevant to inquire into people's perceptions, explanations, and prescriptions with respect to racial differences, it seems also relevant to ask about them as they pertain to other social differences.

5. These problems lead to a final set of questions about how people get recruited to different explanatory styles and about how the distribution of such styles may influence the more general social organization of a society and the way it conducts its affairs.

Implications for Public Policy

We sought to meet the standards of scientific objectivity both in the design and execution of our research and in reporting our findings. We recognize that the topic was not chosen objectively. Once the topic was chosen, however, we made a conscious effort to keep our own values from intruding into the research process.

With the scientific report on the research now complete, we propose, in closing, to assume the mantle of citizens, concerned about the state of race relations in America and about the continuing relative deprivation being suffered by black Americans. In this role, we should like to reflect briefly on what the project has taught about the way in which white racial attitudes may contribute to the current state of affairs. We shall also comment on changes in these attitudes and on the relation of these changes to the past, present, and future condition of blacks in the society.

Since our data tell us only about the state of white racial attitudes in the San Francisco Bay Area, strictly speaking, we should limit our comments to how these attitudes bear on the conditions experienced by blacks in the Bay Area. We believe that the observations have more general applicability, but it will take further research for this to be demonstrated.

We do not believe that white racial attitudes are the exclusive source of the racial problems besetting the society or that these problems can be solved simply by changing attitudes. We do believe, however, that attitudes count. On the one hand, they help people in different ways to accept or to live comfortably with conditions as they are. On the other hand, at different levels of intensity, attitudes can produce discomfort with the status quo and be a stimulus to change.

It is impossible to say how comfortably white Americans have lived with black deprivation throughout American history. The persistence of the deprivation, however, suggests that whatever the discomfort being experienced, it was not enough to cause any massive effort at reform. The exception, of course, was white response to the condition of slavery. While white Americans were divided on that issue, enough were sufficiently uncomfortable about it to play a significant part in slavery's abolition. The deprivations suffered by blacks were not overcome with the end of slavery, however, and since then no comparable effort has occurred on the part of whites to bring about racial equality.

Examining current white racial attitudes affords some insight into the ways that attitudes function to reduce discomfort or even perhaps to foster complacency about the social and economic conditions under which blacks live in the United States. The attitude that most directly lessens discomfort is that blacks are innately inferior to whites.

Given such an attitude, it seems perfectly natural that blacks are underprivileged relative to whites, and that this state of affairs will continue. Given that the differences are innate, nothing can be done to change things and therefore it is useless to try.

The explanation of racial differences as genetically produced was undoubtedly more prevalent in America's past than it is today. Indeed, although survey data are not available, this explanation may have been predominant at one time. It was clearly a rationale for slavery. As we have seen, it is still an element in white thought about blacks. We classified 6 percent of our sample of the Bay Area population as subscribing to a wholly genetic explanation of racial differences. To this proportion may be added another 11 percent for whom a genetic explanation is an element in how they account for racial differences. If anything, these are probably underestimates, given the social constraints against acknowledging a belief that blacks are inferior. It seems fair to conclude, however, that only a minority of whites now think this way about the condition of blacks in America.

Explanations other than the genetic one also permit people to avoid feeling disturbed by the racial situation in America. The major alternative, judging from the number of people who subscribe to it, is to blame the victim, even though to believe that individual blacks are wholly responsible for their condition flies in the face of considerable evidence to the contrary. Those who subscribe to an individualistic understanding of racial differences are either unaware of such evidence or refuse to accept it. Instead, informed by their conviction that individuals exercise control over their destinies, they draw what seems to them the logical inference, namely, that blacks as individuals are not exercising that control wisely. The imagery may not lead its adherents to be entirely comfortable about the relative deprivation suffered by blacks. It is effective, however, in virtually relieving them of any responsibility to turn the situation around. "If only they work hard enough, blacks can succeed like everyone else. After all, some blacks do it, others can too if only they would try."

Individualistic thought has not always been associated with neglect of the condition of blacks in America. An important argument in the fight against slavery was that it restricted blacks from being in command of their own destinies. Among persons who supported the abolition of slavery were those who would be classified as individualistic in their racial thinking today. This early concern was not maintained. Once slavery was ended, blacks were perceived to be as free to make their way in the world as anyone else. If they failed now, it was their responsibility, no one else's.

Judging from the Bay Area data, individualists now outnumber geneticists in the population by a considerable margin. Indeed, individualistic explanations of racial differences have more subscribers than any other mode. Seventeen percent were classified as pure individualists and another 22 percent were in a mixed mode with an individualistic component, for a total 39 percent in all. It seems likely that individualistic thinking about race would be found even more widespread in the nation as a whole.

The belief that God ordained the races to be different also has deep roots in American history. It has probably never been the predominant religious view and, indeed, today most Bay Area residents who acknowledge a belief in God do not subscribe to this explanatory mode. However, this idea is clearly among those that have served in the past and present to help white Americans avoid feeling an obligation to do very much to change the social circumstances in which blacks find themselves. "What God has wrought, let not man put asunder."

Like the genetic mode, the supernatural mode has only a minority of adherents. In our sample we classified 6 per-

cent as pure supernaturalists and another 16 percent in a
mode having a supernatural component. Once again, however, it seems likely that proportionately more adherents
to the supernatural mode would be found in the nation as
a whole than in the Bay Area.

These, then, are the ideas that contribute to white apa-
thy about the black condition today; they are ideas that
have done so now for a period of well over two centuries.
We do not know how many supporters they still command in the national population. In the Bay Area, they
add up to 53 percent of the sample; that is to say, 53 percent adopt a supernatural, a genetic, or an individualistic
explanation of racial differences, alone or in some combination.

Attitudes, we have suggested, can also lead people to be
uncomfortable about existing social arrangements and
consequently to be a stimulant to social change or, at least,
to efforts to bring about social change. Our inquiries indicate that there are two principal ways of interpreting the
social condition of blacks that have these consequences.
One is to believe that black deprivation is environmentally
caused; the other is to attribute it to white racism. In both
cases, blacks are not blamed for their social circumstances.

Neither of these interpretations is new. There were persons in colonial America who believed that as social circumstances permitted blacks would gain equality with
whites. Environmentalists shared with individualists an
opposition to slavery. With the end of slavery, blacks were
left to their own devices by individualists, whereas environmentalists continued to express concern and to extend
a helping hand.

There is no way to judge how many in the population
were environmentalist in their thinking about race in
America's past. It seems clear that they were a minority
but how small a minority is not known. As the proportion
of the educated population has grown, and as social science knowledge about the sources of black-white differ-

ences has increased and been more widely disseminated, an increase has undoubtedly occurred in the proportion of environmentalists in the population. In the Bay Area, we classified 18 percent in the pure environmental mode or as including an environmental component in their racial understanding.

Radical interpretations of the racial situation in America probably have a considerably shorter history than any other. They began to appear in any significant number in the 1930s and, we would guess, reached their zenith in the 1960s. Since then they have probably declined. In the Bay Area, we counted 6 percent as pure radicals and another 6 percent as in a mode with a radical component.

Whites who believe that American society is racist and who are openly critical of this state of affairs have undoubtedly contributed to a climate of opinion in which white concern about the black condition is considered a socially desirable attitude. Whites of this persuasion were also important to the civil rights struggles of the 1950s and 1960s. In terms of concrete achievement, however, it seems apparent that those whose understanding of racial differences we have labeled radical have not seen the realization of their vision. Certainly, there has been no major upturning of existing social arrangements to improve the condition of blacks in the society.

Since the 1930s, the environmentalists and the environmental-radicals have probably had the greatest influence in shaping the positive efforts of whites to improve the social conditions of blacks in the country. The environmentalists have been prominent supporters of the civil rights struggle, and have been at the forefront of the movement to integrate the schools. They have also been the strongest advocates of affirmative action. And from their ranks has come a disproportionate number of white leaders supporting legislation to reduce discrimination in education, housing, and employment.

That the leverage of the environmentalists has not been

greater is due, in part, to the fact that the programs they have supported have not had the success anticipated. Also, because they do not accept the notion that whites today have some responsibility for the black condition, they have been unwilling to support compensatory programs that would favor blacks over whites. And, more generally, they have been unwilling to help where more than a mild sacrifice of their own interests has been required.

Among those whose attitudes we studied, there was one group, the transitionalists, whose understanding of racial differences we were unable to classify. In effect, the transitionalists rejected all the explanations placed before them and did not provide an alternative. Judging from the attitudes they expressed in their answers to the prescriptive questions, they resemble the environmentalists more than any other group. Since they represent a substantial minority of the population—20 percent by our count—the transitionalists have probably helped to get the environmentalists' legislation passed.

Our overall impression is that the cause of racial equality is less well-served by white racial attitudes today than it was at the height of the civil rights struggle in the 1950s and 1960s. Even then, of course, the attitudes did not produce the commitments necessary for dramatic change. More progress, however, was then being made than seems the case at present. To be sure, the black community was making more demands on the white community in those years than now, or at least it was doing so more effectively. Moreover, the white community was less preoccupied with its own economic welfare than it is now.

Taking a longer view, the net change in white racial attitudes since the last century has probably been in a positive direction, however much current attitudes may suggest that there is still a great distance to go. The major achievement has been the decline in genetic thinking about race. Latter-day proponents of genetic thinking do not appear to have had much success in generating a revival. The vestiges that remain are nothing to get complacent about; the Ku Klux Klan has not disappeared. But it seems reasonable to conclude that we are well past the era in which genetic explanations were dominant. Supernatural explanations remain a minority viewpoint and appear likely to continue to do so. So far there have been no signs that the evangelical revival is producing a resurgence of biblical interpretation that casts blacks as God's second-class citizens. In this connection, it should be recalled that it is a particular image of God, not all images, that is associated with supernatural explanations of racial differences.

That individualistic interpretations of the racial situation have succeeded genetic explanations as the dominant mode is not an unequivocal gain. Comparatively speaking, less social stigma is associated with individualistic than with genetic explanations, which perhaps helps to explain why the former now has more subscribers than the latter. Unlike the geneticists, the individualists do not claim blacks are inferior. In fact, the underlying assumption in the individualists' thought is that blacks are inherently equal. But with respect to supporting social programs designed to improve the condition of blacks relative to whites, the geneticists, if anything, are less likely to offer opposition than the individualists.

As widespread as individualistic thinking is, it is unlikely that it is increasing in strength. Such an increase would occur at the expense of a decline in genetic attitudes. Added together, it is difficult to believe that traditional interpretations of racial differences have proportionately as many adherents as they had in the past. The modern modes, we believe, are gaining more supporters. As between the modern modes, however, it is the environmentalists who appear to be growing the most, followed by the environmental-radicals. At best, the pure radicals are doing no more than holding their own. It is also conceivable that they are losing adherents. It can be expected, consequently, that a substantial body of white opinion will continue to support efforts to break down racial barriers in America, but only so long as the costs do not escalate too much. Given that contingency, only a modicum of support is likely to be forthcoming from the white community judging from the present distribution of white racial attitudes.

Appendix A **A Description of the Follow-Up Study**

The follow-up study of racial attitudes is part of a larger program of research begun in 1971. Since that date, the Survey Research Center of the University of California at Berkeley has been coordinating a number of studies relating to social indicators of racial prejudice, political alienation, and the status of women. The data analyzed here were collected in 1973 as part of that series of studies. This particular study was a self-administered mailback survey of the population of the five counties in the San Francisco-Oakland standard metropolitan statistical area (San Francisco, Alameda, Contra Costa, Marin, and San Mateo counties). In this appendix we describe briefly how this sample was selected and how it compares to the estimated characteristics of the population from which it was drawn. We also describe the caseweights used in analyzing this data set.

Preliminary Bay Area Surveys

The sample for the mailback survey was composed of participants in two previous surveys of the Bay Area population. Respondents to these two surveys were chosen through a three-stage, area probability sample, which afforded each noninstitutionalized adult an approximately equal chance of being selected. Both of the earlier surveys consisted of personal interviews with approximately 1,000 respondents.

The first survey that preceded our follow-up study was the Bay Area Survey 2 (BAS 2), conducted in 1972. It contained questions on three substantive areas—racial prejudice, political alienation, and the status of women.[1] The analysis presented in Chapter 3 is based on this survey. Each of the three subprojects of the study was allocated a randomly chosen third of the BAS 2 respondents for follow-up work. The Racial Prejudice Subproject's share was 315 respondents.[2]

The second survey that provided the sampling frame for our follow-up study was the 1972–73 Bay Area Religious Consciousness Survey.[3] That survey was designed to investigate, among other things, certain differences between persons over and under 30 years of age; consequently, the younger group was deliberately over-sampled in order to yield approximately equal numbers of respondents in both age groups. In creating our own sampling frame, we randomly selected only about half of those age 30 or younger, whereas we attempted to recontact all of those over 30. A total of 683 respondents from that survey were recontacted.

Therefore, our total sampling frame for the mailback survey was 998 persons, with 315 from BAS 2, and 683 from the Religious Consciousness Survey. Of these 998 persons, 646 returned our questionnaire. Of these respondents, 504

1. The interview schedule and a detailed discussion of the sampling procedures can be found in *Bay Area Survey 2 Study Codebook* (Berkeley, Calif.: Survey Research Center, University of California, 1975).

2. Twenty of these cases were exchanged with the Political Alienation subproject for an equal number from that set of cases. The cases exchanged were of particular interest to the Political Alienation project; the cases received in return were matched as closely as possible by race, age, sex, and education with those given up.

3. The results of that survey are reported in Robert Wuthnow, *The Consciousness Reformation* (Berkeley, Calif.: University of California Press, 1976). The interview schedule is reproduced there as Appendix D. The sample design is discussed in pp. 6–10.

identified themselves as being white; most of the analysis was carried out on data collected from that group. Approximately 100 white respondents answered the explanatory-mode questions both in BAS 2 and the follow-up study; this group is the basis for the discussion in Chapter 10 of the stability of responses to the mode items.

Comparison of Sample with Population

Although each step of the sampling process was designed to ensure approximately equal probabilities of selection for all adult residents of the Bay Area, our sample does not exactly reproduce all the area's demographic characteristics. We compared the sex, race, education, and age distributions of our respondents with the 1970 Census data for the San Francisco-Oakland metropolitan area.[4] The purpose of this comparison was to anticipate any potential bias in the estimation of other characteristics of our respondents. Sample surveys often have better response rates from whites than from blacks, from women than from men, and from the better educated than from the less well-educated. Given that such biases might result, for example, in overestimating the population of liberals in the population, it is wise to keep such potential problems in mind.

In the case of our sample, there were no substantial differences from the census figures for race and age. The proportions of whites and blacks in the sample were within two percentage points of the census data, although the "other race" category was under-represented (9 percent in the sample; 12 percent in the census data). The age distribution of the sample was somewhat younger than in the

4. The comparison data were obtained from the United States Bureau of the Census, *Public Use Samples of Basic Records from the 1970 Census: Description and Technical Documentation* (Washington, D.C.: U.S. Government Printing Office, 1972).

census figures (36 percent versus 32 percent under age 30; 30 percent versus 34 percent age 50 or over), but the difference was not large enough to cause concern.

The difference in the proportions of men and women, however, was substantial. In our sample, 61 percent are women, compared with a figure of 53 percent for the regional population. Furthermore, our sample is considerably better educated than the population of the region as a whole. Whereas only 33 percent of the population attended school beyond the twelfth grade, 53 percent of our sample did so. Obviously, we could not ignore these discrepancies when estimating the distributions or the effects of variables related to sex or education, as many attitude variables are. In order to compensate for these differences, we have used caseweights throughout our analysis.

What the use of caseweights means, for calculating statistics, is that certain classes of respondents that were over-represented in our sample were assigned weights of less than 1.0, whereas the members of under-represented groups were assigned weights greater than 1.0. The net effect of this weighting procedure was to reduce the influence of the better educated and more liberal respondents in estimations of the proportion of respondents holding modern explanations of racial differences or favoring liberal racial policies.

To calculate the weights we first obtained the census data on the joint age, sex, race, and education distributions in the Bay Area. Then we cross-classified our respondents in terms of these variables. Finally, we divided the proportion of our sample in each cell by the corresponding proportion in the population. The inverse of the resulting ratio was assigned to each case in the cell as its caseweight.

We recognize that this weighting procedure does not eliminate the problem of bias in our sample, but the descriptive results of our analysis are probably more reflective of the Bay Area population with the use of these caseweights. The analytic results of our study—correlations and other relationships among variables—did not seem to depend materially on the use of caseweights, based on a comparison of a number of weighted versus non-weighted analyses. We therefore concluded that since the caseweights did not alter the major analytic conclusions of our study, it was preferable to use the weights for their descriptive value.

The Construction of Summary Measures

This appendix shows how the various summary measures used in analysis were created. It should be noted that in subsection 1 the methodology of constructing the explanatory-mode scales is discussed in great detail. Descriptions of the other scales presume that discussion and only briefly cover the points proper to each of the other scales.

1. CONSTRUCTION OF THE EXPLANATORY-MODE TYPOLOGY

We constructed the mode typology in two steps. First, we analyzed the individual explanatory-mode items and combined them into four scales. Secondly, we placed each respondent into one of the explanatory-mode categories in accordance with his or her scores on the four mode scales. Following the discussion of these two procedures below, we describe a simplified method of constructing a mode typology for those interested in replicating our typology in a less complex, but still adequate, manner.

Creating the Explanatory-Mode Scales

We asked dozens of questions designed to reveal the respondents' explanations for the social and economic dif-

ferences between blacks and whites. We then analyzed all
these items in order to identify and measure the various
dimensions represented in the data. Some of the dimensions were obvious a priori, and we only needed to confirm their existence and to select the best measures of
them; the supernatural and the genetic explanations for
racial differences fell into this category. The individualist
and social explanations, however, were not so easy to dis-
entangle. After extensive factor analyses of both the interitem correlation matrix and the matrix of P-squares, we
settled on the solution described in the text: one dimension
representing the individual versus social explanation of
the obstacles to black advancement, and a second dimension representing the attribution of black versus white
blame for the situation of blacks.

The methodology of item analysis developed for this
study is described in detail elsewhere.[5] The P-squared
statistic, in particular, is described in that reference. Before
giving a detailed account of the four mode scales, however,
we will present a general explanation of our methodology.

The main problem in analyzing a set of attitude items is
to determine which ones seem to be measuring the same
underlying attitude. As a first step we examine the covar-
iation among the items, using common factor analysis
techniques on the matrix of interitem correlations. Items
that do not covary cannot be said to measure the same
thing. That is, people who answer one question in a liberal
way should tend to answer another question in a liberal
way, if those two questions truly measure the same attitude. This criterion is sometimes referred to as the internal
validity of a set of items.

But we cannot stop there. Even if items covary, they
may still mean quite different things to the respondents

5. Thomas Piazza, "The Analysis of Attitude Items," *American Journal of
Sociology* 86 (November 1980):584–603.

and may be related in distinct ways to other variables that
are important to our study (such as education and age). For
example, if one pro-black question is favored by young
people whereas a second question is favored, relatively, by
older respondents, then those two questions would seem
to have distinct meanings and should not be confused. For
purposes of this study, we looked particularly at the relation of items with age, sex, education, father's education,
occupation, income, union membership, rent versus own
one's home, number of children, and southern origin.
Only items judged to have reasonably consistent relations
with all those variables were considered to be measures of
the same underlying attitude. We assessed the degree of
that consistency by calculating an index of proportionality
and by carrying out canonical correlation analyses, as described in the above-cited article.

As a result of this analysis, we concluded that four sets
of items formed reasonably coherent groups, and those
became our four explanatory-mode scales. We created the
scales by recoding all the items in each group to a common
range and then averaging the answered items for each
case. An item with four response categories, for instance,
could be coded from 0 to 3; an item in the same set with
only two categories would then be coded 0 or 3. The component items of each scale are as follows (question numbers refer to the questionnaire included as Appendix D):

Supernatural
    4.b.   John Smith—God
    32.b. SES—God

Genetic
    4.d.   John Smith—Genetic
    32.e. SES—Genetic
    33.   IQ = 5 (IQ = 4 counted as missing)

Social-Awareness
    4.g.   John Smith—Individualist (reversed)
    32.d. SES—Social is most important reason
    33.   IQ = 4 (IQ = 5 counted as missing)

Blame-Whites
- 4.c. John Smith—Keep Down is most important reason
- 32.c. SES—Individualist (reversed)
- 34.a. White Fault

The properties of the four scales can be summarized as follows:

	Range	Mean	S.D.	N
Supernatural	0–3	.86	1.12	489
Genetic	0–3	.72	.91	500
Social Awareness	0–1	.41	.35	502
Blame Whites	0–6	2.30	1.39	504

Note that the supernatural and the genetic scales are heavily skewed—relatively few respondents endorse these explanations. The other two scales are more "normally" distributed.

Creating the Typology

Based on each respondent's score on the four explanatory-mode scales, we assigned him or her to one category of the explanatory-mode typology. (Fifteen respondents who did not have a valid score on all four scales were not assigned.) We attempted various clustering methods and tested alternate cutting points for each mode scale. We evaluated the results of these attempts in terms of how well each typology predicted its component dimensions and other variables of interest.

We followed several procedures to create the typology that we finally settled on. First, we standardized the mode scales with mean equal to 50 and standard deviation equal to 10. Next, we divided up the scales into discrete categories. The genetic and supernatural scales were dichotomized, with a standardized score of 60 or above equal to "high." The social awareness scale was divided into five categories, with cutting points at 40, 50, 55, and 60. The blame scale was also divided into five categories, with cutting points at 42.5, 46.5, 54, and 61.

Once we divided the mode scales into categories, we cross-classified the respondents by the resulting four variables and assigned them to categories of the typology based on that cross-classification. The procedure used can easily be understood by referring to Table B-1, which shows how the combinations of the social awareness and the blame scales were divided up into domains. Each of those two scales was divided into five categories, as described above, and the resulting twenty-five combinations of scores were divided into four domains.

Table B-1 **Scale Combinations for Mode Typology**

BLAME		SOCIAL AWARENESS				
		(Indiv.) 1	2	3	4	(Social) 5
(Blacks)	1	I	I			
	2	I	I			E
	3	I				E
	4				E	E
(Whites)	5		R	R	R	R-E

The five combinations marked I in Table B-1 represent the domain of the individualists. Respondents with those combinations of scores on the social awareness and blame scales were classified as individualists on the mode typology. If they also scored "low" (less than 60) on the supernatural and genetic scales, they were classified as pure individualists. If, on the other hand, they scored "high" on the supernatural scale, on the genetic scale, or on both scales, they were classified, respectively, as individualist-supernaturals, individualist-geneticists, or individualist-supernatural-geneticists.

Similarly, the combinations marked R and E in Table B-1 indicate the domains of the radicals and the environmentalists. Note the R-E cell, which represents the radical-environmentalists. Respondents in these R, E, and RE cells who scored low on the supernatural and genetic scales were assigned, respectively, to the radical, environmentalist, and radical-environmentalist modes. There were about a dozen respondents in the R and E domains who also scored high on the supernatural or genetic scales; they were assigned to the transitional mode.

The unmarked cells in the central part of Table B-1 indicate the domains of the transitionals and of the non-individualist supernatural and genetic types. If respondents in those cells scored low on both the supernatural and genetic scales, they were classified as transitionals. If, on the other hand, they scored high on the supernatural scale, the genetic scale, or both scales, they were classified, respectively, as supernaturalists, geneticists, or genetic-supernaturalists.

All eleven mode types were created as described above. The procedure was admittedly an arbitrary one, but we exercised a great deal of care at each step in order to create a typology that would be a useful summary of the data. There are many combinations of scores on the four mode dimensions, and it is no simple task to cluster all those combinations into a few groups, each representing a distinct social type. Our typology does not pretend to be an absolute crystallization of American perceptions of social reality. Rather, it was designed to summarize and to illuminate the relationship between explanatory mode and policy orientation. We do not claim that our typology is the only way to do this, but we believe that the results presented in the text show that we were at least reasonably successful.

A Simplified Method of Typology Construction

The typology we employed in our analysis represents our best effort to use the entire array of items in our questionnaire. We realize, however, that other researchers who wish to pursue our line of analysis are unlikely to use all our explanatory-mode questions in collecting data. Consequently, we have developed a simplified procedure for creating a typology that uses the responses to only two sets of questions—the John Smith questions and the SES questions. Whereas our original typology uses the responses to eleven different items (combined into four mode scales), the simplified procedure uses only five of those eleven items.

The first step in this procedure is to define five explanatory-mode domains, each on the basis of the response to a single item. The domains are defined as follows (question numbers refer to the questionnaire given as Appendix D):

Supernatural	4.b. = 1	John Smith—God
Genetic	32.e. = 1 or 2	SES—Genetic
Individualist	32.c. = 1 or 2	SES—Individualist
Radical	4.c. is MIR	John Smith—Keep Down is most important reason
Environmental	4.g. = 2	John Smith—Individualist (rejected)

Respondents who answer the above questions in the indicated way are considered to fall within the appropriate domain. For example, only those giving response 1 ("probably a reason") to question 4b are considered to have a supernatural explanatory mode.

After all respondents have been scored on the five domains, the respondents are classified into the appropriate mode category based on those five scores. For instance, those who fall into the supernatural domain but not into any of the other four domains are classified as pure supernaturals; those who fall into both the radical and the environmental domains but not into any of the other three domains are classified as radical-environmentalists. Respondents who do not fall into any of the five domains are classified as transitionals. There will be a few respondents with combinations of modes not allowed in our typology—combinations of radical or environmental with one or more of the three traditional modes; these combinations can be classified as transitionals or can be excluded from the classification, if the researchers desire. This procedure will yield the same eleven explanatory-mode types described in the text.

Compared with the typology used in the text, this more simply constructed typology suffers primarily from some unreliability in scoring respondents on the five mode domains; each of those scores is based on the response to a single questionnaire item. Nevertheless, this procedure allows the researcher to bypass the intermediate steps of combining items into scales and then deciding where to draw the lines between high and low scale scores. The rather simple procedure is, we hope, attractive to researchers who might otherwise abandon any thought of trying to replicate our typology.

Although the simply constructed typology does not—and cannot be expected to—yield results as powerful as the typology used in the text, we found that it does quite well. In our sample, most respondents were classified into the same explanatory mode by both procedures. Furthermore, the power of the typology to predict respondents' scores on the prescription scales was still substantial when the simplified method of typology construction was used. We therefore do not hesitate to recommend this simplified procedure to those researchers who would like to explore this line of analysis but are not in a position to make it a major component of their data collection and analysis efforts.

2. PRESCRIPTION SCALES

Our questionnaire contained twenty-two items designed to assess our respondents' views on social policy
relative to blacks (see questions 36–57 in Appendix D). The
questions dealt with government pressure on business and
labor unions, school integration and busing, special compensatory programs for blacks, open housing laws, and
miscegenation. Our purpose in analyzing these items was
to identify the dimensions that seemed to guide respondents in organizing their policy positions with respect to
blacks. Based on our analysis (using the methods discussed
above in subsection 1), we concluded that there are two
clearly identifiable dimensions along which the responses
to many of these items are ordered.

The first dimension is that of support for, or opposition
to, government intervention to help blacks. Those who fall
at the liberal end of this dimension favor government
pressure on businesses and unions to provide better opportunities for blacks. Those at the other end of this dimension emphasize the rights of private property and
maintain that employers should be free to hire whomever
they wish.

The second dimension is represented by respondents'
positions on miscegenation and on open housing laws. It
seems to reflect the degree to which white respondents
feel a personal affinity toward blacks. Those who seem to
feel such an affinity accept the idea of interracial marriage,
both in general and as it might apply to their own children, and they also support open housing laws. Respondents at the other end of this dimension disapprove of
miscegenation and also oppose open housing laws. We
found it interesting that the item on open housing laws
fell along the same dimension as the miscegenation items.
This seems to indicate that whites' positions about living
near blacks are based on different criteria than support for

such things as affirmative action or better job opportunities for blacks. The housing issue is a more emotional matter, linked to feelings about intermarriage.

The component items of each of these two scales are as follows (question numbers refer to the questionnaire given as Appendix D):

Institutional Intervention

44 ≠ 4	Employers should be free (rejected)
46 = 3 or 4	Government pressure business
49	Private property (disagree)
53 = 1 or 2	Hire black teachers

Personal Affinity

48	Open housing laws (favor)
56	Favor intermarriage—in general
57 = 1	Favor intermarriage—own child

The items in each set above were coded to a common range, and their scores were averaged to create scales. A minimum of two valid items in each set was required for a valid scale score. For presentation in the text the resulting scales were standardized with a mean of zero and a standard deviation of 10. The properties of the unstandardized scales, however, are as follows:

	Range	Mean	S.D.	N
Institutional Intervention	0–3	1.03	.82	499
Personal Affinity	0–6	2.82	1.80	486

3. PERCEPTION MEASURES

A major section of our questionnaire was devoted to the issue of what social structural or characterological differences people perceive to exist between whites and blacks (see questions 16–22 in Appendix D). We uncovered several distinct dimensions along which whites make such judgments. In order to simplify our discussion in Chapter 7, however, we focused on a single six-category typology of social and characterological differences that summarizes the main thrust of the variation along these dimensions. We will first describe how we created that typology and its component measures. Then we will summarize the results of our analysis of the whole set of perception items, so that researchers wishing to measure such perceptions can build on our experience with these items.

Perception Typology and Component Scales

We created the six-category perception typology by cross-classifying a three-category measure of the perception of social structural differences by a two-category measure of the perception of characterological differences. We selected the component items of each of these measures by our usual item analysis procedures, as described above. The items in each set are as follows:

Social Perceptions
     18.a.   Good job
     18.c.   Good housing
     18.d.   Good medical care

Characterological Perceptions
     19.d.   Children to college
     19.l.   Take care of home
     20.h.   Sloppy

The method of combining each set of items into a summary measure was more complex than simply summing or averaging the original coded values of the items. Since we wanted to reduce each measure to a few discrete categories, we recoded the component items and combined them in such a way as to facilitate discussion of each discrete category in substantive terms.

For the social structural measure, we first dichotomized each of the three items. Those respondents who said that whites were more likely (either much or somewhat more likely) than blacks to have a good job were considered as having perceived a social difference (detrimental to blacks); those who said there was no difference or (in a few cases) that blacks were more likely than whites to have a good job were considered as having perceived no social difference. The items on good housing and good medical care were similarly dichotomized. We created the full social structural perception measure by adding up the number of perceived differences; possible scores ranged from zero to 3. For the perception typology, we classified each respondent into one of three categories, depending on the number of items on which he or she perceived a social structural difference. Those who perceived differences on all three items were classified as strongly affirming social structural differences; those who perceived no differences were classified as denying such differences; those who perceived one or two differences were classified in the middle category.

For the character perception measure, we followed a similar procedure. We first dichotomized each of the three component items to indicate whether the respondent perceived a character or value difference that reflected poorly on blacks. We contrasted such persons with those who perceived no such differences or (in a few cases) who perceived differences that favored blacks rather than whites. (Recall that we carried out this analysis using the white respondents only.) To create the full characterological perception measure, we classified each respondent into one of four categories, depending on the number of perceived differences (from zero to 3) unfavorable to blacks. For the perception typology, however, we collapsed this measure into two categories. Those who perceived differences on two or three items were classified as affirming characterological differences; those who perceived one or no differences were classified as rejecting such differences.

The full perception scales, ranging from zero to 3, were used in the graphs at the end of Chapter 6, standardized to have a mean of zero and a standard deviation of 10. The collapsed versions were used in Chapter 7, primarily as components of the six-category perception typology. The properties of the full unstandardized scales are as follows:

	Range	Mean	S.D.	N
Social Perceptions	0–3	2.02	1.12	504
Characterological Perceptions	0–3	.95	.99	490

Other Sets of Perception Items

An extensive analysis of the full set of perception items revealed that they tended to fall along two main dimensions, as summarized in our typology. Within each of these two major categories, however, coherent subsets of items were also identified. These subsets express different nuances of the major dimensions and may be of interest to researchers in this area.

The social structural perception items seem to fall into four subsets. The first two concern the perception of actual social realities affecting blacks—whether blacks are as likely as whites to have the good things in life and whether discrimination still exists today in various areas of life. This perception seems to depend on whether public or private spheres are being considered. The public reality concerns jobs, education, and treatment by the police. The private reality concerns good housing and treatment by storekeepers and taxi drivers. The public reality dimension is the stronger of the two and is analogous to the social structural perception summary measure used in the text.

The other two subsets of social structural perception items deal with opportunity—whether whites have a better chance than blacks (or vice versa) to obtain various good things in life, specifically well-paid jobs, residences of choice, and good medical services. We asked the questions twice—first asking respondents to compare whites and blacks, and then asking them to compare the average black with *poor* whites. Our item analysis indicated that responses to these two sets of questions were not uni-dimensional. Two related, but distinct, dimensions are present—one for the white-black comparison and another for the poor-white/black comparison. The items in all four social perception subsets are as follows:

Public Reality
    18.a.   Good job
    22.c.   Discrimination in education
    22.f.   Discrimination by police

Private Reality
    22.a.   Discrimination in housing
    22.b.   Discrimination by taxi drivers
    22.d.   Discrimination by storekeepers

White-Black Opportunity
    16.a.   Well-paid job
    16.d.   Living where one pleases
    16.f.   Good medical services

Poor-White/Black Opportunity
    17.a.   Well-paid job
    17.d.   Living where one pleases
    17.f.   Good medical services

The character perception items seem to fall into three subsets. The first subset concerns perceived differences between whites and blacks in certain matters that reflect middle-class cultural values. This subset is the strongest characterological subset and was used in the text for the perception typology. The second subset concerns values that a good Weberian might call the spirit of capitalism—ambition, valuing money, wanting one's own business. The third subset focuses on perceived differences between whites and blacks in the value they place on having a good time and having an exciting sex life. Although most whites do not see any differences along this third dimension, we found some systematic variation that was related to other variables of interest. The items in the three characterological subsets are as follows:

Middle-Class Values
  19.d.   Children to college
  19.l.   Take care of home
  20.h.   Sloppy

Spirit of Capitalism
  19.b.   Have own business
  19.c.   Earn lot of money
  20.j.   Ambitious

Seek Pleasure
  19.g.   Good time today
  19.j.   Exciting sex life

4. CONTACT MEASURE

Interracial contact is often hypothesized to have some bearing on whites' attitudes toward blacks. We therefore included several questions on this topic in our study (see questions 58–65 in Appendix D). It turned out that interracial contact had some effect on our personal affinity measure, but that the effect was not strong, once explanatory mode was controlled (eta-squared reduced from .13 to .05). (The corresponding eta-squares on institutional intervention were .07 and .01.) As a result, not much attention is paid to contact in the text. Nevertheless, we did analyze the contact items with care and did succeed in creating a summary measure of interracial contact that was used to calculate the eta-squares given above. Since some researchers may be interested in the results of our work on these items, a brief summary is included here.

We thought at first that it would be relatively easy to classify the contact items into such categories as voluntary or involuntary contact on the basis of interitem correlations and relationships with other relevant variables. Different kinds of contact, however, are not as susceptible as attitude items to this type of clustering. In a sense, each kind of interracial contact is somewhat independent of other kinds, and each has its own "story." As a result, these items are not easy to summarize, and they certainly cannot simply be summed or averaged into an ordinary scale.

In order to summarize the information contained in the responses to the contact items, we finally adopted a method of classifying white respondents into categories on the basis of two criteria—a subjective component and a behavioral component. The subjective component ranks respondents according to their own definition of the closeness of their contact with blacks. The ranking is as follows, with relevant questionnaire numbers given in parentheses:

Subjective Component
1 Any close black friends (61.a) and call 2+ blacks by first name (62)
2 Call 2+ blacks by first name (62) but have no close black friends (61.a)
3 Neither

The behavioral component is intended to clarify the subjective one, because the latter conceals important differences. To say that one has close black friends, for instance, can mean different things to different people. Since we are interested in interracial contact as a behavioral factor, whose effects should be compared to those of attitudes, we obviously need some assurance that the reported level of contact has some objective referent. Two of our items were used to provide such a referent, and the following behavioral ranking was created:

Behavioral Component
1 Have been entertained by blacks (64) and have entertained blacks (63)
2 Have entertained blacks (63) but have not been entertained by blacks (64)
3 Neither

The subjective and the behavioral rankings were combined into a single contact classification. A full cross-classificaticn of the two components generates nine classes. We found, however, that those nine cells can be collapsed to five, based on relationships to several other variables. These five categories are as follows, with subjective and behavioral rankings in parentheses:

Contact Classification
1   Close friend/Been entertained (1,1)
2   2+ first name/Been entertained (2,1)
3   Close or 2+ first name/Have entertained (1,2) or (2,2)
4   Close or 2+ first name/Not entertained (1,3) or (2,3)
5   No close or 2+ first name/entertained or not (3,1) or (3,2) or (3,3)

The values (2,1) for the second category, for instance, mean that respondents classified into that category were ranked in class 2 of the subjective component, as described above, and in class 1 of the behavioral component.

This contact classification seems to summarize most of the useful information contained in the responses to the several contact items in our questionnaire. Although we did not find interracial contact to be a strong predictor of policy prescriptions, and therefore did not make much use of this classification, it could be quite useful in other contexts.

5. PSYCHOLOGICAL SCALES

There has been extensive speculation about the psychological roots of racial prejudice. Although we were aware of this literature, we could not explore the matter thoroughly in the present study. We did, however, include two blocks of social psychological items so that this area would not be overlooked completely. The first block of items (question 72 in Appendix D) was taken from Selznick and Steinberg and includes their adaptation of some of the usual authoritarianism and anomie items.[6] The second block (question 84) is composed of new items.

Our analysis of this whole set of items yielded three subsets, two of which were used in abbreviated form in the text. The first subset is a version of authoritarianism, the second includes anomie-type items, and the third reflects the respondents' interest in the stars and luck. Items included in each set are as follows, with an asterisk indicating that the item was used in creating a summary measure:

Authoritarianism
*72.c.	Weak and strong
*72.f.	No arguments
84.e.	Communists in schools

Anomie
*72.k.	Nothing worthwhile
*72.1.	Live for today
72.h.	Simple answers
84.1.	Nuclear war

Stars and Luck
72.e.	Read stars
84.b.	Stars tell future
84.p.	Good and bad streaks

In the end, we could devote only limited attention to these items. The stars and luck subset was only weakly related to other variables of interest and was not used at all. Both the authoritarianism and anomie subsets were retained because of their links to prejudice in the literature, even though only authoritarianism was strongly related to explanatory mode and policy prescriptions. In retaining these two classic subsets, however, we decided to use only the traditional items (indicated above with asterisks) and not the new items that we created. Since we were going to call these subsets by their traditional names, we

6. Gertrude J. Selznick and Stephen Steinberg, *The Tenacity of Prejudice* (New York: Harper and Row, 1969).

did not want to obscure the issue by including new items.

One consequence of this decision was that we were left with only two items in each subset that met our item analysis criteria for scaling. We proceeded to make do with what we had, although the reader should be aware that the resulting scales are only rough approximations of the respondents' location on these dimensions. Concretely, each item was scored as zero or one, excluding the "don't knows," and was summed with the other item in its set. The properties of the resulting unstandardized scales can be summarized as follows:

	Range	Mean	S.D.	N
Authoritarianism	0–2	.70	.72	392
Anomie	0–2	.79	.77	440

6. CONCEPT OF PREJUDICE

We developed two substantial blocks of items to measure our respondents' conceptions of what prejudice means. One block of items (question 11 in Appendix D) presented practices that could be construed as racist to varying degrees, and the respondent was asked whether each practice was "all right" or not. The second block of items (questions 66–69) presented more of such practices, but asked the respondent whether he or she would label the practice as prejudice, allowing for responses ranging from "definitely prejudice" to "definitely not prejudice." Although we made only minimal use of these items in the text because of our desire to simplify the presentation of the main points of our study, the results of this analysis are quite interesting and are therefore summarized here.

We uncovered two main dimensions along which our white respondents seem to judge whether or not a given practice should be construed as prejudice. The first of these dimensions could be termed *pseudo-neutrality*. It involves the perception of latent bias in such apparently neutral practices as the use of IQ tests for school tracking and job screening. Those who regarded such practices as acceptable tended to be sympathetic to whites having problems with affirmative action (question 66.b.) but unsympathetic to black efforts to overcome past discrimination (question 69.b.). This dimension is strongly related to education, with the more highly educated being relatively likely to perceive latent bias in ostensibly neutral practices. Similarly, this dimension is strongly related to our environmentalist explanatory mode.

The second dimension we found could be called *symbolic insensitivity*. It is expressed by those who regard it as non-prejudicial to call a black man "boy" or to consider blacks inferior to whites or to hold that blacks do not work as hard as whites. What is notable is that positions on these symbolic issues are possibly undergoing a generational change, as indicated by a very strong effect of age on this dimension. Older respondents do not consider these symbolic affronts to be manifestations of prejudice, whereas younger respondents do so consider them. Furthermore, as we might expect, the genetic explanatory mode is strongly related to this dimension. The items in each of these subsets are as follows:

Pseudo-Neutrality
  11.a.   School tracking by IQ tests
  68.d.   IQ tests for bricklayers
  69.b.   No sympathy for Jones (a black)

Symbolic Insensitivity
  68.a.   Blacks inferior
  68.c.   Call a black "boy"
  68.n.   Blacks don't work as hard

Some of these items are obviously quite similar to certain explanatory-mode items. Both sets of items involve the interpretation of social reality, and in many ways they are parallel manifestations of those patterns of thought that we were trying to summarize and to formalize in our explanatory-mode typology. This very similarity is the reason why we did not discuss the concept of prejudice in the text. Although such a discussion would have enabled us to flesh out in more detail the meaning of each explanatory mode, we would have made our overall analytic model more complex than we wished. Furthermore, an examination of the joint effects of explanatory mode and concept of prejudice on policy prescriptions revealed that explanatory mode was the stronger predictor. Nevertheless, these items on the concept of prejudice are worth looking at, and we encourage other researchers to consider using them in further research on racial attitudes.

Appendix C *The Effect of Explanations on Prescriptions Where Perceptions Are Shared*

This appendix presents, in more detail than could be accommodated in the text, the results of analysis pursued to test the proposition that where the same perception is subject to different explanations, the nature of that explanation will have a significant influence on prescriptions.

It will be recalled that respondents were classified into six perception groups based on their scores on the characterological and social structural scales, as follows:

1. Deny both characterological and social structural differences.

2. Affirm characterological but deny social structural differences.

3. Deny characterological and strongly affirm social structural differences.

4. Deny characterological and weakly affirm social structural differences.

5. Affirm characterological and strongly affirm social structural differences.

6. Affirm characterological and weakly affirm social structural differences.

The procedure we follow is to examine, for each of these perception groups, how much, if at all, their mode of explaining the differences they perceive is related to their scores on the two prescription scales—institutional intervention and personal affinity.

We begin with respondents who deny both characterological and social structural differences. That such respondents have explanations of racial differences may seem a contradiction. If no differences were acknowledged, what is there to explain? In this regard, it is to be remembered that the questions designed to tap explanatory modes took for granted that there are social structural differences between the races and asked respondents simply to account for the stated differences. Respondents holding to the view that the differences stated are nonexistent could have said so and refused to answer the questions. Virtually no one took this course who denied that there were any differences between the races in answer to other questions. Instead, these respondents answered the explanatory-mode questions as they were asked. That they did so may be explained, at least in part, as a result of their not taking the questionnaire seriously or, perhaps, of their being unaware of their own inconsistencies. Another explanation, of course, is that the people who are the most disposed to deny both characterological and social structural differences are those whose explanatory mode is individualistic. For the individualists, the denial of group differences may be entirely in accord with their mode of accounting for differences since for them the differences being explained, and therefore acknowledged, are individual, not group, differences.

In examining the data, we find that of the sixty-six respondents classified as denying both kinds of differences, fifty (76 percent) are either pure individualists or in a mixed traditional mode having an individualistic component. (These modes account for only 40 percent of the total sample.) Using the rule of thumb that a cell ought to have at least ten cases to warrant a statistic being calculated, not enough cases are classified in any other mode to warrant a stable statistic being calculated for them.

Both the pure individualists and the individualists in a mixed mode score less than the average respondent on the two prescription scales. Relatively, however, as can be seen from the figures reported immediately below, the pure individualists score less conservatively on the two scales than the individualists in a mixed mode. This finding is in accord with what we found earlier when we examined the bivariate relation between explanations and prescriptions. Occupants of the mixed traditional modes were consistently the more conservative in their prescriptive responses.

Scores on:	Mixed modes with an individualist component	Pure individualists
Institutional intervention	−9.1 (29)	−6.9 (21)
Personal affinity	−6.5 (24)	−1.4 (21)

(Scores are deviations from mean scores of entire sample.)

Substantially fewer respondents—only twelve, in fact—acknowledge characterological differences but unequivocally deny social structural differences, and of the twelve not one respondent accounts for the differences perceived in a modern mode. (It is also of interest that none of these twelve respondents is a supernaturalist, although given the total number of supernaturalists in the sample, this could have occurred by chance.) Nine of the twelve cases are pure individualists or in a mixed mode having an individualistic component. Given the number of cases, no analysis is possible. It is to be recalled, however, that this perception group as a whole scored considerably below the average respondent on both institutional intervention and personal affinity.

Of the 138 respondents who deny characterological but strongly affirm social structural differences, 98 (71 percent) are occupants of the transitional or one of the modern modes. (This figure compares with 45 percent of the total sample occupying these modes.) The individualist is the only traditional mode with more than 10 respondents in this classification. The scores on the two prescription scales of the five mode types for which comparison is possible are as follows:

Scores on:	Indivi-dualists	Transi-tionalists	Environ-mentalists	Radicals	Radical-environ-mentalists
Institutional Inter-	−2.9	3.9	8.8	10.5	12.8
vention	(14)	(31)	(27)	(20)	(20)
Personal Affinity	1.0	2.9	8.7	11.7	9.2
	(14)	(31)	(27)	(20)	(18)

(Scores are deviations from mean scores of entire sample.)

As was found earlier for the total sample, the radical-environmentalists are the strongest supporters of institutional intervention with the radicals and the environmentalists, in that order, following not far behind. The transitionalists show significantly less support for institutional intervention than any of the modern modes although they are more supportive than the average respondent. In turn, the individualists, more opposed than the average respondent to institutional intervention, score significantly lower on institutional intervention than the transitionalists or the occupants of the modern modes.

The results are roughly parallel on personal affinity. This time, however, the radicals score as slightly more liberal than the radical-environmentalists. This result parallels the result for the total sample. We attributed it earlier to the radicals responding more emotionally than the radical-environmentalists to the social structural differences they perceive. Otherwise, the modern modes all show more personal affinity than the transitionalists. Once again, the individualists show the least support, although they do show more affinity than the average respondent. This is consistent with earlier findings concerning the individualists, which showed that they were more in opposition to institutional action to help blacks than to exhibit personal affinity for blacks.

Respondents who weakly affirm social structural differences but deny characterological differences exist in sufficient numbers to allow meaningful comparison in three pure modes—the individualistic, the transitional, and the environmental—and in those mixed modes having an individualistic component. The scores of these modes on the two scales are as follows:

Scores on:	Mixed modes with an individualist component	Indivi-dualists	Transi-tionalists	Environ-mentalists
Institutional	−6.5	−2.7	2.9	6.5
Intervention	(16)	(24)	(29)	(13)
Personal Affinity	−6.8	−2.8	3.8	7.4
	(16)	(23)	(29)	(15)

(Scores are deviations from mean scores of entire sample.)

These figures tell basically the same story as the earlier comparisons. Modes make a difference in the prescriptions subscribed to, even among people sharing the same perceptions. The environmental mode is associated with the most liberal responses on the two scales, whereas the most conservative stance is adopted by those in the mixed modes having an individual component. The transitionalists and individualists fall in between, with the former being closer to the environmentalists in their responses and the individualists closer to the occupants of the mixed modes. In this instance, the individualists are relatively no less conservative on personal affinity than on institutional intervention, a result that contrasts with their usual practice, and which we cannot explain.

Turning finally to those who both affirm characterological and social structural differences, it is necessary, once again, to distinguish the weak from the strong affirmers of social structural differences. Among the strong affirmers, there are enough cases to enable comparison of those in the environmental, the transitional, and the individualistic modes, and in the mixed traditional modes.

Scores on:	Traditional mixed mode	Indivi-dualists	Transi-tionalists	Environ-mentalists
Institutional intervention	−4.5	−2.6	.2	5.8
	(19)	(14)	(21)	(12)
Personal affinity	−5.6	− .1	− .1	6.3
	(18)	(14)	(21)	(12)

(Scores are deviations from mean scores of entire sample.)

Modes continue to make a significant difference in prescriptive responses and in the expected direction except for the equal scores on personal affinity between the individualists and the transitionalists. The tendency for individualists to be relatively more opposed to the practice of institutional intervention than to the expression of feelings of personal affinity is once again in evidence in these figures.

The last perception group to be considered comprises those who acknowledge characterological and weakly affirm social structural differences. None of the modern modes is represented in this perception category, nor, once again are there enough pure supernaturalists to allow their inclusion in the comparison. For the first time, however, there are enough geneticists to be included. Moreover, individualists-geneticists and individualists-supernaturalists exist in sufficient numbers to warrant presenting the results for them.

Scores on:	Ind.-Gen.	Ind.-Sup.	Indivi-dualists	Geneti-cists	Transi-tionalists
Institutional intervention	−9.9	−6.3	−8.3	−7.8	1.7
	(11)	(12)	(10)	(10)	(14)
Personal affinity	−11.3	−7.7	−1.5	−6.2	2.4
	(10)	(13)	(10)	(10)	(14)

(Scores are deviations from mean scores of entire sample.)

Looking first at the scores on institutional intervention, we find that the transitionalists, as would be expected based on what we have learned about them so far, are more supportive than any of the traditional modes. Opposition to institutional intervention is strong for both the individualists and the geneticists. That individualists are slightly more in opposition than the geneticists is in accord with previous findings and theoretical expectations, although the differences between them are not statistically significant. Of the two mixed traditional modes, the one that combines a genetic with an individualistic perspective shows even more opposition to institutional intervention than the pure geneticists or pure individualists. Opposition is slightly muted among the individualist-supernaturalists. This finding reflects the earlier one that a supernaturalist understanding of racial differences produces somewhat greater support, or at least less opposition to institutional intervention than do the individualistic or geneticist explanatory styles.

Scores on personal affinity do not parallel precisely those on institutional intervention, but the deviations are in accord with what we have learned about the prescriptive orientations of the different modes. Once again, the individualists' tendency to be relatively less conservative on personal affinity than on institutional intervention is manifest. Indeed, in this instance, the transitionalists show slightly less personal affinity than the individualists. The geneticists score quite low on personal affinity and the occupants of the two mixed modes score even lower. It is to be noted that the individualist-supernaturalists score significantly lower than the individualists on personal affinity whereas they score higher on institutional intervention. This reflects the earlier finding that supernaturalists, while inclined relative to the individualists to support institutional efforts to combat racial discrimination, are less inclined to feel personal affinity with blacks.

These results provide consistent evidence that what a

particular perception of racial differences implies for the prescriptive postures that people adopt is strongly dependent upon how the perceived differences are accounted for. The same perception can have sharply different prescriptive consequences depending upon the way in which it is explained.

The Status of Perceptions

Does this mean, then, that perceptions have no relevance to racial attitudes? We reported the answer to this question in the text. However, in order not to burden the text with somewhat tedious details, we present here the evidence on which the answer was based.

Once explanations are taken into account, do perceptions continue to be related to prescriptions independently? Or is their association with prescriptions wholly a function of their association with explanations?

Our ability to answer this question is circumscribed because of the paucity of cases in some of the explanatory modes and because the occupants of some modes share similar perceptions. We are unable, for example, to examine the relation between supernaturalists' perceptions and prescriptions simply because there are too few supernaturalists in any perception category to allow comparisons. Further, we are unable to examine the relation between the perceptions and prescriptions of geneticists, radicals, and radical-environmentalists because all the occupants of these modes are concentrated in a single perception group. It is possible, however, to inquire how closely, if at all, differences in perception are related to the prescription scores of individualists, transitionalists, and environmentalists since there are enough cases and some variation exists in how the occupants of these modes perceive racial differences.

We consider the environmentalists first because the results for them are the most straightforward. Table C-1 presents the environmentalists' scores on the two prescription scales, according to whether they perceive characterological and/or social structural differences between the races.

Table C-1 **Scores on Institutional Intervention and Personal Affinity by Perceptions for Environmentalists (in deviations from mean score)[a]**

CHARACTEROLOGICAL DIFFERENCES	SOCIAL STRUCTURAL DIFFERENCES		
	Denied	Weakly Affirmed	Strongly Affirmed
Institutional Intervention			
Affirmed	[b]	[b]	5.8
	(0)	(2)	(12)
Denied	[b]	6.5	8.7
	(3)	(13)	(27)
Personal Affinity			
Affirmed	[b]	[b]	6.3
	(0)	(2)	(12)
Denied	[b]	7.4	8.7
	(3)	(13)	(27)

[a] Standard deviation = 10
[b] Too few cases for stable statistic.

There are empty cells in Table C-1, forestalling comparison of some perception types. Insofar as comparison is possible, it appears that perceptions influence prescriptions independently of the way the perceptions are explained. Among the environmentalists who strongly affirm social structural differences, those who deny characterological differences score higher on both institutional intervention and personal affinity than those who deny these differences. Among environmentalists who deny characterological differences, those who strongly affirm social structural differences score higher on both prescription scales than those who weakly affirm social structural differences. The differences are not as strong as those associated with explanatory modes. Nevertheless, given this evidence alone, we have good reason to include perceptions as an independent factor in measuring racial attitudes.

The results are not quite as sharp or consistent for the transitionalists. For them, as can be seen in Table C-2, the perception of characterological differences is associated consistently with lower scores on both prescription scales. The effects of the perception of social structural differences, however, are not consistent. In half of the four possible comparisons, the strong affirmers score higher on prescription than the weak affirmers. The opposite result is obtained in the other two comparisons. Moreover, the results are not consistent among either those affirming or those denying characterological differences. Aside from being inconsistent, perception of social structural differences makes for less variation in prescription scores than does the perception of characterological differences. In sum, for the transitionalists, the perception of characterological differences appears to be related to prescriptions independently of mode. However, the effects of social structural differences on prescriptions at best are slight and not in a consistent direction.

For individualists, as can be seen in Table C-3, their scores on institutional intervention are not affected by whether they affirm or deny characterological differences where they strongly affirm social structural differences. There is an effect among weak affirmers, with those affirming characterological differences considerably more resistant to institutional intervention than those denying these differences. The perception of social structural differences also appears to affect institutional intervention scores. Among those who affirm characterological differences, those who weakly affirm social structural differences are more opposed to institutional intervention than

Table C-2   **Scores on Institutional Intervention
and Personal Affinity by
Perceptions for Transitionalists
(in deviations from mean score)**[a]

CHARACTEROLOGICAL DIFFERENCES	SOCIAL STRUCTURAL DIFFERENCES		
	Denied	*Weakly Affirmed*	*Strongly Affirmed*
Institutional Intervention			
Affirmed	[b]	1.7	.2
	(2)	(14)	(19)
Denied	[b]	2.9	4.0
	(5)	(29)	(31)
Personal Affinity			
Affirmed	[b]	−2.4	−1.0
	(2)	(14)	(21)
Denied	[b]	3.8	2.9
	(5)	(29)	(31)

[a] Standard deviation = 10
[b] Too few cases for a stable percentage.

Table C-3   **Scores on Institutional Intervention
and Personal Affinity by
Perceptions for Individualists
(in deviations from mean score)[a]**

CHARACTEROLOGICAL DIFFERENCES	SOCIAL STRUCTURAL DIFFERENCES		
	Denied	*Weakly Affirmed*	*Strongly Affirmed*
Institutional Intervention			
Affirmed	[b]	−8.2	−2.6
	(3)	(10)	(14)
Denied	−6.9	−2.7	−2.9
	(21)	(24)	(14)
Personal Affinity			
Affirmed	[b]	−1.5	−1.0
	(3)	(10)	(14)
Denied	−1.3	−2.8	1.0
	(21)	(23)	(14)

[a] Standard deviation = 10
[b] Too few cases for stable score.

the strong affirmers. Among those who deny character-ological differences, whether social structural differences are weakly or strongly affirmed has no effect on institutional intervention scores. Those who deny social structural differences, however, are considerably more conservative than the two affirming groups.

The results on personal affinity are, if anything, even less definitive than those on institutional intervention. The greatest personal affinity is exhibited by those who deny characterological and strongly affirm social structural differences. Other than that, scores on personal affinity are scarcely affected by perception, except that those who deny characterological and weakly affirm social structural differences exhibit less personal affinity than any other perception combination.

By virtue of the empty cells, with comparisons possible for only three modes and the results for the three modes inconsistent, we can draw no firm conclusions concerning the status of perceptions as a component of racial attitudes except that they appear considerably less important in determining prescriptions than do explanatory modes. The strongest suggestion offered by the findings is that the perception of characterological differences may be associated with a conservative stance on prescriptions, independently of explanatory mode. At least this is the direction of the relationship in six out of the eight comparisons that Tables C-1 to C-3 allow. However, this result would probably be subject to considerable specification if a larger sample were available to extend the comparisons. As regards social structural differences, the findings show that how they are perceived makes less of a difference to prescriptions than whether characterological differences are acknowledged or not. Other than that, the wisest conclusion to be drawn is that the independent status of such perceptions, insofar as they are an element in white racial attitudes, remains unresolved.

(_____)
(1-4)
5-6/
7-8/11

The questions in this first section are mostly about some of the problems facing us in today's world. Our purpose in asking them is to learn what people in different walks of life feel are the causes of these problems. Knowing more than we do about people's understanding of problems can help in trying to deal with them better.

1. We begin with the problem of suffering in the world. Here are some reasons that people have given to explain why there is suffering. For each reason, please place an "X" in a box to show whether you think it is a major reason for suffering, a minor reason, or not a reason for suffering at all.

	Major Reason for Suffering 1	Minor Reason for Suffering 2	Not a Reason for Suffering at All 3	
a. People at the bottom are exploited by those at the top.	☐	☐	☐	9/
b. It's because we don't know enough yet about the scientific laws governing life .	☐	☐	☐	
c. People are being punished for what they did in a previous life	☐	☐	☐	
d. Suffering comes about because people are just naturally selfish	☐	☐	☐	
e. Suffering is just part of life.	☐	☐	☐	
f. Suffering is a result of social arrangements that make people greedy for riches and power.	☐	☐	☐	
g. Suffering is the work of the devil	☐	☐	☐	
h. People don't take care of themselves as they should .	☐	☐	☐	16/

i. Any other reason for suffering *(PLEASE WRITE IN SPACE BELOW)*

17/

_____.

Please go back now and choose the <u>one</u> reason which you think is most important for explaining suffering and circle the letter of that reason below:

a	b	c	d	e	f	g	h	i

18-19/

271

-2-

2. Twin brothers grow up--one to become a successful lawyer, the other to
    become a criminal and to spend most of his life in jail. As you think
    about this and similar stories you've heard, how do you explain them?

    *(Place an "X" next to the answer below which comes closest to your own
    explanation. If none do, please write in your explanation in the space
    provided.)*

    1. ☐ Such things are decided by God for reasons we cannot understand.   20/

    2. ☐ There really is no way to explain such things, although I think
            of them as decided by fate rather than God.

    3. ☐ One brother was just born with better genes than the other.

    4. ☐ The explanation probably lies in the way they were brought up;
            even though they were twin brothers, there would be differences
            in the way their parents raised them or in the kinds of friends
            they made.

    5. ☐ One brother used his will power to work hard and to make himself
            successful; the other didn't.

    6. ☐ None of the above explanations suits me. My explanation is:

        _____

        _____

3. One of the tragedies of life is when people, through no fault of their
    own, are suddenly killed in an accident; for example, passengers being
    killed in an airplane crash. Here are some of the kinds of thoughts that
    pass through people's minds when such a tragedy occurs. Which one of
    them comes closest to expressing what you think when such accidents
    occur? *(Check one answer)*

    1. ☐ It's the will of God.   21/

    2. ☐ The day we die is fated; everybody's number comes up sooner or
            later.

    3. ☐ It's just bad luck.

    4. ☐ My first thought is to wonder whether the pilot or some mechanical
            failure in the airplane is to blame.

    5. ☐ None of the above comes close to expressing my thought. What I
            tend to think is that:

        _____
                            (Please write out)
        _____

-3-

4. John Smith is a 32 year old black man. He and his family live in a
fine house in the suburbs. He has an important job as a manager in
an industrial firm and earns an income of $20,000 a year.

There's a lot of talk at the plant where Smith works about how a
black man like Smith could have become so successful. Here are
some of the reasons offered.

*(Please read each reason and place an "X" in column I if you think
it might be a reason for Smith's success. If you feel it probably
isn't a reason for Smith's success, place a check in column II.)*

		I Probably a Reason for Smith's Success	II Probably not a Reason for Smith's Success	
		1	2	
a.	Nowadays most firms want to have a few blacks around. John is probably one of these token blacks	☐	☐	22/
b.	The reason John Smith prospers is probably because he respects God and lives the kind of life that God rewards	☐	☐	
c.	John was talented and intelligent enough to get by the whites who were trying to keep him down. If he had been white with his abilities, he would probably have a better job and be earning even more . . .	☐	☐	
d.	Black people as a group are somewhat down on the intelligence scale, but there are a few capable individuals like John Smith .	☐	☐	
e.	There is a lot less discrimination in America than there used to be and it is not at all surprising to find more and more successful black people.	☐	☐	
f.	A large part of it might be due to the fact that John Smith's family and friends were different from most black people in that they encouraged him to develop his talents	☐	☐	
g.	John Smith became so successful because, despite what some people say, anybody who has ambition and works hard in America can make it	☐	☐	
h.	John was probably willing to 'knuckle under' and do whatever his white employers told him	☐	☐	29/

Suppose now you had to choose one of these reasons as probably the most important
reason for Smith's success; circle the letter of the reason you would choose:

30-31/

| a | b | c | d | e | f | g | h |

-4-

5. Some people live to a ripe old age, while others die in the prime of life. Many other people have offered the following reasons as to why they think this is so. Which comes closest to your view?

32/

1. ☐ It's in the hands of God.

2. ☐ It's mostly because some people are in a position so that they can buy medical services and others can't.

3. ☐ It's mostly a matter of the survival of the fittest.

4. ☐ It's mostly a matter of good or bad luck.

5. ☐ It mostly depends on how people take care of themselves.

6. ☐ It's mostly because the medical profession has prevented the government from making medical care equally available to all people.

6. We read more and more these days about alcoholism and about people's lives being ruined from drinking too much. Where does most of the fault lie for people drinking too much? *(CHECK ONE ANSWER)*

1. ☐ It's a person's own fault.   33/

2. ☐ It's the fault of the kind of high pressure world we live in.

3. ☐ It's mostly the fault of the liquor industry making drinking too attractive.

4. ☐ It's no one's fault really; it's just that some people are born with weak characters and others with strong characters.

5. ☐ The fault lies with people turning more and more away from God.

6. ☐ It's mostly the fault of the group a person grows up in; some groups just drink a lot more than other groups.

7. ☐ None of these. It's mostly the fault of _____

_____
(Please write out)

-5-

7. People interviewed in a previous study of ours have suggested that
   American Jews seem to be better off on the average than other Americans.
   The people interviewed offered the following reasons as to why they
   think this is so. Which comes closest to your view?

1. ☐ The Jews are God's Chosen People.   34/

2. ☐ Jews use their wealth and power to keep other Americans down.

3. ☐ Jewish people tend to work harder than other Americans and,
      as a result, are more successful.

4. ☐ Jewish traditions emphasize those things that you require to
      succeed in America.

5. ☐ Jews are better off because social arrangements in America
      have worked in their favor.

6. ☐ Jews are genetically superior to other Americans.

7. ☐ None of the above comes close to my view. I think _____

   _____

8. All in all, as you assess your feelings about Jews, which of the
   following statements comes closest to representing the way you
   feel about them? *(PLEASE CHECK ONLY ONE.)*

1. ☐ Frankly, looking inside myself, I tend to feel somewhat hostile   35/
      toward Jews.

2. ☐ There are many individual Jews whom I admire but I feel that I
      do harbor some ill feelings toward Jews in a general way.

3. ☐ I believe I can honestly say that I have no ill feelings about
      Jews at all though I am not disposed to favor them over other
      groups.

4. ☐ Not only do I bear no resentment towards Jews, but I feel
      particularly drawn to them in a positive way.

5. [ ] None of the above comes close to representing my feelings. I
      feel _____

   _____

9. Here's one more "explanation" type of question before we turn to other
matters. This time, we'd like you to tell us how much you agree or
disagree with each of the following explanations as to why there are
still so many poor people in America.

*(Please place an "X" for each reason indicating whether you agree
with it strongly, agree somewhat, disagree somewhat, or disagree
strongly.)*

	Agree Strongly 1	Agree Somewhat 2	Disagree Somewhat 3	Disagree Strongly 4	Can't Say 5	
a. The poor are poor because the wealthy and powerful keep them poor	☐	☐	☐	☐	☐	36/
b. The poor simply aren't willing to work hard; they wouldn't be poor if they really tried not to be	☐	☐	☐	☐	☐	
c. God gave people different abilities so that the work of the world will get done	☐	☐	☐	☐	☐	
d. The poor are poor because social arrangements in America don't give all people an equal chance	☐	☐	☐	☐	☐	
e. Poor people are born without the talent to get ahead	☐	☐	☐	☐	☐	
f. Poor people are used to being poor because they grew up with it and it is a way of life for them	☐	☐	☐	☐	☐	41/

Please go back now and choose the ONE reason which you think is most important in explaining poverty, and circle the letter of that reason just below:

a b c d e f	42/

-7-

10. There's a lot of discussion these days about how people ought to act in their daily lives. It is not always clear what things ought to be admired and which ones we should disapprove of.

How do you feel about people doing each of the following things--would you admire them for it, think it was all right, be mildly disapproving, or be strongly disapproving?

(For each item, place an "X" in the column that best describes how you feel about that item.)

If people are like this, I would:

		Admire Them 1	Think It's All Right 2	Be Mildly Disapproving 3	Be Strongly Disapproving 4	
a.	Carry a knife as protection against being robbed . . .	☐	☐	☐	☐	43/
b.	Take very good care of one's home . .	☐	☐	☐	☐	
c.	Live for today and face tomorrow's problems if and when they come . .	☐	☐	☐	☐	
d.	Stay on welfare rather than take a job which pays less than welfare does	☐	☐	☐	☐	
e.	Put work before pleasure	☐	☐	☐	☐	
f.	Give into one's sexual impulses .	☐	☐	☐	☐	
g.	Act dishonestly if it doesn't hurt anybody	☐	☐	☐	☐	
h.	Stand up for one's rights even if this means getting into a fight	☐	☐	☐	☐	50/

-8-

11. Here are some things that happen regularly in American life. How do
    you feel about these things? Do you think they are all right or not?

    *(For each item, place an "X" in the column that best describes how
    you feel about that item.)*

		All Right 1	Not All Right 2	Can't Say 3	
a.	All students in a school are given an I.Q. (Intelligence) test and assigned to classes according to how well they did on the test .	☐	☐	☐	51/
b.	The biggest country club in town refuses to let any blacks have memberships in the club	☐	☐	☐	
c.	A construction firm advertises some job openings for manual laborers but announces that it will only consider applicants who have a high school education	☐	☐	☐	
d.	A local real estate company sells houses to people regardless of their race	☐	☐	☐	
e.	All of the women who clean floors for a large bank are black	☐	☐	☐	
f.	A home for the aged run by local residents of Greek ancestry permits only those of Greek ancestry to enter the home	☐	☐	☐	
g.	A school board in a mostly black area which has few black teachers announces that it is going to hire more black teachers, even though they can get better qualified white teachers	☐	☐	☐	
h.	All of the employees of bakeries run by a black religious group are black	☐	☐	☐	58/

-9-

12. Here are some statements about the place of men and women in our society.

(Place an "X" in the column following each statement to say whether you agree strongly, agree somewhat, disagree somewhat, or disagree strongly with each statement.)

	Agree Strongly 1	Agree Somewhat 2	Disagree Somewhat 3	Disagree Strongly 4	
a. Raising children should be a woman's main responsibility in life	☐	☐	☐	☐	59/
b. On the average, men are more interested in women's bodies than in their minds	☐	☐	☐	☐	
c. When it comes to caring for babies and small children, men <u>by nature</u> are less patient and giving than women	☐	☐	☐	☐	
d. Women don't get along with each other as well as men do on the job	☐	☐	☐	☐	62/

13. These statements are about children. Once again, please place a check in the column following each statement to say whether you agree strongly, agree somewhat, disagree somewhat, or disagree strongly with each statement.

	Agree Strongly 1	Agree Somewhat 2	Disagree Somewhat 3	Disagree Strongly 4	
a. Without children, the average husband and wife wouldn't have very much to share or to talk about together	☐	☐	☐	☐	63/
b. There's something wrong with a woman who doesn't want to have children .	☐	☐	☐	☐	
c. Many husbands and wives drift apart because the wife pays too much attention to the children .	☐	☐	☐	☐	65/

-10-

14. Imagine you had a daughter who developed a serious interest in a career.
     Which of the following statements comes closest to how you would feel if
     your daughter decided <u>not to marry and have children</u>, but rather to
     devote her life to her work?   66/

1. ☐ I'd disapprove and I'd try hard to persuade her to change her
        mind.

2. ☐ I'd disapprove, but I wouldn't try to persuade her to change her
        mind.

3. ☐ I'd approve but have some misgivings.

4. ☐ I'd approve wholeheartedly.

5. ☐ None of the above expresses my view. Instead, I'd _____

    _____

15. How comfortable would you feel about a woman holding each of the jobs
     listed below--comfortable, somewhat uncomfortable, or very uncomfortable?

How comfortable would you be if a woman were:	Comfortable 1	Somewhat Uncomfortable 2	Very Uncomfortable 3	
a. Your car mechanic	☐	☐	☐	67/
b. Your congresswoman	☐	☐	☐	
c. Your pilot or co-pilot on a cross-country flight . . .	☐	☐	☐	
d. Your surgeon for an eye operation	☐	☐	☐	
e. Your defense attorney . . .	☐	☐	☐	
f. A bulldozer operator on nearby construction	☐	☐	☐	
g. The President of your country	☐	☐	☐	73/

-11-

II.

The main purpose of our study, you will remember, is to learn how white and black Americans feel about each other these days. Your honest answers to the following questions will help to make clear what major problems must still be solved in this area and how our country can best go about solving them.

16. One of the things that many blacks complain about is that compared to whites they are treated unequally in America. Some whites feel that this is not true and that blacks have more advantages than whites, at least in some ways. How do you feel?

    (Please place an "X" in the box following each statement to indicate whether whites or blacks on the average have the greater chance to do each of the following things in America today.)

		Whites Have Greater Chance 1	Blacks Have Greater Chance 2	No Difference 3	Can't Say 4	
a.	Getting a well-paid job . . .	☐	☐	☐	☐	9/
b.	Getting a good education . .	☐	☐	☐	☐	
c.	Getting financial help when in need	☐	☐	☐	☐	
d.	Living where one pleases . .	☐	☐	☐	☐	
e.	Being treated fairly by the police	☐	☐	☐	☐	
f.	Getting good medical services	☐	☐	☐	☐	
g.	Being treated fairly by store-keepers	☐	☐	☐	☐	15/

-12-

17. Now instead of comparing the average black person with the average white person, compare the average black person with the average poor person who is white. Which of them do you think has the greater chance to do each of the following things in America today?

		Poor Whites Have Greater Chance 1	Average Black Has Greater Chance 2	No Difference 3	Can't Say 4	
a.	Getting a well-paid job . .	☐	☐	☐	☐	16/
b.	Getting a good education .	☐	☐	☐	☐	
c.	Getting financial help when in need	☐	☐	☐	☐	
d.	Living where one pleases .	☐	☐	☐	☐	
e.	Being treated fairly by the police	☐	☐	☐	☐	
f.	Getting good medical services	☐	☐	☐	☐	
g.	Being treated fairly by storekeepers	☐	☐	☐	☐	22/

18. Sometimes there is a difference between having the chance to do something and actually doing it. How would you compare the average black and the average white person with respect to their actually having each of the following things?

(Please mark an "X" to indicate whether you think the average black or the average white is the more likely to have each of the following things.)

		Blacks are:		Whites are:			
		Much More Likely To Have 1	Somewhat More Likely To Have 2	Somewhat More Likely To Have 3	Much More Likely To Have 4	No Difference 5	
a.	Good job	☐	☐	☐	☐	☐	23/
b.	Good education . .	☐	☐	☐	☐	☐	
c.	Good housing . . .	☐	☐	☐	☐	☐	
d.	Good medical care	☐	☐	☐	☐	☐	26/

-13-

19. So far we've asked about how black and white people differ in the opportunities open to them in America. This question asks how much they differ in what they consider important in life.

   a. For example, thinking of the average black family as compared to the average white family, which one do you think would be more likely to think it important to someday own a summer house on a lake?

   1. ☐ Much more important for black family   27/

   2. ☐ Somewhat more important for black family

   3. ☐ Somewhat more important for white family

   4. ☐ Much more important for white family

   5. ☐ No difference probably

   Now, how about the things listed below. Would they be more important for the average black or the average white family?

	Much More Important to Black Family 1	Somewhat More Important to Black Family 2	Somewhat More Important to White Family 3	Much More Important to White Family 4	No Difference 5	
b. Owning their own business	☐	☐	☐	☐	☐	28/
c. Earning a lot of money	☐	☐	☐	☐	☐	
d. Seeing that their children go to college	☐	☐	☐	☐	☐	
e. Owning a big car .	☐	☐	☐	☐	☐	
f. Having good police protection in their communities . . .	☐	☐	☐	☐	☐	
g. Having a good time today	☐	☐	☐	☐	☐	
h. Going to church . .	☐	☐	☐	☐	☐	
i. Participating in sports	☐	☐	☐	☐	☐	
j. Having an exciting sex life	☐	☐	☐	☐	☐	
k. Being involved in community activities	☐	☐	☐	☐	☐	
l. Taking very good care of one's home	☐	☐	☐	☐	☐	38/

-14-

20. Here's a question somewhat like the last one. This time, please read
    down the following descriptions of people and for each description,
    indicate by marking an "X" whether you think it applies more to black
    or more to white people in America.

| | | Applies More to: | | No | Can't | |
		Blacks 1	Whites 2	Difference 3	Say 4	
a.	Warm and friendly	☐	☐	☐	☐	39/
b.	Poor	☐	☐	☐	☐	
c.	Willing to work hard . .	☐	☐	☐	☐	
d.	Likely to cheat or steal	☐	☐	☐	☐	
e.	Religious	☐	☐	☐	☐	
f.	Intelligent	☐	☐	☐	☐	
g.	Likely to commit sex crimes	☐	☐	☐	☐	
h.	Sloppy	☐	☐	☐	☐	
i.	Good at sports	☐	☐	☐	☐	
j.	Ambitious	☐	☐	☐	☐	
k.	Good sense of humor . . .	☐	☐	☐	☐	
l.	Oversexed	☐	☐	☐	☐	
m.	Honest	☐	☐	☐	☐	51/

-15-

21. Here's the same list of descriptions as in the last question. Please go
    over the list once again but this time, indicate by an "X" how you think
    most Americans would answer--would most Americans think the description
    applies more to black people or more to white people?

Most Americans Would Think Description:

		Applies More to: Blacks	Whites	No Difference	Can't Say	
		1	2	3	4	
a.	Warm and friendly	☐	☐	☐	☐	52/
b.	Poor	☐	☐	☐	☐	
c.	Willing to work hard . . .	☐	☐	☐	☐	
d.	Likely to cheat or steal .	☐	☐	☐	☐	
e.	Religious	☐	☐	☐	☐	
f.	Intelligent	☐	☐	☐	☐	
g.	Likely to commit sex crimes	☐	☐	☐	☐	
h.	Sloppy	☐	☐	☐	☐	
i.	Good at sports	☐	☐	☐	☐	
j.	Ambitious	☐	☐	☐	☐	
k.	Good sense of humor	☐	☐	☐	☐	
l.	Oversexed	☐	☐	☐	☐	
m.	Honest	☐	☐	☐	☐	64/

22. Here are some ways that black people in America have been discriminated
    against in the past. To what extent do you think these kinds of dis-
    crimination exist today--a great deal, a fair amount, a little, or not
    really at all?

		Great Deal	Fair Amount	A Little	Not at All	
		1	2	3	4	
a.	Blacks not being able to live where they want to even when they have the money	☐	☐	☐	☐	65/
b.	Blacks being passed up by white taxi cab drivers in favor of a white customer down the street	☐	☐	☐	☐	
c.	Black children being given a poorer education in public schools than white children	☐	☐	☐	☐	
d.	Black shoppers being taken advantage of by white storekeepers	☐	☐	☐	☐	
e.	Blacks being sentenced to longer jail terms than whites for the same offense	☐	☐	☐	☐	
f.	Black neighborhoods getting poorer police protection than comparable white neighborhoods	☐	☐	☐	☐	70/

$$(\underline{\quad}_{(1-4)} \underline{\quad})$$
5-6/
7-8/13

23. This question is a sort of a quiz. Its purpose, however, is not to
    test you since very few people will know the correct answers to most
    of these questions. Rather, we are trying to find out what more needs
    to be done to teach Americans of all groups what other groups are like.

    *(Please read each question and then check the answer which you think
    comes closest to being correct. Even if you don't know an answer,
    please make a guess as to which answer is correct.)*

a. What proportion of the population of the San Francisco Bay Area is black?

                                                        1. ☐   6 per cent   9/
    ☐ I am sure   2. ☐ 11 per cent
    ☐ I am fairly sure } that the answer is: 3. ☐ 16 per cent
    ☐ I would guess   4. ☐ 25 per cent
                                                        5. ☐ 40 per cent

b. In 1971, 6 out of every 100 males in the Bay Area wanting work were
   unemployed. What do you think the unemployment rate is for black
   males?

                                                        1. ☐   3 out of 100 10/
    ☐ I am sure   2. ☐   6 out of 100
    ☐ I am fairly sure } that the answer is: 3. ☐ 11 out of 100
    ☐ I would guess   4. ☐ 15 out of 100
                                                        5. ☐ 20 out of 100

c. In 1970, blacks were 11 per cent of the total population of the United
   States. What proportion of those arrested for serious crimes in the
   United States in 1970 were black?

                                                        1. ☐   4 per cent   11/
    ☐ I am sure   2. ☐ 11 per cent
    ☐ I am fairly sure } that the answer is: 3. ☐ 17 per cent
    ☐ I would guess   4. ☐ 26 per cent
                                                        5. ☐ 36 per cent

d. In 1969, 9 out of every 100 white families in the United States had
   incomes which were below the poverty level. How many black families
   do you think were below the poverty level?

                                                        1. ☐   5 out of 100 12/
    ☐ I am sure   2. ☐ 10 out of 100
    ☐ I am fairly sure } that the answer is: 3. ☐ 20 out of 100
    ☐ I would guess   4. ☐ 30 out of 100
                                                        5. ☐ 40 out of 100

-17-

23. (continued)

e. In 1971, 20 out of every 100 white families in the United States had women as the head of the household. How many black families do you think had women as head of the household?

			1. ☐ 20 out of 100	13/
☐ I am sure			2. ☐ 35 out of 100	
☐ I am fairly sure	that the answer is:		3. ☐ 45 out of 100	
☐ I would guess			4. ☐ 55 out of 100	
			5. ☐ 65 out of 100	

24. Some people feel that blacks in America have their own culture or way of life, that their religion, language, dress, food, music, ways of doing things are different from white ways of doing things. Others feel that there are no differences or that blacks, because they tend to be poor, seem to be different but really aren't. What's your view?

1. ☐ Blacks live pretty much the same as whites.   14/

2. ☐ Blacks live differently because they tend to be poor, not because they are black.

3. ☐ Blacks have their own way of life.

25. Here now are some observations about how black people live and about black-white relations. We'd like you to tell us whether you think each statement is true or false. If you're not sure, please guess.

(Please mark your answer for each statement with an "X".)

	I'm Sure It's True 1	I Guess It's True 2	I Guess It's False 3	I'm Sure It's False 4
a. The average black child does as well in school in America as the average white child	☐	☐	☐	☐ 15/
b. Poor black children are more likely than poor white children to carry knives and other dangerous weapons to school . .	☐	☐	☐	☐
c. In black families women are more likely to make the important decisions than men .	☐	☐	☐	☐
d. More black people on the average have family troubles than white people do	☐	☐	☐	☐
e. When blacks are given the opportunities to improve their economic position, they make good use of them	☐	☐	☐	☐
f. Today when an employer has to decide between two equally qualified applicants, he is likely to choose the black rather than the white applicant	☐	☐	☐	☐
g. A white person has a better chance to get a fair trial in this country than a black person	☐	☐	☐	☐
h. Whites are more likely than blacks to be racist	☐	☐	☐	☐ 22 /

26. Some black leaders have said that blacks are proud of their blackness and want to gain acceptance for themselves as a group having their own style of life--dress, music, and religion.

a. How many black Americans do you think feel this way?

23/

1. ☐ Almost all
2. ☐ A majority
3. ☐ About half
4. ☐ A minority
5. ☐ Almost none

b. How do you personally feel about this idea?

1. ☐ I am in favor of it.   24/

2. ☐ I'd favor it if it could be worked out.

3. ☐ I'm against it because I don't think it could work.

4. ☐ I'm against it whether it could work or not.

27. Other black leaders have said that blacks basically want to live the same way that white Americans do.

a. How many black Americans do you think feel this way?

1. ☐ Almost all   25/

2. ☐ A majority

3. ☐ About half

4. ☐ A minority

5. ☐ Almost none

b. How do you personally feel about this idea?

1. ☐ I am in favor of it.   26/

2. ☐ I'd favor it if it could be worked out.

3. ☐ I am against it because I don't think it could work.

4. ☐ I am against it whether it could work or not.

-20-

28. One black group has proposed that the U.S. government give black people
enough land in now sparsely populated parts of America to set up their own
country.

a. How many black Americans do you think feel this way?

    1. ☐ Almost all   27/

    2. ☐ A majority

    3. ☐ About half

    4. ☐ A minority

    5. ☐ Almost none

b. How do you personally feel about this idea?

    1. ☐ I am in favor of it.   28/

    2. ☐ I'd favor it if it could be worked out.

    3. ☐ I am against it because I don't think it could work.

    4. ☐ I am against it whether it could work or not.

29. Some black ministers have been known to say that the best hope for
black people is to turn back to God and be concerned about what will
happen to them in the next life rather than in this one.

a. How many black Americans do you think feel this way?

    1. ☐ Almost all   29/

    2. ☐ A majority

    3. ☐ About half

    4. ☐ A minority

    5. ☐ Almost none

b. How do you personally feel about this idea?

    1. ☐ I am in favor of it.   30/

    2. ☐ I am against it.

-21-

30. One black organization feels that the best way for blacks to get their rights in America is to use to the fullest the legal channels provided them under American law.

a. How many black Americans do you think feel this way?

1. ☐ Almost all   31/

2. ☐ A majority

3. ☐ About half

4. ☐ A minority

5. ☐ Almost none

b. How do you personally feel about this idea?

1. ☐ I am in favor of it.   32/

2. ☐ I'd favor it if it could be worked out.

3. ☐ I am against it because I don't think it could work.

4. ☐ I am against it whether it could work or not.

31. Other black leaders have said that there will have to be a lot of violence before black people get equal rights in America.

a. How many black Americans do you think feel this way?

1. ☐ Almost all   33/

2. ☐ A majority

3. ☐ About half

4. ☐ A minority

5. ☐ Almost none

b. How do you personally feel about this idea?

1. ☐ I am in favor of it.   34/

2. ☐ I'd favor it if it could be worked out.

3. ☐ I am against it because I don't think it could work.

4. ☐ I am against it whether it could work or not.

-22-

III.

The purpose of this short section is to learn how Americans from different walks of life explain differences between races.

32. Most people--blacks and whites alike--agree that on the average a white person in America is more likely to have a good income, to be well educated, and to have a regular job. Here are some of the reasons that have been given as to why on the average blacks are not as well off as whites in America.

(Please read over all of the reasons first and then go back and mark an "X" to indicate how much you agree or disagree with each one.)

	Agree Strongly 1	Agree Mildly 2	Disagree Mildly 3	Disagree Strongly 4	Can't Say 5	
a. Rich and powerful white people control things in America and because they can make more money by doing so, they act to keep black people down	☐	☐	☐	☐	☐	35/
b. The differences are brought about by God; for reasons we cannot now know, God made the races different as part of a divine plan	☐	☐	☐	☐	☐	
c. It's really a matter of some people not trying hard enough; if blacks would only try harder they could be just as well off as whites	☐	☐	☐	☐	☐	
d. A history of slavery and being discriminated against have created conditions that make it difficult for black people to work their way out of the lower classes	☐	☐	☐	☐	☐	
e. Blacks come from a less able race and this explains why they are not as well off as whites in America	☐	☐	☐	☐	☐	
f. Because they have different life styles, black Americans teach their children values and skills which are different from those which are required to be successful in American society	☐	☐	☐	☐	☐	40/

(Please go back now and choose the one reason which you think is most important for explaining black-white differences and circle the letter of that reason below.)

a	b	c	d	e	f

41/

33. Here are some reasons people have given to explain why blacks don't seem to do as well on intelligence tests as whites. Which comes closest to your view?

42/

1. ☐ White people purposely designed intelligence tests to favor themselves.

2. ☐ God gave different gifts to different races for reasons we cannot understand.

3. ☐ Black people score less well than white people because they do not try hard enough.

4. ☐ The tests are made for middle-class white people and the tests turn out to be unfair to black people.

5. ☐ By nature, black people just are less intelligent on the average than white people.

6. ☐ In general, black people don't put much value on doing well on intelligence tests; they're more interested in other things.

-24-

We'd like now to try a different way to learn how people explain black-white differences. Please answer all parts of question 34 and then tell us whether you think question 32, or question 33, or question 34 does a better job of getting at your true feelings.

34a. Thinking still of the fact that the average black person is less well off than the average white person, how much do you think this is the fault of white people living today?

1. ☐ It's mostly the fault of white people living today.   43 /

2. ☐ It's partly the fault of white people living today.

3. ☐ It's not at all the fault of white people living today.

IF YOU THINK IT'S PARTLY OR MOSTLY THE FAULT OF WHITE PEOPLE, ANSWER THE QUESTIONS IN THIS BOX.

---

b. Would you say that:

    1. ☐ All white people are at fault.   44 /

    2. ☐ Not all, but a good majority are at fault.

    3. ☐ A sizeable minority are at fault.

    4. ☐ A handful of white people are at fault.

c. Do the white people who are at fault act intentionally to keep black people down or do they do so unknowingly and without really meaning to?

    1. ☐ Mostly intentionally.   45 /

    2. ☐ Mostly unknowingly and without meaning to.

---

d. How much do you think it is the fault of black people that they don't do as well as whites?

1. ☐ It's mostly black people's fault.   46 /

2. ☐ It's partly black people's fault.

3. ☐ It's not black people's fault at all.

IF YOU THINK IT'S PARTLY OR MOSTLY BLACK PEOPLE'S FAULT, PLEASE ANSWER THE QUESTIONS IN THIS BOX.

---

e. Would you say that:

    1. ☐ All black people are at fault.   47 /
    2. ☐ Not all, but a majority are at fault.
    3. ☐ A sizeable minority are at fault.
    4. ☐ A handful are at fault.

f. In what ways are black people at fault? (CHECK AS MANY AS APPLY)

    1. ☐ They don't work hard enough   48 /
    2. ☐ They are too militant; anger white people.
    3. ☐ They don't fight for their rights.
    4. ☐ They refuse to give up ways of living which keep them from competing well with whites.
    5. ☐ Other: _____
                   (Please write in)

-25-

Some people believe that the differences between whites and blacks are the result of forces largely outside of man's control. Some say that the differences were ordained by God. Others say that the differences are genetic, produced by natural forces which at some time in history made the races different.

34e. How do you feel about the idea that for reasons which we cannot know, God made the races different?

1. ☐ I am convinced that this is true.   49/

2. ☐ I lean to believing that this is true.

3. ☐ I am doubtful but would leave the possibility open.

4. ☐ I really don't believe this.

34f. How about the genetic argument; that the forces of nature have created the differences between races that we find today.

1. ☐ I am convinced that this is true.   50/

2. ☐ I lean to believing that this is true.

3. ☐ I am doubtful but would leave the possibility open.

4. ☐ I really don't believe this.

35. Comparing now all of question 34 with all of questions 32 and 33, which one do you think allowed you to best express what you believe to be the reasons for racial differences?

1. ☐ Question 32 ⎫   51/
2. ☐ Question 33 ⎬ because _____
3. ☐ Question 34 ⎪   _____
4. ☐ None of them ⎭   _____
                          _____

-26-

IV.

A lot of things have been proposed and tried to bring about equality between the races in America. In this section we'd like to get your reaction to some of these things.

36. Which of the following statements comes closest to expressing your view about how much government should be doing to help black people in the United States? (Check one)

1. ☐ Nothing more; government has done too much already.   **52** /

2. ☐ Nothing more; what government is doing now is enough.

3. ☐ No new laws are necessary; but the present laws against discrimination should be strictly enforced.

4. ☐ New and tougher laws against racial discrimination should be passed and strictly enforced.

5. ☐ The government needs to do more than fight discrimination; it should use tax money to insure better jobs, housing and education for black people even if this means discrimination in reverse.

6. ☐ I think the federal and state governments in America are racist and it is unrealistic to expect them to help black people.

7. ☐ The government shouldn't be doing anything at all; it should be left up to individuals.

37. Generally speaking do you favor or oppose busing to bring about racial balance in public schools?

1. ☐ I am strongly opposed.   **53** /

2. ☐ I am mildly opposed.

3. ☐ I am mildly in favor.

4. ☐ I am strongly in favor.

5. ☐ No opinion.

38. How about school integration? Generally speaking, are you in favor or opposed?

1. ☐ I am strongly opposed.   **54** /

2. ☐ I am mildly opposed.

3. ☐ I am mildly in favor.

4. ☐ I am strongly in favor.

5. ☐ No opinion.

-27-

So far, we do not have the scientific evidence to know for sure whether children--white or black--get a better or worse education in integrated schools.

39a. Suppose it were found that integrated schools didn't make any educational difference for either black or white children but that schools did help to make for better relations between black and white youngsters. If this were found, how then would you feel about school integration?

1. ☐ Strongly approve   55/
2. ☐ Mildly approve
3. ☐ Mildly disapprove
4. ☐ Strongly disapprove

b. IF STRONGLY OR MILDLY APPROVE: How would you feel about busing to achieve integration?

1. ☐ Strongly approve   56/
2. ☐ Mildly approve
3. ☐ Mildly disapprove
4. ☐ Strongly disapprove

40a. Now, suppose it were found that integrated schools improved the education of black students but made no difference in the education of white students. If this were found, how would you then feel about school integration?

1. ☐ Strongly approve   57/
2. ☐ Mildly approve
3. ☐ Mildly disapprove
4. ☐ Strongly disapprove

b. IF STRONGLY OR MILDLY APPROVE: How would you feel about busing to achieve integration?

1. ☐ Strongly approve   58/
2. ☐ Mildly approve
3. ☐ Mildly disapprove
4. ☐ Strongly disapprove

41a. Now suppose it were found that integrated schools improved the education of black students but that white students tend to do better in all white schools. If this were found, how would you then feel about school integration?

    1. ☐ Strongly approve   59 /

    2. ☐ Mildly approve

    3. ☐ Mildly disapprove

    4. ☐ Strongly disapprove

    b. IF STRONGLY OR MILDLY APPROVE: How would you feel about busing to achieve integration?

        1. ☐ Strongly approve   60 /

        2. ☐ Mildly approve

        3. ☐ Mildly disapprove

        4. ☐ Strongly disapprove

42. Even though the evidence is spotty, most people do have an opinion about the educational effects of integrated schools.

    a. On the average do you think that whites get a better education in integrated schools or in all or mostly white schools?

        1. ☐ Much better in white schools   61 /

        2. ☐ Somewhat better in white schools

        3. ☐ No difference

        4. ☐ Somewhat better in integrated schools

        5. ☐ Much better in integrated schools

        6. ☐ I have never thought about this and have no opinion.

    b. How about black students. On the average do you think that they get a better education in integrated schools or in all or mostly black schools?

        1. ☐ Much better in black schools   62 /

        2. ☐ Somewhat better in black schools

        3. ☐ No difference

        4. ☐ Somewhat better in integrated schools

        5. ☐ Much better in integrated schools

        6. ☐ I have never thought about this and have no opinion

-29-

43. How would you feel about the following things being done by a school to try and improve educational opportunities for black children?

a. Offering special classes to parents to teach them how they can help their children do better in school.

    1. ☐ I would be in favor if the classes were open to all parents.   63/

    2. ☐ I would be in favor even if such classes were only open to black parents.

    3. ☐ I would be against this either way.

b. Paying youngsters who are doing poor school work if they do better.

    1. ☐ I would be in favor if this were done for all students doing poor work.   64/

    2. ☐ I would be in favor even if this were done only for black students doing poor work.

    3. ☐ I would be against it either way.

c. Hiring more qualified black teachers.

    1. ☐ I would be in favor of the school actively looking for black teachers but not of hiring a less qualified black instead of a more qualified white.   65/

    2. ☐ I would be in favor even if this meant not hiring some more highly qualified white teachers.

    3. ☐ I would be against it either way.

d. Setting up a black studies program.

    1. ☐ I would be in favor if the program were open to all students.   66/

    2. ☐ I would be in favor even if this program were only open to black students.

    3. ☐ I would be against it either way.

e. Allowing for community control of schools so that in black areas, black parents would have more say in how the schools are run.

    1. ☐ I would be in favor.   67/

    2. ☐ I would be opposed.

    3. ☐ I don't know enough about community control programs to say.

-30-

44. Generally speaking, how do you feel about laws which make it
    illegal for an employer to refuse to hire a person for an
    available job just because of that person's race?

    1. ☐ I approve such laws but think we ought to go further   68 /
           in enforcing them.

    2. ☐ I approve such laws but think we have gone too far
           in enforcing them.

    3. ☐ I approve such laws but don't know enough to judge
           how they are being enforced.

    4. ☐ I am against such laws; employers should be free
           to hire whomever they want.

45. Many black people and some whites too feel that employers ought to
    favor black over white applicants for jobs in order to make up for
    the past when whites were favored over blacks. How do you feel?

    1. ☐ I favor such a policy until the employment rate for   69 /
           blacks is as high as it is for whites.

    2. ☐ I favor such a policy but only if blacks are preferred
           when they are as well or better qualified as whites.

    3. ☐ The color of a man's skin shouldn't count; people should
           be hired only on the basis of how qualified they are
           on the job.

    4. ☐ The decision should be up to the employer; if black
           employers want to hire only blacks, they should be
           able to; similarly, white employers should be able
           to hire whom they please.

46. How actively do you think the federal government ought to press business
    to have a fair proportion of blacks in all kinds of jobs?

    1. ☐ Government shouldn't do anything; this is a matter which   70 /
           should be left to business to decide for itself.

    2. ☐ Government should make it clear that it favors such a
           policy but leave it up to individual businesses to decide
           how to follow the policy.

    3. ☐ Government should refuse to give government contracts where
           companies are not following such a policy.

    4. ☐ We've reached a stage where laws should be passed to allow
           levying fines on businesses which do not follow such a policy.

    5. ☐ None of the above expresses my view. I think government should:

    _____
                      (Please write in)

-31-

47. How actively do you think government should press for unions with
    all white members to open up to blacks?

    1. ☐ Government ought not to interfere in this area.   9/

    2. ☐ Government should make it clear that it favors such a
           policy but leave it up to individual unions to decide
           how to follow the policy.

    3. ☐ Government should refuse to give government contracts
           where employees of a company belong to such a union.

    4. ☐ Legislation should be passed making it possible to levy
           fines on unions which do not admit blacks to membership.

    5. ☐ None of the above expresses my view. I think government
           should:

    _____
                    (Please write in)

48. Shifting now to the subject of housing, how do you feel about laws
    which say that it is illegal for anyone who puts his property up for
    sale to refuse to sell to a person just because of that person's
    race?

    1. ☐ I strongly favor such laws.   10/

    2. ☐ I mildly favor such laws.

    3. ☐ I mildly disapprove such laws.

    4. ☐ I strongly disapprove such laws.

49. Many people do oppose laws such as this one. One person has told us,
    for example, "It isn't that I wouldn't sell my house to a black family.
    It's just that I don't like being told what I must do with my private
    property. I feel that since it's my property I should have the right
    to sell to anyone I want to."

    How do you feel about this person's opinion?

    1. ☐ I strongly agree.   11/

    2. ☐ I mildly agree.

    3. ☐ I mildly disagree.

    4. ☐ I strongly disagree.

-32-

50. Another person who opposes such laws told us, "It isn't fair to my
    neighbors if I sell my house to a black family. Really, I'm making
    the choice for them because after I sell my house, I won't be living
    in this neighborhood any more."

    How do you feel about this person's opinion?

    1. ☐ Strongly agree   12/
    2. ☐ Mildly agree
    3. ☐ Mildly disagree
    4. ☐ Strongly disagree

51. It has been proposed by some people that the government ought to help
    build low cost housing in suburban areas. They say that this would
    help to bring black and white people in contact and to break down
    black ghettoes in the inner city.

    How do you feel about this idea?   13/

    1. ☐ I think it's a good idea; I favor it.
    2. ☐ I agree with what these people want to do; but their
         idea wouldn't work. It would just mean bringing
         ghettoes into the suburbs.
    3. ☐ It just doesn't make sense to try to make middle class
         people mix with lower class people whether they are
         black or white; they have different values and just
         wouldn't get along.

52. A white student in an integrated school comes home to report to his
    parents that he has been robbed of his lunch money by three black
    students. This is the third time this has happened during the school
    year and by now the white student is feeling pretty hostile toward
    black people generally. If you were a parent in such a situation,
    which of the following things do you think you would do? *(CHECK
    AS MANY AS APPLY.)*

    1. ☐ Nothing, let your child handle the situation himself.   14/
    2. ☐ Explain to my son why such things happen in a way so that
         he understands that it is wrong to be prejudiced.
    3. ☐ Go to the principal and complain without giving names of
         the black students.
    4. ☐ Go to the school principal, give the names of the black
         students, and ask that they be punished.
    5. ☐ I would (also) _____
                              (Please write in)
         _____

53. Half of the children attending public school in a town are black and half are white. However, out of 100 teachers in the school, only ten are black. Black parents ask the school board to hire only black teachers whenever a vacancy occurs until half of the teachers are black. In such a situation, which of the following things do you think the school board should do? *(CHECK ONE ANSWER.)*

1. ☐ Do what the black parents want even if this means hiring some teachers who aren't fully qualified.   15/

2. ☐ Make every effort to try to get more black applicants and then hire qualified black teachers even if they may be less qualified than white applicants.

3. ☐ Make every effort to try to get more black applicants but hire only on the basis of qualifications.

4. ☐ Stick with the present policy of hiring the best teachers from among those who apply.

5. ☐ None of these things. I think the school board should:

_____
(Please write in)

54. An employer does his best to increase the number of black workers in his factory, but his white workers begin to complain that the new black workers aren't carrying their load. In such a situation, what do you think the employer should do? *(CHECK AS MANY AS APPLY)*

1. ☐ Stop hiring blacks altogether.   16/

2. ☐ In the future hire only blacks who are qualified.

3. ☐ Let all workers--white or black--who aren't carrying their load go.

4. ☐ Try to persuade white workers to accept the present situation.

5. ☐ I would (also) _____
(Please write in)

-34-

55. Frank and Lucille Jones live in an all white community and own their
    own home. Frank's company transfers him to a job in another city.
    The Jones' put their house up for sale and decide to sell it to a middle
    class black family who want to buy it and are willing to pay the price
    asked. Jones' neighbors hear about this and find a white family who
    are willing to buy the house and even pay $1,000 more than the Jones
    would get from the black family. What do you think you would do if
    you were in the Jones' situation?

    1. ☐ Sell to the black family.   17/

    2. ☐ Sell to the white family.

    3. ☐ It would depend on whether I was a close friend of
           my neighbors.

56. Which of the following statements comes closest to your personal feel-
    ings about marriage between blacks and whites?

    1. ☐ Blacks and whites should marry their own kind.   18/

    2. ☐ It's not a good idea for blacks and whites to marry
           because their children will suffer.

    3. ☐ People should marry anyone they choose regardless of race.

57. Suppose you had a child who wanted to marry a black person who had
    a good education and a good job. How would you feel about this?

    1. ☐ I would approve.   19/

    2. ☐ I would disapprove but keep silent.

    3. ☐ I would object.

    4. ☐ I would not care either way.

    5. ☐ I don't know.

-35-

V.

The purpose of this section of the questionnaire will be to find out how much or how little black and white people come into contact with each other. Getting accurate information on this topic is difficult. Please write in the margin wherever you think a question might not be getting an accurate picture of your situation.

8. Are there any black families living on either side of the street on which you now live?

   1. ☐ None that I know of   20/

   2. ☐ Yes, one family

   3. ☐ Yes, two families

   4. ☐ Yes, three families

   5. ☐ Yes, four families

   6. ☐ Yes, five families

   7. ☐ Yes, more than five families. (How many altogether would you estimate? _____)

59. How many black children attend public school in your neighborhood?

   1. ☐ I would guess that out of every 100 children in school,   21-22/
             _____ are black . (Write 0 if none are black.)

   2. ☐ I don't really know.

60. Are you presently employed?

   1. ☐ No   23/

   2. ☐ Yes ...... How many blacks are employed at your place of work? *(Please fill in numbers)*

                      Out of about _____ employees, I would   24-27/
                      estimate that _____ are black.

-36-

61a. Do you have any really close friends who are black?

   1. ☐ Not a really close friend, no.   28/

   2. ☐ Yes, one

   3. ☐ Yes, two   } Please answer questions in box below.

   4. ☐ Yes, three or more

---

  b. Thinking now of your closest black friend, how long have
     you known each other?

     1. ☐ Less than three months   29-30/

     2. ☐ From 4 to 6 months

     3. ☐ Between 7 and 12 months

     4. ☐ About _____ years *(Please fill in number)*

  c. Where did you meet?

     1. ☐ In the neighborhood   31/

     2. ☐ At work

     3. ☐ At church

     4. ☐ Elsewhere: _____
                     (Please write in)

---

62. How many blacks, if any, do you know well enough to call by their first
    names?

   1. ☐ None   32/

   2. ☐ One

   3. ☐ Two

   4. ☐ Three

   5. ☐ Four

   6. ☐ Five to ten

   7. ☐ More than ten

-37-

63. Have you ever entertained a black person in your home?

    1. ☐ No   33/

    2. ☐ Once

    3. ☐ Twice

    4. ☐ Three times

    5. ☐ Four times

    6. ☐ Five to ten times

    7. ☐ More than ten times

64. Have you ever been entertained by a black family in their home?

    1. ☐ No   34/

    2. ☐ Once

    3. ☐ Twice

    4. ☐ Three times

    5. ☐ Four times

    6. ☐ Five or more times

65. During the time you were growing up, did you have any very close friends who were black?

    1. ☐ No not really   35/

    2. ☐ One

    3. ☐ Two

    4. ☐ Three

    5. ☐ Four

    6. ☐ Five or more

-38-

VI.

Most Americans feel that it is wrong to be prejudiced. There seems to be a lot of disagreement, however, about what it means to be prejudiced. Our purpose in this section is to find just how much disagreement there is and what it is about.

66. John Brown works as a machinist but is presently out of a job. He feels that the country has gone overboard in helping blacks mostly at his expense. It's in his kind of neighborhood that the government has built low cost housing for blacks. He's had his house broken into and robbed. He finds it hard to get jobs because employers would rather hire a black man. He feels that if it cost all those middle class "do-gooders" as much as it has cost him, they wouldn't be so eager to help blacks either.

a. Based on knowing this much about him, would you say that John Brown is:

1. ☐ ´A highly prejudiced person   36/

2. ☐ Somewhat prejudiced

3. ☐ Slightly prejudiced

4. ☐ Not really prejudiced at all

b. Whether you think Brown is prejudiced or not, to what extent did you find yourself feeling sympathetic toward him?

1. ☐ Very sympathetic   37/

2. ☐ Somewhat sympathetic

3. ☐ Somewhat unsympathetic

4. ☐ Very unsympathetic

c. Do you agree or disagree that efforts to reduce discrimination and prejudice put more of a burden on poorer than more well-to-do white people?

1. ☐ Agree   38/

2. ☐ Disagree

67. To begin, a white person believes that black children do less well on intelligence tests on the average than white children. Would you say that such a belief is:

1. ☐ Definitely a sign of prejudice 39/
2. ☐ Possibly a sign of prejudice
3. ☐ Probably not a sign of prejudice
4. ☐ Definitely not a sign of prejudice
5. ☐ Can't say because ______________

____

____
(Please say why)

68. In the same manner please go through the following statements and say how much you think they are or are not a sign of racial prejudice.

		Definitely Prejudice 1	Possibly Prejudice 2	Probably Not Prejudice 3	Definitely Not Prejudice 4	Can't Say 5	
a.	Suppose someone believes that blacks generally are inferior to whites	☐	☐	☐	☐	☐	40/
b.	Black students demand that certain classes dealing with black subjects be open to blacks only	☐	☐	☐	☐	☐	
c.	An older white man addressing a young black aged 25 as "boy".	☐	☐	☐	☐	☐	
d.	All applicants for 20 jobs as brick layers are required to take an intelligence test and the job is given to the 20 applicants who score the highest with no attention paid to race, creed, or color	☐	☐	☐	☐	☐	43/

	Definitely Prejudice 1	Possibly Prejudice 2	Probably Not Prejudice 3	Definitely Not Prejudice 4	Can't Say 5
e. A black person who believes that he can never be treated fairly by a white person .	☐	☐	☐	☐	☐ 44/
f. Having a police force that is 98% white in a community that is 30% black	☐	☐	☐	☐	☐
g. A private club that is restricted to whites only	☐	☐	☐	☐	☐
h. A white gambler rubbing a black person's hair to bring himself luck	☐	☐	☐	☐	☐
i. A white American missionary telling the members of an African tribe that only if they believe in Christ can they go to heaven	☐	☐	☐	☐	☐
j. A black social club which refuses to admit whites	☐	☐	☐	☐	☐
k. A white person who refuses his house to sell to anyone who is black	☐	☐	☐	☐	☐
l. A bank which requires a very good credit rating before making a loan . .	☐	☐	☐	☐	☐
m. A large company strictly follows a policy of never considering a person's race or religion in hiring	☐	☐	☐	☐	☐
n. A person who believes that blacks on the average don't work as hard as whites	☐	☐	☐	☐	☐ 53/

-41-

69. Richard Jones is a black man who owns a body repair shop. He follows
     a policy of hiring only blacks even though most of his customers are
     white. He defends his policy by saying that he is only doing in
     reverse what many white owned firms did in the past and what some
     still do. He also points out that the body repair workers union in
     town doesn't admit blacks.

  a. How would you judge Jones' policy of hiring only blacks to work
     for his business?

     1. ☐ Highly prejudiced   54/

     2. ☐ Somewhat prejudiced

     3. ☐ Slightly prejudiced

     4. ☐ Not prejudiced at all

  b. Whether you think the policy is prejudiced or not, to what
     extent did you feel sympathy toward what Jones is doing?

     1. ☐ Very sympathetic   55/

     2. ☐ Somewhat sympathetic

     3. ☐ Somewhat unsympathetic

     4. ☐ Very unsympathetic

-42-

VII.

This section of the questionnaire includes a variety of questions about your attitudes on topics other than black-white relations. This information is important if we are to compare how different kinds of people think and feel on the topics asked about in earlier sections of the questionnaire.

70a. Suppose Congress were to pass a law saying that groups who disagree with our form of government could not hold public meetings or make speeches. Would you be in favor or against such a law being passed?

    1. ☐ In favor   56/

    2. ☐ Opposed

b. As far as you know, would the Congress have the right to pass such a law under the Constitution?

                                                    57/

    1. ☐ Yes

    2. ☐ No

    3. ☐ Don't know

71a. How would you feel about Congress passing a law saying that the President must be a man who believes in God? Would you be in favor or opposed?

    1. ☐ In favor   58/

    2. ☐ Opposed

b. As far as you know, would the Congress have the right to pass such a law under the Constitution?

    1. ☐ Yes   59/

    2. ☐ No

    3. ☐ Don't know

-43-

72. For each statement, please indicate whether you agree or disagree by
marking an "X" in the column under the appropriate answer.

		Agree 1	Disagree 2	Don't Know 3	
a.	No weakness or difficulty can hold us back if we have enough will power	☐	☐	☐	60/
b.	Sex crimes, such as rape and attacks on children, deserve more than mere imprisonment; such criminals ought to be publicly whipped, or worse	☐	☐	☐	
c.	People can be divided into two distinct classes--the weak and the strong	☐	☐	☐	
d.	Much of our lives is controlled by plots hatched in secret places	☐	☐	☐	
e.	Reading the stars can tell us a great deal about the future	☐	☐	☐	
f.	I don't like to hear a lot of arguments I disagree with	☐	☐	☐	
g.	A little practical experience is worth more than all the books put together	☐	☐	☐	
h.	The answers to this country's problems are much simpler than the experts would have us think	☐	☐	☐	
i.	Getting to the top is more a matter of luck than of ability	☐	☐	☐	
j.	Most people in government are not really interested in the problems of the average man	☐	☐	☐	
k.	You sometimes can't help wondering whether anything is worthwhile anymore	☐	☐	☐	
l.	Nowadays a person has to live pretty much for today and let tomorrow take care of itself	☐	☐	☐	71/

73a. Suppose a man admitted in public that he did not believe in God. Do you think he should be allowed to teach in a public high school?

  72/

  1. ☐ Yes

  2. ☐ No

b. Do you think he should be allowed to hold public office?

  73/

  1. ☐ Yes

  2. ☐ No

c. Do you think that a book he wrote should be removed from public libraries?

  1. ☐ Yes 74/

  2. ☐ No

74. Darwin's theory of evolution says that human beings evolved from lower forms of animal life over many millions of years. Which of the following statements comes closest to expressing your belief in this theory?

  1. ☐ The theory is almost certainly true 75/

  2. ☐ The theory is probably true

  3. ☐ The theory is probably false

  4. ☐ The theory could not possibly be true

  5. ☐ I have not really thought about this before

-45-

(___ (1-4) ___)
5-6/
7-8/15

75. To what extent do you think your life is influenced by each of the following?

(For each one, please mark an "X" to show whether you think it determines your life almost entirely, has a strong influence on your life, has a small influence, or has no influence at all.)

	Determines My Life Almost Entirely	Has a Strong Influence	Has a Small Influence	Has no Influence At All
	1	2	3	4
a. The way you were brought up .	☐	☐	☐	☐
b. God or some other supernatural force	☐	☐	☐	☐
c. Luck	☐	☐	☐	☐
d. The characteristics you were born with	☐	☐	☐	☐
e. What people in power decide .	☐	☐	☐	☐
f. Will power	☐	☐	☐	☐

Now please go back and choose the <u>one</u> thing that you think has the <u>greatest influence</u> in deciding the course of your life and circle the letter of your choice below:

a	b	c	d	e	f

15/

76a. Which of the following statements comes closest to expressing your
     belief about God? *(CHECK ONE)*

   1. ☐   I don't believe in God.   16/

   2. ☐   I don't believe or disbelieve in God, I just don't
         think it is possible for me to know whether there
         is a God or not.

   3. ☐   I am uncertain but lean toward not believing in God.

   4. ☐   I am uncertain but lean toward believing in God. *(If
         you choose this answer, please answer the questions
         in the box below.)*

   5. ☐   I definitely believe in God. *(If you choose this answer,
         please fill out the questions in the box below.)*

   6. ☐   I am uncomfortable about the word "God" but I do
         believe in some kind of transcendent force or energy.
         *(If possible, please say what you think this force
         is like.)*

         _____

         _____

   7. ☐   None of the above expresses my views. What I believe
         about God is: _____

         _____

IF YOU BELIEVE IN GOD OR LEAN TOWARD BELIEVING, PLEASE ANSWER THE QUESTIONS
IN THE BOX BELOW:

b. Do you picture God as having a human form?
   1. ☐   Yes   17/
   2. ☐   No. How do you picture God? _____

         _____

c. Which of these statements comes closest to your view about God's
   influence on your life?
   1. ☐   God has left each of us completely free to decide our   18/
         life for ourselves.
   2. ☐   Most of our life is decided by God.
   3. ☐   Other. What? _____

         _____

d. Do you feel that God influences history?
   1. ☐   No   19/
   2. ☐   Yes. How? _____

         _____

e. Do you feel that God answers prayers?
   1. ☐   Yes   20/
   2. ☐   No

77. Which of the following comes closest to your view about life after death? *(CHECK ONE)*

    1. ☐ I don't believe there is a life after death.   21/

    2. ☐ I'm unsure whether or not there is life after death.

    3. ☐ I believe that there must be something beyond death, but I have no idea what it may be like.

    4. ☐ There is life after death with rewards for some people and punishment for others.

    5. ☐ There is life after death but no punishment.

    6. ☐ The notion of Reincarnation expresses my view of what happens to people when they die.

    7. ☐ None of the above. I think: _____

    _____

78. How often do you do each of the following?

	Every Day 1	Several Times a Week 2	About Once a Week 3	Several Times a Month 4	About Once a Month 5	Several Times a Year or Less 6	Never 7	
Pray	☐	☐	☐	☐	☐	☐	☐	22/
Meditate . . .	☐	☐	☐	☐	☐	☐	☐	
Read the Bible	☐	☐	☐	☐	☐	☐	☐	
Attend church or synagogue meeting . . .	☐	☐	☐	☐	☐	☐	☐	25/

79. People who believe in astrology claim that the stars, the planets, and our birthdays have a lot to do with our destiny in life. How do you view this claim? *(CHECK ONE)*

    1. ☐ I am a firm believer in astrology.   26/

    2. ☐ I am somewhat doubtful, but lean to believing in it.

    3. ☐ I am very doubtful, but still think it's a possibility.

    4. ☐ Count me as a disbeliever.

-48-

80. How well informed are you about astrology?

1. ☐ Very well informed.   27/
2. ☐ Fairly well informed.
3. ☐ Only slightly informed.

81. Whether they believe in astrology or not, many people are
interested in their horoscopes. How interested are you?
                                                            28/
1. ☐ Very interested.
2. ☐ Fairly interested.
3. ☐ Slightly interested.
4. ☐ Not interested at all.
5. ☐ Frankly, I don't really know what a horoscope is.

82. Which of these statements comes closest to your view of extra
sensory perception (ESP)?

1. ☐ I never heard of it.   29/
2. ☐ I am sure it exists.
3. ☐ I am not sure, but I think it probably exists.
4. ☐ It probably doesn't exist.
5. ☐ I am sure it doesn't exist.

83. Have you ever had an experience which you think is an example of
extra sensory perception?

1. ☐ No   30/

2. ☐ Yes. Could you briefly describe your experience?

_____

_____

-49-

84. For each of the following statements, please indicate whether you
strongly agree, agree, disagree, or strongly disagree. Mark an "X"
in the appropriate column.

		Strongly Agree 1	Agree 2	Disagree 3	Strongly Disagree 4	Can't Say 5	
a.	This country is run by a small group of powerful men	☐	☐	☐	☐	☐	31/
b.	Knowledge of the movement of stars and planets can tell us a lot about the future	☐	☐	☐	☐	☐	
c.	Hard work can get a person almost anything he wants in this society	☐	☐	☐	☐	☐	
d.	Working on the thirteenth floor of an office building will bring bad luck	☐	☐	☐	☐	☐	
e.	There are a large number of Communists in our school system	☐	☐	☐	☐	☐	
f.	Success in the business world is pretty much a matter of luck	☐	☐	☐	☐	☐	
g.	Airplane crashes are largely a matter of fate	☐	☐	☐	☐	☐	
h.	Spiritual experiences can help us to understand a lot of things that control our lives	☐	☐	☐	☐	☐	
i.	How far you get in this society is largely determined by your environment	☐	☐	☐	☐	☐	39/
j.	God has taken a part in important events in human history .	☐	☐	☐	☐	☐	
k.	Success in school is largely a matter of being born smart . .	☐	☐	☐	☐	☐	
l.	Our political leaders have little chance of avoiding a major nuclear war	☐	☐	☐	☐	☐	
m.	Science can help us to overcome all of our important problems	☐	☐	☐	☐	☐	
n.	Mental illness is largely a person's own fault	☐	☐	☐	☐	☐	
o.	Automobile accidents are basically a matter of bad luck . . .	☐	☐	☐	☐	☐	
p.	Life seems to be a series of good and bad streaks	☐	☐	☐	☐	☐	
q.	Fortune tellers seem to tell you a good deal about the future .	☐	☐	☐	☐	☐	47/

-50-

We'd like you to imagine yourself in the situations described below and to tell us as honestly as you can how you think you would act in each of them.

85. You are driving a lonely road within the speed limit in a city which has a leash law. Suddenly a dog runs in front of your car and before you can stop you hit him, knocking him unconscious. Frankly, what do you think you would do in such a situation?

    1. ☐ Probably keep going.   48/

    2. ☐ Most likely call the police and tell them where the animal was.

    3. ☐ Take the animal to the closest vet and try to contact the dog's owner.

    4. ☐ Truly don't know.

    5. ☐ Other. What? _____

       _____
                        (Please write in)

86. A co-worker and close friend of yours has been in an accident and is laid up for a long time in bed. He lives off his insurance and savings but finally these run out. He calls you up and asks for a loan of money each week until he gets well. The loan he asks for is in an amount you could afford although it will mean pinching pennies. What do you think you would do in this situation?

    1. ☐ Suggest that he try to get the loan from a bank.   49/

    2. ☐ Lend him the money but ask for interest.

    3. ☐ Lend him the money without interest.

    4. ☐ Truly don't know.

    5. ☐ Other. What? _____

       _____
                        (Please write in)

87. Imagine that you are boarding a bus and you overhear the driver say to the person ahead of you, "Sorry, I don't carry any change, unless you have a quarter, you'll have to get off." In such a situation, what do you think you would do?

    1. ☐ Give the person a quarter.   50/

    2. ☐ Offer to change a dollar for the person.

    3. ☐ Probably do nothing.

    4. ☐ Truly don't know.

    5. ☐ Other. What? _____
                        (Please write in)

88. You are walking along through a park in bright daylight and suddenly
    from behind some bushes, someone screams, "Help, help, he's trying
    to kill me." In such a situation, what do you honestly think you
    would do?

    1. ☐ Probably keep walking.   51/

    2. ☐ Start looking for a policeman or a phone booth to call
          the police.

    3. ☐ Run behind the bush and be of whatever help you could.

    4. ☐ Truly don't know.

    5. ☐ Other. What? _____

          _____
                         (Please write in)

89. Here are a set of paired statements, each offering a different view-
    point about getting ahead in the world. (Please read each pair of
    statements, and mark an "X" to say which one of these statements comes
    closer to expressing how you feel.)

A. 1. ☐ Leadership positions tend to go to capable people who   52/
          deserve being chosen.

    2. ☐ It's hard to know why some people get leadership positions
          and others don't; ability doesn't seem to be the important
          factor.

B. 1. ☐ Women should try to get the best training possible for   53/
          what they want to do.

    2. ☐ Women should pull together in women's rights groups and
          activities to get what they want.

C. 1. ☐ When I make plans, I am almost certain that I can make them   54/
          work.

    2. ☐ It is not always wise to plan too far ahead because many
          things turn out to be a matter of good or bad fortune
          anyhow.

D. 1. ☐ Many women have only themselves to blame for not doing better 55/
          in life. If they tried harder, they'd do better.

    2. ☐ When two qualified people, one female and one male, are consid-
          ered for the same job, the female won't get the job no matter
          how hard she tries.

E. 1. ☐ As far as world affairs are concerned, most of us are the   56/
          victims of forces we can neither understand nor control.

    2. ☐ By taking an active part in political and social affairs,
          people can control world events.

-52-

89. (Continued)

F. 1. ☐ Men and women just have different places in life, and that's   57/
        the way it's likely to stay.

    2. ☐ People may be prejudiced against women but it's possible
        for women to gain equality in American society.

G. 1. ☐ People are lonely because they don't try to be friendly.   58/

    2. ☐ There's not much use in trying too hard to please people;
        if they like you, they like you.

H. 1. ☐ Many women who don't do well in life do have good training,   59/
        but the opportunities just always go to men.

    2. ☐ Women may not have the same opportunities as men, but
        many women haven't prepared themselves enough to make
        use of the opportunities that come their way.

I. 1. ☐ I have often found that what is going to happen will   60/
        happen.

    2. ☐ Trusting to fate has never turned out as well for me as
        making a definite course of action.

J. 1. ☐ Women would be better off and the cause of equal rights   61/
        for women would be advanced if they were less pushy about it.

    2. ☐ The only way women will gain their civil rights is by
        constant protest and pressure.

K. 1. ☐ One of the major reasons we have wars is because people   62/
        don't take enough interest in politics.

    2. ☐ There will always be wars, no matter how hard people
        try to prevent them.

L. 1. ☐ The best way for women to be sure of getting equal   63/
        rights is through pressure and social action.

    2. ☐ The best way for women to be sure of getting equal
        rights is for each individual woman to work hard and
        get a good education.

-53-

The following questions about your background complete the questionnaire.

90. How long have you lived in the Bay Area? (This means anywhere in Alameda, Contra Costa, Marin, Napa, San Francisco, San Mateo, Santa Clara, Solano, or Sonoma counties.)

    1. ☐ Less than 6 months   64/
    2. ☐ 6 to 11 months
    3. ☐ 1 or 2 years
    4. ☐ 3 to 5 years
    5. ☐ 6 to 10 years
    6. ☐ 11 to 20 years
    7. ☐ More than 20 years

91. How long have you lived at this address?

    1. ☐ Less than 6 months   65/
    2. ☐ 6 to 11 months
    3. ☐ 1 to 2 years
    4. ☐ 3 to 5 years
    5. ☐ 6 to 10 years
    6. ☐ 11 to 20 years
    7. ☐ More than 20 years

92. Do you own your own home or do you rent?

    1. ☐ Own   66/
    2. ☐ Rent
    3. ☐ Other

93. How do you feel about living in the Bay Area?

    1. ☐ Very satisfied   67/
    2. ☐ Fairly satisfied
    3. ☐ Not too satisfied
    4. ☐ Not at all satisfied
    5. ☐ No opinion

-54-

94. Are you single, married, separated, divorced, or widowed?

    1. ☐ Single   68/

    2. ☐ Presently married and living with spouse.

    3. ☐ Separated

    4. ☐ Divorced

    5. ☐ Widowed

95a. How many children do you have?

    1. ☐ None   69/

    2. ☐ One

    3. ☐ Two

    4. ☐ Three   ANSWER **95b.**

    5. ☐ Four

    6. ☐ Five

    7. ☐ Six or more

95b. How many of your children are:

_____ Twelve years old or younger.   70/
       (Fill in the blank with the exact number; write 0 if none
        of your children fall into this age category.)

_____ Thirteen to twenty-one years old.   71/
       (Fill in the blank with the exact number; write 0 if none
      of your children fall into this age category.)

_____ Over twenty-one.   72/
       (Fill in the blank with the exact number; write 0 if none
      of your children fall into this age category.)

96. What is the highest grade or year you completed in school?
(Circle the highest grade.)

                                                          73-74/

    Grade School: K 1 2 3 4 5 6 7 8

    High School: 1 2 3 4

    College: 1 2 3 4 5+

-55-

(___ (1-4) ___)
5-6/
7-8/16

97. How far did your mother and father go in school? Also, if you are married, how much education did your spouse have?

(Please check the answer that comes closest to describing the amount of education that your mother, your father and your spouse completed.)

Mother   Father   Spouse (if married)

☐	☐	☐	Elementary school or less	9-10/
☐	☐	☐	Some junior high school	11-12/
☐	☐	☐	Junior high school graduate	
☐	☐	☐	Some senior high school	13-14/
☐	☐	☐	Senior high school graduate	
☐	☐	☐	Some community or junior college	
☐	☐	☐	Community or junior college graduate	
☐	☐	☐	Some college or university	
☐	☐	☐	College or university graduate	
☐	☐	☐	Postgraduate study	
☐	☐	☐	Postgraduate degree	

98. In what state of country were you living around the time when you were 16 years old?

_____   15-16/

99. When you were 16 years old, were you living on a farm, in a small city, in a suburb of a large city, or in a large city?

17/

1. ☐   On a farm

2. ☐   In a small city

3. ☐   In a suburb of a large city

4. ☐   In a large city

5. ☐   Other. Where? _____

00. In what country was your father born? _____   18-19/

01. In what country was your grandfather and grandmother on your father's side born?

a. Paternal Grandfather was born in: _____   20-21/

b. Paternal Grandmother was born in: _____   22-23/

-56-

102. In what country was your mother born? _____ 24-25/

103. In what country was your grandfather and grandmother on your mother's side born?

    a. Maternal Grandfather was born in: _____ 26-27/

    b. Maternal Grandmother was born in: _____ 28-29/

104. Please look over the following list of clubs and organizations and indicate by a check mark whether or not you belong to each type of organization.

		Belong To	
		Yes 1	No 2
a.	Church-connected groups	☐	☐
b.	Fraternal lodges or veteran's organizations .	☐	☐
c.	Business or civic groups	☐	☐
d.	Professional groups	☐	☐
e.	Parent-teachers Association	☐	☐
f.	Youth groups (Scout Leader, Little League coach or Manager, etc.)	☐	☐
g.	Community center	☐	☐
h.	Neighborhood improvement associations	☐	☐
i.	Social or card playing groups	☐	☐
j.	Sports teams	☐	☐
k.	Country clubs	☐	☐
l.	Political clubs or organizations	☐	☐
m.	Issue or action oriented groups	☐	☐
n.	Charity or welfare organizations	☐	☐

30/

43/

105a. Are you working at the present time, are you in your own business, are you unemployed, or something else?

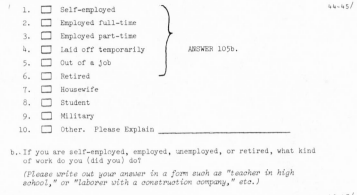

                                                                   44-45/

    1.   ☐   Self-employed

    2.   ☐   Employed full-time

    3.   ☐   Employed part-time

    4.   ☐   Laid off temporarily   ANSWER 105b.

    5.   ☐   Out of a job

    6.   ☐   Retired

    7.   ☐   Housewife

    8.   ☐   Student

    9.   ☐   Military

   10.   ☐   Other. Please Explain _____

  b. If you are self-employed, employed, unemployed, or retired, what kind of work do you (did you) do?

    (Please write out your answer in a form such as "teacher in high school," or "laborer with a construction company," etc.)

                                                                        46-47/

_____

IF MARRIED, PLEASE ANSWER QUESTIONS IN THIS BOX

106a. Is your (husband/wife) working at the present time, self-employed, unemployed or what?

                                                                  48-49/

     1.   ☐   Self-employed

     2.   ☐   Employed full-time

     3.   ☐   Employed part-time   ANSWER 106b

     4.   ☐   Laid off temporarily

     5.   ☐   Out of a job

     6.   ☐   Retired

     7.   ☐   Housewife

     8.   ☐   Student

     9.   ☐   Military

    10.   ☐   Other. Please Explain _____

  b. If your (husband/wife) (is/was) self-employed, employed, unemployed, or retired, what kind of work (does/did) (he/she) do? (Write out your answer as indicated above in question 105 b.)

                                                                      50-51/

107a. What kind of work did you father (head of household) do when you
were 16 years old?

*(Please write out your answer in a form such as "teacher in high
school," or "laborer with a construction company," etc.)*

_____   52~53/

b. Was he/she self-employed at that time?

1. ☐ Yes   54/

2. ☐ No

108. Which of the following best expresses your present religious
preference? *(Please check only one.)*

☐ No religious beliefs   55~56/

☐ Agnostic

☐ Atheist

☐ Humanist

☐ Eastern Orthodox

☐ Mormon

☐ Protestant. (Please specify your denomination in as much
detail as possible. For example, if Baptist, are you
American Baptist, Southern Baptist or something else; if
Lutheran, are you American Lutheran Church, Lutheran Church
in America, Lutheran Church-Missouri Synod, or something
else; if Presbyterian, are you United Presbyterian, Presbyterian, U.S.A. or are you something else?)

_____
                    Denomination

☐ Roman Catholic

☐ Jewish

109. In what religion were you raised?

☐ In no religion   57~58/

☐ Protestant. Which denomination? _____

☐ Roman Catholic

☐ Eastern Orthodox

☐ Jewish

☐ Other. Please specify: _____

-59-

110a. Do you belong to a labor union?

    1. ☐   Yes   59/

    2. ☐   No

  b. Does your (husband/wife) belong to a labor union?

    1. ☐   Yes   60/

    2. ☐   No

    3. ☐   I am not married

111. If you were asked to use one of **four** names for your social class, which would you say you belong in--the lower class, working class, middle class, or upper middle class?

    1. ☐   Upper middle class   61/

    2. ☐   Middle class

    3. ☐   Working class

    4. ☐   Lower class

    5. ☐   Other. What class is that? _____
                                        (Write in)

    6. ☐   None; I don't believe in classes

    7. ☐   Can't say

112. How would you describe your politics when you were sixteen--would you say that you were a radical, a liberal, a conservative, a strong conservative, or were you middle-of-the-road?

    1. ☐   Radical   62/

    2. ☐   Liberal

    3. ☐   Middle-of-the-road

    4. ☐   Conservative

    5. ☐   Strong conservative

    6. ☐   Don't know

113. How would you describe your politics now--would you say that you
are a radical, a liberal, a conservative, a strong conservative,
or are you middle-of-the-road?

   1. ☐ Radical   63/

   2. ☐ Liberal

   3. ☐ Middle-of-the-road

   4. ☐ Conservative

   5. ☐ Strong Conservative

   6. ☐ Don't know

114. Generally speaking do you usually think of yourself as liberal Democrat, a moderate Democrat, a moderate Republican, a conservative
Republican, an Independent, or as something other than these?

   1. ☐ A liberal Democrat   64/

   2. ☐ A moderate Democrat

   3. ☐ A moderate Republican

   4. ☐ A conservative Republican

   5. ☐ An Independent

   6. ☐ Other. Please name: _____

115. How would you describe your father's politics at the time when you
were sixteen--were they radical, liberal, conservative, strongly
conservative, or middle-of-the-road?

   1. ☐ Radical   65/

   2. ☐ Liberal

   3. ☐ Middle-of-the-Road

   4. ☐ Conservative

   5. ☐ Strongly conservative

   6. ☐ Don't know

116. How would you describe your mother's politics at the time when you
were sixteen--were they radical, liberal, conservative, strongly
conservative, or middle-of-the-road?

   1. ☐ Radical   66/

   2. ☐ Liberal

   3. ☐ Middle-of-the-Road

   4. ☐ Conservative

   5. ☐ Strongly conservative

   6. ☐ Don't know

117. Please check the figure that comes closest to your present yearly
     family income before taxes. (This figure should include dividends,
     interest, salaries, wages, pensions, and all other income.) If
     you are uncertain, please indicate your best guess.

     ☐ None   67-68/
     ☐ Less than $2,000
     ☐ $2,000 to $2,999
     ☐ $3,000 to $3,999
     ☐ $4,000 to $4,999
     ☐ $5,000 to $5,999
     ☐ $6,000 to $6,999
     ☐ $7,000 to $7,999
     ☐ $8,000 to $8,999
     ☐ $9,000 to $9,999
     ☐ $10,000 to $10,999
     ☐ $11,000 to $11,999
     ☐ $12,000 to $14,999
     ☐ $15,000 to $19,999
     ☐ $20,000 to $24,999
     ☐ $25,000 and over

118. What is your sex?

     1. ☐ Female   69/
     2. ☐ Male

119. What is your race: 70/
     1. ☐ White
     2. ☐ Black
     3. ☐ Mexican-American
     4. ☐ Other Spanish-American
     5. ☐ Oriental, Chinese, Japanese, Korean
     6. ☐ Other. Please specify: _____

120. What was your age at your last birthday?

                                                                71-72/
     _____
            Age

            THANKS AGAIN FOR YOUR TIME AND EFFORT

Index

Adorno, T. W., 13
Affective expression of prejudice, 9
Affirmative action. *See*
    Compensatory programs;
    Prescriptions, as element of
    racial attitudes
Age: and explanatory modes,
    152–154, 157, 161, 170, 172, 179,
    182, 214; and mode-prescription
    relation, 183, 184, 185; and
    symbolic insensitivity, 255
Amerman, Helen E., 155-156n
Anomie: and explanatory modes,
    173, 176–178; measures of, 177,
    253–254; and mode-prescription
    relation, 188
Anti-Semitism, 15. *See also* Jews
Apostle, Richard A., 6n
Ashmore, Richard D., 173n
Attribution theory, 16n
Authoritarianism: and
    explanatory modes, 173–176,
    177, 178, 182, 215; measures of,
    13, 174, 175, 253–254; and
    mode-prescription relation, 183,
    184, 185; and prescriptions, 183
Authoritarian Personality, The
    (Adorno et al.), 13n, 174

Bauer, Raymond, 2–3, 4
Bay Area Religious Consciousness
    Survey, 232
Bay Area Survey (BAS): compared
    to follow-up study, 71–74, 105,
    192–196; consistency of

responses in, 44–48; generality
    of modes in, 48–53, 67, 204; on
    IQ test differences, 41, 45–47,
    73–74, 192, 195–196; limitations
    of, 39, 41, 47, 48, 57, 62–63, 67;
    "over-under statistic" used in,
    58, 59; on perception-
    explanation relation, 62–65, 67;
    purposes of, 36–37, 38, 39, 41–
    42, 49, 55; sample in, 38, 39,
    231–232; on socioeconomic
    status differences, 40, 42–43, 47,
    71–73, 192–196; structure of, 37,
    38–42, 49–51, 62–63
Beal, George M., 3n
Behavioral measures, 9, 191, 197,
    217
Bennett, Lerone, Jr., 149n
Binder, Frederick, 149n
Black family, attitudes toward, 30,
    31, 63, 64
Blacks' racial attitudes, 191, 200–
    204, 219. *See also* Racial
    attitudes
Bogardus, Emory S., 13n
Bogardus Social Distance Scale,
    13, 14
Braly, Kenneth, 10
Brooks, Ralph M., 3n

Campbell, Angus, 10n
Campbell, Donald T., 15–16n
Caseweighting, 234–235
Catholicism. *See* Roman
    Catholicism

333

attitudes: behavioral measures of, 191, 197, 217; causal relation to explanatory modes, tested, 181–190; definition of, 9, 13, 18; explanations related to, 18–19, 33–35, 55–62, 95–109, 111–114, 143–147, 181–190, 199–200, 211, 213, 257–268; in initial interviews, 20–21, 22, 33–35, 36; and institutional intervention, 110–113, 138–145, 184–189 *passim*, 213, 244, 245, 258, 259–268 *passim;* measures of, 56–57, 87–95, 110–113; perceptions related to, 18–19, 116, 117, 136–147, 212–213, 257–268; and personal affinity, 88, 110–113, 138–143, 143–146, 184–189 *passim*, 244–245, 258, 259, 260–268 *passim;* and personal cost, 92–93, 197–200, 209, 228; and political orientation, 188–190; weakness of measures based on, 13–14, 15, 55. *See also* Discrimination
Prochansky, H., 7n
Protestantism, 161–165, 214. *See also* Religion; Religious Affiliation
Prothro, J. W., 10
Pseudo-neutrality, 254–256
Psychological factors: and explanatory modes, 173–179, 182, 215; scales to measure, 174, 175, 177, 252–254. *See also* Anomie; Authoritarianism
Pure modes: and age, 152, 153; described, 96–104; and educational level, 160; frequency of, 82–83; and perceptions, 124–126, 127–132; and prescriptions, 96–104, 108, 112; respondents assigned to, 82–83, 240, 241. *See also names of various modes*

Questionnaire: limitations of, 9; used in follow-up study, 269–359

Racial attitudes: affected by personal cost, 92–93, 197–200, 209, 228; and age, 152–154, 157, 161, 214; among Blacks, 191, 200–204, 219; behavioral indicators of, 191, 197; and educational level, 101, 154–160, 183, 214; generational shift in, 154, 156–157, 179, 192, 228–230, 255; historical, 224, 225, 226–227; and psychological factors, 173–179, 182, 183, 215; and religion, 23–24, 34, 125, 129, 151, 161–167, 214; and social change, 222–223, 226, 228–230; use of term, 8, 17–18, 36, 216. *See also* Explanations, as element of racial attitudes; Perceptions, as element of racial attitudes; Prescriptions, as element of racial attitudes; Racial prejudice
Racial prejudice: behavioral expression of, 9, 191, 197; change in, over time, 1, 6, 11, 14, 136, 149, 215, 228–230; definitions of, 7–8, 10, 17–18, 19, 137; elements of, defined, 8–10, 13–14, 15–17, 18, 19, 36; measures of, 6, 7, 10–15, 115–116, 136, 137, 215, 219, 254–256; and psychological factors, 173–179, 182, 183, 215; recognition of, 88, 93–94, 98, 100, 101, 103, 105, 107, 108, 254–256; use of term, 7–8, 17–18, 36, 67, 93n, 215–216. *See also* Discrimination; Explanations, as element of racial attitudes; Perceptions, as element of racial attitudes; Prescriptions, as element of racial attitudes; Racial attitudes
Racial Stereotype Index, 10
Racial Stereotyping, Measure of, 10
Racism: literature on, cited, 8n; perceived by radical mode, 28, 61, 105, 107; use of term, 36n. *See also* Racial prejudice; Radical mode
Radical-environmentalist mode: and age, 152, 154; control agents in, 106–107; described,

128031